Praise for *Beyond the Game:*

"For sportswriting that is about those human qualities sports supposedly embodies—courage, regret, desire, heart, guts, spleen—you can't beat *Sports Illustrated* scribe Gary Smith. . . . The best of [his stories] have been gathered into *Beyond the Game.*"
—Scott Dickensheets, *The Las Vegas Sun*

"All the delicious digs about sportswriters—even the justly deserved—duck into hiding when Gary Smith takes the stage. There is sportswriting, and there is Smith's writing. . . . Journalism doesn't get any better. . . . A provocative, evocative storyteller."
—Steve Duin, *The Oregonian* (Portland)

"Vivid and passionate . . . These fifteen pieces set a new standard for sportswriting. Whether the reader is a die-hard fan or a lover of gifted storytelling, he or she will find Smith's book impossible to put down." —*Publishers Weekly* (starred review)

"[A] master storyteller . . . These aren't sports stories but tales that endure, stories about the human spirit and what happens in those doubtful moments between shame and glory, triumph and tragedy." —Gene Sapakoff, *The Post and Courier* (Charleston, SC)

"[Smith] covers sports but seldom will he tell you what the score was or who won. His focus is on the players as people. . . . These essays are wonderful reading, without exception."
—*Booklist* (starred review)

"Smith's language brings us close to the action. . . . Along the way, his prose surprises in every line."
—Jonathan Pitts, *The Baltimore Sun*

Beyond the Game

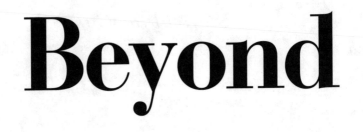

Beyond

the Game

The Collected Sportswriting
of Gary Smith

Grove Press / New York

Published simultaneously in Canada
Printed in the United States of America

FIRST PAPERBACK EDITION

These stories originally appeared in *Sports Illustrated*.
Photograph on p. x courtesy of *The New York Daily News*.

Library of Congress Cataloging-in-Publication Data

Smith, Gary, 1953–
    Beyond the game : the collected sportswriting of Gary Smith / Gary Smith.
      p. cm.
    ISBN 0-8021-3849-7 (pbk.)
      1. Sports—United States.   I. Title.
    GV707 .S62 2000
    796—dc21   00-040606

Design by Laura Hammond Hough

Grove Press
841 Broadway
New York, NY 10003

01 02 03 04 10 9 8 7 6 5 4 3 2 1

This book is dedicated
with loving gratitude to my parents,
Jean and Harry Smith.

Contents

Preface

Explain yourself. Tell us what you do that makes your stories unique. That's what the editors of this book asked me to do here at the start.

I hate explanations, and maybe that's a clue right there. When the music's right, no one needs an explanation, and when it's not, no one wants one. But I suppose that leaves a lot of white space. So I'll add this:

Sport comes to us in boxes—the perimeters of our TV screens or the boundary lines of fields and courts. As much as I enjoy what goes on inside those boxes, I've always had the urge to bust out of them. I've always had the feeling that the most compelling and significant story was the one occurring beyond the game—before it, after it, above it, or under it, deep in the furnace of the psyche. Conventional journalism couldn't always carry me up to those rafters or down into those boiler rooms, so I had to break out of a few of my own little boxes, as well. Thankfully, *Sports Illustrated* gave me the time and space to do that.

What I do may not work for everyone. My father recently admitted that he fell asleep on the first readings of my stories, but *swore* he loved the second go-rounds. I was shocked, and if I weren't a merciful man, he'd be long gone from that dedication page.

He's just one man, though. I hope you enjoy this collection.

Damned Yankee

Everything you will read on the next 23 pages revolves around one photograph. The rest of the old man's past, you must understand, is all but gone. The framed baseball pictures were smashed by his hammer. The scrapbook thick with newspaper clippings was fed to the furnace in the basement of the Sears, Roebuck in Paramus, New Jersey. The trophies, with their figurines of ballplayers and eagles and angel-like women, were placed on a portable table in the middle of a ball field and annihilated, one a day, by the old man's rifle arm. Have you ever heard the popping sound an angel makes when it's struck by a fastball?

Surely the other artifacts that survived are too few and too baffling to be trusted. The death certificate of a seven-year-old boy . . . the tattered letter from the New York Yankees front office . . . the 1955 Louisville Slugger with the name John misspelled on the barrel. Without the photograph, who could watch the gray-whiskered man with no laces in his shoes rummage through his trailer and not wonder if his tale is too fantastic to be true?

This story first appeared in 1997.

But then John Malangone, with a funny look on his face, a mixture of pride in the thing he's holding and an eagerness to be rid of it, thrusts in front of you the picture, snapped on a sunny spring training day 32 years ago. You stare. No. It wasn't a dream. The old man hasn't gone mad. If it hadn't been for the horror, he really might have filled Yogi Berra's shoes. Look at the picture. Just look at it.

> *"Kid! Come over here. Wanna take your picture."*
> *"Who, me? You don't want my picture."*
> *"Come on! Gonna put you right between the two Hall of Fame catchers, Dickey and Cochrane. You're gonna be plastered all over the* Daily News.*"*
> *"The* Daily News? *Naw, get somebody else."*
> *"Somebody else? You crazy, rookie? You're gonna be a helluva star."*

How many of us possess a photograph of the very instant when our lives reached the top of the hill and then, with the click of the camera—*because* of the click of the camera—began their descent? Look closely at John Malangone, in the middle. It's 1955. He's 22. Touching his glove, anointing him, are the fingertips of perhaps the two greatest catchers in the history of baseball: Mickey Cochrane, on the left, a 51-year-old Yankees scout and camp instructor, and Bill Dickey, a 47-year-old Yankees coach. John has just homered in an intrasquad game. He's fresh from leading the winter league in Venezuela in home runs, RBIs and doubles. Casey Stengel has tabbed him "the probable successor to Yogi," even though Berra would be the Yankees' regular starting catcher for four more seasons.

John remembers the words the tall photographer uttered just before he took the picture. John remembers the panic spreading through his stomach as he squatted between Cochrane and Dickey, the fear that someone on his block in East Harlem would see this picture in the next day's paper and call the *Daily News* and tell what occurred on that summer evening 18 years before, insist that what John really deserved was a seat in a chair humming with a couple of thousand volts. John remembers everything, because memory is the whip he has used to flog himself for 60 years. . . .

Orlando Panarese was blond and he was bashful and he was handsome and he was seven, and when he and John trampolined on the bed they usually shared, they jumped so high they nearly banged their heads. It was perfect, having your best buddy be your uncle. Having your mom's little brother living just one floor up in a tenement on 114th Street, so your family was his family and all of you, aunts and uncles and cousins and grandparents, ended up on the roof with Uncle Duffy's pigeons every summer Sunday, playing checkers and eating linguini with red sauce bare-chested, if you were a boy, to save your mother from spending Monday scrubbing shirts. So you could float in and out of each other's apartments at any hour and end up in pj's pounding each other with pillows while Mom and Grandma rolled pasta or talked another cup of coffee to death. *Zi*, John called Orlando, shortening the Italian word for uncle. They would slip downstairs at sunrise, while Grandma Panarese dressed for church, and earn apples for her by helping the Italian fruit peddlers pry open their crates. "*Grazie*, Orlando. *Grazie*, John," she would say when they delivered the apples to her, bowing formally to the little boys.

They were upstairs talking, Mom and Grandma, that July evening in 1937. They couldn't keep their eyes on five- and seven-year-old-boys all day, could they? Eleven years had passed since Grandma had lost her first Orlando, her eight-year-old son who was tagging along with his older brothers to the movies when one of them fibbed, "Go home, Orlando, Mommy's calling you," and the little boy turned back to cross the street and was killed by a truck. A mother can't run scared every minute for 11 years, can she?

John found the broken umbrella rusting in the basement of his six-floor tenement. He and the boys on his block pulled off one of its metal spokes and lashed it, with rope, to a shorn-off broomstick handle. Excellent. A javelin. A new contest for the first-generation Italian-American children teeming on the streets of East Harlem. John took the javelin, paced down 114th Street and eyed his goal: the pile of sand the peddlers would shovel onto the wooden ramp leading into the stables next to John's apartment building, so their horses wouldn't slip in their own urine. The other boys stood in a group in front of the candy store and watched.

John reached back and threw himself, all of himself, into that javelin. Maybe it flew a little off the side of his hand, and maybe it went farther than anyone thought a boy his size could throw it. Every time he has seen it happen ever since—on the sides of water glasses, on cabinet doors, on outfield walls—he has squinted and tried to discern whether it was a misjudgment of his might or a flaw in technique. But he knew, as he watched the javelin arc, that he was in trouble, and he knew when he heard the boys gasp that it had hit someone, and he knew when he approached the tight circle of children and frantic adults and saw two small feet protruding—one sock of solid color and one sock striped—that it was Uncle Orlando. Because when he looked down at the ground, the other striped sock and the other solid one were on his own feet.

A boy turned to John. "You're in trouble," he said.

"Spell that name for me."
"Huh?"
"Your last name, kid. You pronounce it Mal-an-go-nee, right? Gotta make sure they spell it right when they run this picture. M . . . a . . . Is it two l's or one in Malangone?"
"Uh . . . yeah . . . two . . . two l's."

He remembers cringing that day as the photographer scribbled in his notepad. Another secret they were closing in on. Another secret that each line drive off his bat, each shotgun throw from his arm to rub out a runner stealing second was leading them closer and closer to discovering: The 22-year-old Yankees hotshot couldn't read or write. Oh, they would find out why, sure as the sunshine beating on his shoulders as he crouched between Cochrane and Dickey.

He had shoved it out of his mind since the day he had signed, but now, as the shutter clicked, he could smell it: the beginning of the end. The story of the lovable homegrown Italian boy laying siege to the position of the lovable, aging Italian Hall of Fame catcher, the story of a kid as strong as thunder and flakier than snow, able to awaken from a dead sleep in December and out-malaprop Berra, out-Yogi Yogi—you don't think the New York tabloid wretches, the chroniclers of the greatest dynasty in base-ball history, are going to crawl all over that? You don't think they're going to find out how his brain shut down because of the accident and how neither he nor all the letters and numbers he stared at could ever stay still after the *next* shock?

You can't figure on anything in life. You can't figure on a javelin flying through the air and hitting someone's skull, let alone your uncle's. And then, once it does, you can't figure on him pull-ing it out with his own hands, and, oh, thank God, standing up. And walking home with the help of his mother, barely bleeding because it's a puncture wound, and looking all right for a few days, *thankyouthankyouGod . . .* until the small red swelling appears. Nobody ever told John that the wound became infected and that Orlando was taken to a hospital and that he underwent surgery to relieve the swelling but that the infection kept spreading because the use of penicillin was still four years away; Jesus, it's so easy to hoodwink a five-year-old boy. Nobody told him anything, not even what all the commotion was upstairs in Grandma's apartment and why all the adults looked so sunken-eyed. They forgot all about John for a moment, and he wandered up the steps and through the door and into a room where he saw a box surrounded by white drapes and flowers. He stared at it, too short to see its freight. He moved closer, closer. He stepped up onto the kneeler. Orlando . . . ? God, he looked beautiful. Why was he sleeping there? *Zi, what's wrong? ZI, WAKE UP!*

That was how John learned what his right arm had done. That was when he screamed, and his right eardrum popped, and his tongue nearly went down his throat, and the corner of his mouth and his right hand went numb—for the first time. That was when he lost half of his hearing and, for nearly a year, every word of English he had learned. That was when Grandma burst into the room and found the catatonic boy and shrieked at God, "No, not this one too!" And rushed him to the room in her apartment that she had turned into a chapel and held him near the candles and the crucifix and the statues of St. Anthony and Mother Mary and

Baby Jesus, her fumbling fingers pouring olive oil into a small bowl
and dropping into it a piece of wool torn from mattress stuffing,
then striking a match to light the wool and warm the oil, and thrust-
ing her thumb into the liquid and using it to rub tiny signs of the
cross on the boy's forehead, his nose, his chin, his temples and
behind his ears, murmuring ancient words that had been passed
down to her, until her eyelids slowly sagged and a great yawning
fatigue overcame her, as it always did when she healed the old way.

"Shhhh. Don't say a word," they said to each other when the
boy finally fell asleep. "He's quiet now. Don't say a word about
any of this—ever—do you hear me? He's only five. He'll forget
everything if no one ever says a word."

Go back to the photograph. Perhaps you see it now: the un-
certainty in John's smile, in his eyes. Perhaps you see what John
sees when he looks at that picture today. "Half of that boy is missing," he says. "That's just a body there. That's just a shadow I was
casting. That's just a shell."

The police arrived at John's apartment after Orlando's death.
The five-year-old boy climbed out the back window and hid on
the fire escape until they were gone. He had evaded them, he
thought. *For now.* But then a kid on the street called him Killer.
A woman who saw her daughter talking to John cried, "Stay away
from him!" One of the Mafia members who ruled his block
slapped him on the back and said, "Ya got one under ya belt,
kid!"

And then no one saw him. The alleyways behind the tall tenements became his home. On his way to and from school he could
go for blocks scrambling over the tall mesh fences that separated
one building from the next, never seeing the sun except when he
darted over a cross street to the next alley. He could go for hours
hurling balls in the shadows at a clock he drew in chalk on an alley
wall, aiming first at 1 o'clock until he nailed it on the button, then
one by one around to 12, over and over and over, taming the arm
that had betrayed him. Then he would line up two dozen bottles,
hurling anything when his rubber ball had disintegrated—rotten
apples, oranges, stones—exulting silently when the bottles exploded

and the noise shattered off the walls. Soon he was turning his back on his target, spinning and blindly throwing, throwing, throwing. . . . When at last he grew weary, he would grab a stick and imagine that he was conducting an orchestra, sending waves of beautiful music swelling up the tenement walls.

When it snowed and the block was empty, the boy would emerge. The people would hear a relentless scraping noise, and when they peered out, the sidewalk up and down 114th Street between First and Second Avenue would be bare.

He risked exposure only in exchange for exhaustion. He would race to the coal yards three blocks away, and for a quarter, but not really for the quarter, he would take some malingerer's shovel and do the man's task all day. He would endlessly wax and polish the Mob's black Chryslers, long after they were already gleaming, in the alley behind their clubhouse. He went to the basement where the old paisanos made wine, and he hand-cranked the press until his arms screamed. He stood on three empty soda cases and pounded the speed bag in the Silver Star boxing club, just down the street from his apartment building. He mucked the peddlers' stables, wrung water from neighboring women's wet laundry with his thickening wrists, wrung so tightly he sometimes ripped the clothing, trying so hard to please everyone around him and to fatigue the creature into tongue-hanging silence.

The creature?

Yeah. You know. The thing. The hunchback, just behind John's shoulder. Can't you see it in the photograph? The one that could show up at any moment when John wasn't throwing or shoveling or mucking or wringing or punching. The beast he would suddenly hear laughing faintly and mumbling so softly that John had to lean to make out the words. *You. . . . You killer, you. . . . You know what you deserve. . . .* He would shut his eyes, clutch his head, cover his ears, and still he'd sense it, still he'd hear it. It looked like . . . yes, almost exactly like Quasimodo, the terrifying humped creature with half a sunken face whom John kept returning to the Cosmo Theater to stare at in *The Hunchback of Notre Dame* . . . only somehow the eyes and nose and mouth of the hunchback stalking John were his own.

His head would begin to throb. His throat would tighten; he couldn't swallow, he couldn't breathe! His right ear would pop and begin to ring, his throwing hand would go numb, the right edge of his mouth would curve up, his arms shiver, his equilibrium vanish, his vision tunnel and blur. And now, upon whatever surface his eyes fled to, he would see and hear the javelin arcing through the air, making that terrible swishing sound, and then the coffin, looming larger and larger as if he were a small boy again, stepping nearer and nearer to it, and then, Orlando's beautiful face inside it. And John's fist or his baseball bat would lash out at the image, and suddenly there was a hole in the wall or the cabinet or the wardrobe in his bedroom, and his mother was scurrying to find someone to patch it before his hot-tempered father came home.

"Why?" he would hear his father scream at his mother. "Why did you leave him alone that day? It's your fault!" But never, ever, was the subject mentioned when John was in the room. The boy might go two nights, three nights in a row without sleep, and when at last he dozed he would dream that he was running down 114th Street, racing against the javelin, reaching up to catch it before it landed, and then he would awaken, shouting "Orlando!" in a puddle of urine and sweat.

He knotted two dark socks together and tied them around his head, covering his ears, to keep out that maddening swishing sound whenever the wind blew, or whenever he tried to outrun the son of a bitch, all the way from East Harlem to Greenwich Village. . . .

Still mumbling. Still there.

Maybe he could drown the bastard. Maybe if he jumped into the Harlem River off the Willis Avenue Bridge and stayed underwater for one minute . . . two minutes. . . .

Still laughing. Still there.

Maybe if he stuck his grandmother's sewing needle into his throwing arm. . . .

He felt nothing. Still there.

Maybe if he careened down the ramp off the Triborough Bridge on a bicycle with no chain or brakes, he could shatter the hunchback.

He broke his leg.

Maybe he had to pinpoint the demon's location first. Maybe if he turned swiftly when he walked through snow, he could see footprints, the same way the police finally located and killed the Invisible Man in the next movie that obsessed John at the Cosmo. Maybe fabric would reveal the creature's whereabouts, as it did in the film. Maybe if John stood in front of a mirror nonchalantly and suddenly tossed one of his grandmother's black veils over his shoulder it would land on the demon's head and then John could whirl and throttle it. Maybe if he heaved a handful of his mother's baby powder over his shoulder. . . . No! Nothing! Damn him!

There were only two things to be done. Hurry to the arms of his mother, Josephine—she hugged him, soothed him without ever saying what she was soothing away and led him to her own mother, who would stop the pounding in his forehead and temples by rubbing them with warm olive oil. Or he could race to Mount Carmel church and go up into its tower to sit with the bells just like the hunchback did in the movie to escape his enemies. Inside the church where the demon couldn't pursue John, he would light a votive candle and pray feverishly, "Make him stop, God! Make him go away! Please, God, I'll do your work, I'll help people, please!"

He would give the shoes off his feet to a beggar. He planned to become a priest, choke the demon with the collar, but he couldn't even cut it as an altar boy. Instructions bewildered him; he just couldn't concentrate. He would turn the wrong way on the altar, forget what part of the Mass was coming next, spill the wine, exasperate the priest. It was the same story in school, where the letters and numbers swam, and he would end up in the back of the classroom, the perennial dope, lovable but hopeless.

No one could stay mad at him—except his father, the barber. Sylvester Malangone would come home and find his wife gone again, always upstairs with her mom; her guilt over her son's killing of her mother's son had turned her into Grandma's slave. Sylvester's jealous rage would begin to boil, and at the slightest excuse he would seize the thick barber's strap he kept on a hook and rip into his eldest son, John, knowing that the thumps and cries would bring his wife racing downstairs in tears, back where she belonged.

After the rat the beatings grew worse. John awoke to an earth-
quake one night when he was 10; his father heaved the mattress
right off the bed on which John and his brother, Sylvester Jr., were
sleeping, and lunged for a rat of terrifying size. Now John's dad
had the rodent where he wanted it, shrieking behind the radiator,
just enough space between the radiator's ribs to insert one of the
boys' bed slats and pin the rat against the wall. The shrieking grew
ghastly, almost human, and sweat erupted from the father's pores
as his two sons cowered behind him, but he drove the slat home
and blood spattered them, and the father swooned and cried out
and began to shake. He ended up in a straitjacket at Bellevue, and
when he came home a month later, his fury at John had grown
even larger.

Five decades would pass before John would learn that his
father, too, carried a terrible secret. Fifty years of silence and rage
until John learned about the day that his dad, then just a seven-
year-old boy, had been so happy to see his own mother coming
home from another long day at a sweatshop that he and his two
brothers had thrown a bear hug around her legs on the street, top-
pling her backward onto the jagged edges of a steel garbage can,
causing a wound that became infected, just like Orlando's, and
killed her. And John, when he finally heard the story, understood
instinctively that everything he had turned in on himself, his father had turned outward—upon John, the son who had also killed
a loved one accidentally.

The beatings stopped all at once when John was 15. His father
grabbed the strap one day, enraged at John's younger brother for a
change, after the boy had knocked the family's radio off the counter
and broken it, and cocked his arm behind his ear to let the boy have
it, when . . . *huh?* The barber yanked down, and yanked again, but
it was as if the strap were nailed to a ceiling beam. He looked over
his shoulder and saw John clutching the strap with one hand. "You
son of a bitch!" Sylvester Sr. shouted. "So *you* want it!" And he
yanked and yanked, until it dawned on him that his boy was a
5' 10", 195-pound man, arms and thighs like a stevedore's from all
the frantic shoveling and mucking and punching, and his strap would
remain where it was for all time if John so willed it.

The barber grew small before John's eyes. John let go of the strap. His father opened a window and flung the strap into the alley.

Sylvester Sr.'s eyes widened: Out the door John darted, returning in seconds and placing the strap back on its hook.

He needed the lashes. They made him feel good.

You can't see Paul Krichell. He was just a few feet out of the picture that day, wearing a proprietor's grin. "You make me proud, John," Krichell told him just after the *click*. It wouldn't be long now, the 72-year-old scout realized, until the press began pestering him for details of that improbable spring day in 1950 when he strolled onto the field at East Harlem's Jefferson Park in his sunglasses, straw hat and white cotton jacket, looking for someone else.

He had positioned himself on the first base line that day to assess a player from Ben Franklin High. Krichell was the man who had found Lou Gehrig, Charlie Keller, Red Rolfe, Phil Rizzuto, Whitey Ford and a fleet of others, a calm, assured gentleman who knew that everyone knew he was Krichell, the great Yankees scout.

He took no notice of John as the teenager finished laying the strip of lime down the leftfield line. John, academically ineligible, had never played on the team. He was in the hammer-and-nail class at Ben Franklin, the 1940s version of special ed, and served as a gofer for the varsity coach. "Wanna throw, Paulie?" John asked.

"Sure!" said Paulie Tiné.

The two boys had met six years before: Paulie with the disfigured face and John with the disfigured soul, clinging to each other with the static electricity of pain. Paulie was two years older, his cheeks ravaged by a case of acne so severe that John believed him when he claimed he had been burned in a fire. Alleys? Sounded good to Paulie. Baseball all day across the East River at Randall's Island, or on the field at Jefferson Park that was farthest from 114th Street, where no one would likely recognize them? Suited Paulie just fine. The moment that kids from John's block showed up, Paulie would scent his buddy's fear and say, "I'll race ya, John!" The moment girls started pointing at Paulie and shrieking, and hiding behind each other's backs, calling him the Mummy or the

Phantom of the Opera, John would say, "I'll race ya, Paulie!"
And lickety-split they were off, almost faster than shame, Paulie
a heartbeat ahead at first and then John pulling even as they
neared the 107th Street Pier and headed straight for the edge,
diving blindly into the East River—goners if there had been a
log or a boat below.

Has there ever been a friend so loyal as Paulie? When John
couldn't read a sign, Paulie lied, "Don't worry, John. I can't read
that either." When John threw a BB from deep left, Paulie pogoed
across the field, screaming, "Didja see that throw? *John Malangone!
What an arm!*" He was the admiring audience John had never had,
couldn't have—not after what happened when a cop talked him
into joining the Police Athletic League at 13 and he froze on the
mound in his first and only game, unable to throw a single pitch
for fear he would kill the batter. But even to Paulie, John never
told his secret.

They were throwing to each other for distance on an adja-
cent field when Krichell's hungry eyes roved. *What?* Did he just
see what he thought he just saw? One kid had just thrown the ball
from home plate and hit the leftfield fence, near the sign that said
368! Krichell's legs began to move.

"How old are you kid?" Krichell asked.

"Seventeen," replied John.

"Where do you play?"

John hesitated. Loaded question.

"Anyplace!" Paulie piped.

"Come to Yankee Stadium tomorrow. We're having a tryout."

"How do I get there?" asked John.

Krichell's eyebrows took a slow walk. An East Harlem teenage boy who didn't know where the Stadium was? What hole had
this kid been hiding in? "What's your address, kid? We'll pick
you up."

The tryouts had been going on for weeks, the legion of young
prospects already whittled from hundreds to 40, when John entered the Stadium believing he was about to participate in a
distance-throwing contest. The Yankees' coaches blinked at the
lefthander's glove, one of Paulie's that John had been jamming onto

the wrong hand for years, and gave him a righthander's mitt. The first day John sat the entire practice game with Paulie at his side. The second day he was sent to the mound in the seventh. For three scoreless innings he threw blurs. As the Yankee brass stood to leave in the bottom of the ninth, he approached the batter's box. The first pitch came in . . . and went out, ricocheting in the upper deck's empty seats, whack, whack, whack.

"What do you think about playing pro ball?" Krichell asked moments later.

"Sure!" crowed Paulie.

Half the block was out on 114th Street three days later, surrounding the big black car, as word went from window to window: The Yankees are here. *What for?* To sign Malangone. *Malangone?*

Mark this sentence with your thumb. Go back to the photograph. Take a look at the *ain't-he-hot-stuff?* look on Cochrane's face. Priceless. See, Mickey smelled smoke, but he had no idea he was crouching beside a volcano. Just smoke, because he knew the whiff of pain and anxiety well. He had suffered a nervous breakdown in 1936, lost a son in World War II. Sure, this kid he was tutoring, Malangone, was an original—first player Mickey had ever seen run to the outfield during dead time and hit fungoes to himself. But when it was quiet and the kid was unaware, gazing into space, Mickey saw fear and mistook its source. "You're gonna make it," he kept reassuring John. "You're locked in. Stop worrying. If not this year, next year for sure."

Hell's bells, the kid had the goods. "Stronger than a bull," recalls Johnny Blanchard, one of John's catching rivals in the Yankees' farm system. "A rifle arm. Power out the ying-yang. He was a big Yogi Berra."

For the first two years the Yanks hid John on local sandlot teams, converting him from a pitcher to a catcher to take advantage of his stick, watching with a wary eye as he piled up MVP trophies in weeklong tournaments. They were fearful it would be discovered that they had signed him before he had graduated, but were unable to send him away to one of their farm teams; he would

keep freezing on the train platform when it came time to leave his
mother's arms, his grandma's healing fingers. Finally, in the spring
of 1952, just shy of John's 20th birthday, Paulie poured him onto
a bus and he went to Trois Rivieres in the Canadian Provincial
League.

"Listen up, men!" Trois Rivieres manager Frank Novosel
barked to his team as their bus rolled through Montreal, hours after
he had made his final cut. "The guys on this bus are the guys who've
made the ball club. This is the group that's going all the way. You
got it? There's no turning back now, men! No turning back!"

And suddenly, with those words, John felt the shivers and the
sweats again, the ringing and mumbling in his ear, the choking in
his throat, the numbness in his throwing hand. The hunchback had
crossed the border! He rose, struggling to breathe—no, not here,
on a moving bus with nowhere to run. He stumbled to the front.
He knew what happened when he felt trapped.

It was the same feeling he had coming out of anesthesia after
a double hernia operation just a few years before, when he reached
down and felt the surgeon's clips and thick bandages all over his
groin and abdomen and suddenly became sure they were the beast's
hairy hands and fingernails. He screamed and ripped open the entire incision, trying to tear the creature from his groin, then reached
up and tore at his face. A nurse rushed through the door and shrieked:
blood was everywhere. He hurled her across the room. Two orderlies charged in. Two orderlies flew out. It took six men to straitjacket
him, and he lost so much blood that he nearly died.

And now his new teammates and the Trois Rivers bus driver
blinked at him, unaware of such terms as *panic attack* and *post-
traumatic stress disorder;* in 1952 there were only lunatics and
maniacs. "I need a church!" John panted.

"What're we here for?" the bussie grunted. "To play or pray?"

"Take him to a church!" growled Novosel. "When *you* can
hit like him, we'll go where *you* want to go."

A few turns, a few blocks, and the most glorious sight in John's
life appeared: Montreal's huge cathedral, St. Joseph's Oratory.
Between games, for the rest of the season, he was at church, praying and holding holy oil over the candles he had lit and rubbing it

where Grandma had. He hit .302 with 17 home runs and 90 RBIs that season. The fans loved him. One day he might be missing a sock, the next a belt, then a hat. He played without shoelaces. "My feet are tight," he told the skipper. Truth was, he couldn't concentrate enough to tie a bow.

Just before the team's last game, the manager pulled him aside. "The Yankees have called you up for four days," said Novosel. "You probably won't get to play, but you'll get a taste of the big leagues. Then you're going to Venezuela for winter ball. Congratulations!"

"Skip, can't I stay here with you?"

"Are you crazy, son?"

The picture's a damn lie, and Bill Dickey knows it. Go back and look—you couldn't have caught it on the first glance or the second. Sure, Dickey's smiling, but it's only for form's sake. He's smiling at nothing. He isn't looking at the kid.

Dickey didn't care what Stengel or Cochrane thought, or how many four-baggers John hit. He didn't give a flip that John was fresh from two years in the Army, where he'd won a medal for saving a drowning soldier. He didn't give a damn that the glove on John's left hand was given to him four days earlier by Berra himself. Nobody with a head like Malangone's was going to inhabit the soil behind the plate that Dickey, for 17 years with the Yankees, had made holy.

And he was right. He just didn't know how right until that photo hit page 66 of the *Daily News* on February 23, 1955—Malangone misspelled with two l's in the caption beneath it—jangling John's telephone with calls from relatives, friends, Louisville Slugger and Bazooka, and stirring his darkest fear: A locker in The House That Ruth Built was awaiting him, and with it, a chair just up the river at Sing Sing.

Suddenly the disintegration began, and no one in Yankee management could figure out why. So innocently, it started. "Just sign your name here," said the Louisville Slugger representative, handing John a form. "We'll use that signature on your new line of bats." John froze, uncertain how to spell even his first name,

terrified that the world would learn he was illiterate. He stalled,
begged Paulie to jump on a plane to St. Petersburg to sign for
him, but a snowstorm in New York had canceled all flights, and
besides, Paulie had already bailed him out that spring, driving to
Tennessee to retrieve John when he misread the road signs on the
way from New York to Florida and got lost for three days. *Jhon*,
he finally scrawled on the Slugger form. Someone at the company
noticed at the last minute and tried to etch over it, but his teammates snickered and Yankee brass scowled when the bungled bats
appeared. John snickered too. That was always the best way to
cover his confusion: Giggle, play the buffoon, *act* crazy, man, so
no one suspects you're *going* crazy!

He came to the plate in an intrasquad game brandishing a
rake instead of a bat. He noticed a motorboat with keys in the
ignition, jumped in and gunned it for a joyride, forgetting to untie
the rope. The dock and the boat both splintered. The Yankees' front
office got a call.

John bought a motorcycle. He wrecked it one day later. In
retaliation for a prank, he cackled and hurled oranges at his teammates in the Yankees' hotel, splattering seeds and juice, shatter-
ing an exit sign. "I did it, Skipper," John volunteered at the next
morning's team meeting.

"Why, John?" asked Casey Stengel.

"I was warming up, Skipper."

"Yeah?" said Casey, rolling his eyes. "Who was your catcher?"

On the golf course just outside the hotel, John noticed a pond
full of golf balls. He filched a dozen pillowcases and filled them
with balls, placing them in the lobby beside the baskets of oranges
and grapefruits for the guests. Stengel got another belligerent call.
Finally, a day passed without trouble, and John mock-swooned in
relief onto his roommate's bed. A slat splintered in half and tore
right through the roommate's expensive suitcase, and the roomie
went straight to the brass. What more did John have to do to make
the Yankees see what he saw when he looked in the mirror?

Sooner or later, Dickey knew, Stengel and the front office had
to see what he saw: that the catcher was the nerve center of a ball
game, and that you couldn't have a guy there, no matter how

powerful his arm or catcherlike his body, who flashed signs that were incomprehensible to his pitchers.

John's teammates—the nonpitchers, at least—loved to gather around him in lounge chairs beneath the stars that spring and re-enact his latest fiasco. They crooned the song they always crooned to guys about to walk the plank—*Dear John . . . I sent your saddle home*—and were agog that day after day, by sheer dint of talent, his saddle remained right where it was. They marveled at Malangonese, a language in which an RBI might be an IBM, and treading water was *threading* water. The great Joe DiMaggio, John addressed as Charley. Correcting him was pointless. "O.K., tank you," John would say in his thick Noo Yawk accent. "I got it now. Got it down to a *teeth.*"

One evening during that pivotal spring of '55, the players were buzzing about the change that had come over pitching coach Phil Page. "Didn't you hear what happened?" a player told John. "He killed his friend over the winter in a hunting accident."

John blanched. Then came the cold sweat, the hair rising from his flesh. He lurched away from the group, hesitated and then bolted for Page's room. Finally, for the first time in his life, he was going to tell someone his secret. Finally there was someone who would understand, someone whom John could perhaps even help. He rapped on the coach's door. Page opened it. John's mouth opened. Nothing came out.

"What do you want?" the coach demanded.

"Maybe I . . ." John stammered. "Maybe I can help you."

Page's eyes narrowed. The buffoon, he thought, was mocking him. "You?" he said. "You can't help yourself." He shut the door, and the words that might have saved John never left their vault.

Camp broke. The confounded Yankee chiefs assigned John to the Double A Birmingham Barons. The Barons had a new man-ager. His name was Phil Page. A few days later, as the Barons played their way from Florida to Alabama in a string of exhibi-tions, John was sitting in the stands an hour before a game and needed to use the rest room. Confused by the lettering on the doors, he waited and watched. A door opened. A woman emerged. John headed through the other door, not realizing that the ladies' room had two doors. A woman screamed. Page refused to believe it was an honest mistake.

Only a couple of weeks had passed since the click of the camera, and now John and his Mercury were lost on the road again, in search of the Class B Tars in Norfolk, Virginia. A place where he and the hunchback could hit .326 without running the risk of being called up to Yankee Stadium.

It grows more and more unnerving, the idyllic photograph—doesn't it? A few weeks later John walked into a doctor's office in Norfolk. "My nerves are bad," he told the physician. "I think too much."

"Take off your clothes," the doctor told him. "I'll be right back." While the doctor was gone, John fled. For four years, from Norfolk to Portsmouth to Montgomery to Knoxville to Amarillo to Charlotte to Winston-Salem and back to Knoxville, he fled. Every city, his ritual was the same. First, he would search for a church, a place to drop a 50 and run the whole rack of candles. Second, he would find lodging, preferably in a migrant worker's shack on a farm a few miles from his teammates, so they wouldn't know what happened when he chanced to see an umbrella or a pair of striped socks, so they wouldn't notice him roaming the roads at night gathering rocks to throw at poles and trees. Then he would look for a day job simonizing cars or hauling blocks of ice or collecting golf balls at a driving range, anything to demolish dead time. Dead time was killer time; why was baseball so riddled with it? He would count mosquitoes during games, do push-ups, run sprints, squeeze his crucifix, rattle off Hail Marys, do anything to stave off another flashback, meanwhile losing all track of minor things such as strikes, balls, outs, base runners, signals, score. *You don't tag up with two outs, Nuts 'n Bolts, you run on anything! Get your head in the goddam game!* He was cut from the team in mid-game in Winston-Salem—what's a manager to do with a guy who rips two straight doubles and gets picked off both times?

He couldn't possibly explain it to anyone, not even himself. Each time he slunk out of the office of another furious manager, he felt humiliated . . . and *relieved.* Relieved because when he went a week or two without punishment his guilt would eat at him like acid; he was cheating, getting away with something he didn't deserve. And yet he lived in dread of pushing the Yankee brass too far, of being separated once and for all from the game he loved, from the rickety minor league clubhouses and stadiums where he was so popular.

For years he tiptoed this precarious ledge between stardom and banishment. One night he would leave a gaping hole in Norfolk's centerfield fence, attempting to snag a fly ball in his Mercury at 40 mph. The next night he would batter the plywood-bandaged wall with line drives. He would go AWOL for two weeks. He would hit .356 at Winston-Salem. He would ground out and continue running up the rightfield line, all the way to the fence, and smash it with his fist. No one ever dreamed that he was swinging at a flickering image of a javelin, a coffin, a child's face.

He lived for those weeks when Paulie would join him. In between he befriended the old black groundskeepers and locker room janitors in all those Southern towns, helping them to rake the field, dig mud from cleats, scrub the floor. They too were outcasts, and they never tried to get too close. In '57 he married a knockout from East Harlem named Rosemary Chique, whom he had met—where else?—in a church. He turned everything over to her: checkbook, money and responsibility for the children they would have. Even when things were great, when it was just the two of them and her skin on his skin felt like heaven's grace, the mumbling might start: *What about Orlando? You're alive right now, too alive, but he's just dust beneath the ground.* John would have to turn and roll away, the life all gone from him.

And then in the spring of '59, still without a single big league at-bat, his career was over. It ended in a flash when he wiped out his third motorcycle, broke his leg and knew that he had finally run out of ways to make absolutely certain that he failed.

Thirty-two years walked by. The photograph remained forever young, hanging on a wall in the house John and Rosemary bought in Little Ferry, New Jersey, right across the street from St. Margaret's church. But everything else changed.

Paulie was shot on the street by a mugger and died on the operating table, calling John's name. John stood on the 107th Street Pier and screamed back Paulie's.

John's father died of lung fibrosis. "You never forgot, did you, John?" the old man said just before he expired, and the two of them cried. But they never spoke of *what* John never forgot.

Rosemary bore John five children through their on-again, off-again marriage, but he was afraid to hold them or play with them, afraid he would hurt them and lose them . . . and so, of course, for long periods of time, he did. He always seemed to be gone, working two full-time jobs, repairing and installing New York City fire hydrants from dawn till midafternoon, running to his mother's house in the Bronx for an hour and then off to his night job as a mechanic in Sears' automotive department. They called him the Santa Claus of Sears, he gave away so many repair jobs, still hoping against hope to convince God to call off the beast. But, of course, John needed the beast, so who could say that any of its visits came without a whistle from somewhere deep inside John?

He turned to drinking and totaled five cars, but he and the demon always walked away. When his despair, at last, was more than the candle racks at St. Margaret's could bear, he took it to a therapist in the early 1980s. He spoke of grief, of anxiety, of the ticket to the bigs that he had torn to bits, of everything but the hunchback and the secret. "You're reminiscing too much," the therapist told him. "You need to get rid of all those trophies, plaques and pictures."

He began the destruction with sledgehammer blows of his bat, but that was too impersonal, too swift. He needed to involve the killer that hung from his right shoulder; he needed to make sure he was still in command of it. The children playing at Moonachie Park in northern New Jersey kept looking at each other and shaking their heads. Day after day, a gray-whiskered man wearing a wool pullover hat in the dead of summer because of what the wind did inside his ear, wearing a coat because the warmth took him back to his grandmother's candles, would set up a table in front of home plate and place a trophy on it. Then he would lay cobblestones to steady the trophy and blocks of wood to shield all of it

but the metal figurine. He would walk 30 or 40 strides away with
a bucket of balls. Only the finest, most accurate 55-year-old arm
in the country could hit the tiny target from that distance. Only
John Malangone could nail his past right on the head.

There's no need to leave you, dry-mouthed, on that ball field,
because that's not how the story ends. On a February day in 1991,
a 53-year-old man from Manhattan named Ron Weiss got directions to the Sears in Paramus, New Jersey, where John worked.
Ron's son had just been cut from his school baseball team. Ron's
life had just been shaken by his retirement after 30 years as a phys-
ed teacher and coach. Ron's heart was still racked by regret that
he had never taken a shot at the big leagues. And the one shiny
thing that he kept clutching was a compliment from a teammate
on a sandlot team he had played for in 1965, an anvil-armed power
hitter who had told Ron that his infield play reminded him of a
couple of guys he had rubbed elbows with a few years back, a
couple of guys named Tony Kubek and Bobby Richardson.

Ron ignored John's reluctance. Ron kept coming back, asking John to turn his son into a ballplayer, asking John to be a friend.
"You don't know who I am," John finally said. "You can't trust
me with your son."

"Why not?"

Perhaps it was because Ron was virtually a stranger. Perhaps
it was because of Ron's childlike trust. How do you figure that after
a lifetime of holding it in, a guy whom John had given an offhand
attaboy 26 years earlier would be the one to whom he would finally spill his secret? The javelin, the coffin, the demon, everything. And mercy, Ron didn't recoil, not an inch.

They went together to John's mother. The 80-year-old woman
began to sob when Ron spoke Orlando's name. "You're gonna get
him sick!" she told the stranger.

"Mom," said John, "I've been sick for a long time." She cried
some more, and they talked through their tears and their shudders for hours. When they finished, John wanted to dance.

He and Ron took another trip, to the Manhattan Bureau of
Records. They asked for the death certificate of Orlando Panarese,

and John nearly vomited as he waited to see if the word after *Cause of Death* was *Murder*. The clerk handed Ron the medical examiner's report. Ron cleared his throat and read: "I further certify that I have viewed said body and from Partial Autopsy and evidence, that . . . the chief and determining cause of his death was Brain Abscess following perforating fracture of the scalp, skull and brain: that the contributing causes were Accidental." John hugged Ron. John wept.

He needed to tell someone from the Yankees his secret. He tracked down Johnny Blanchard at the Plaza Hotel in Manhattan, where Blanchard had gone to sign autographs. John told him everything. "I was paralyzed," says Blanchard.

A week without the hunchback passed, then another. The damnedest craving came over John. "Ron," he said, "ya know what I wanna do now? I wanna play ball. Play ball with a clear mind, for the first time in my life. C'mon, let's join a team."

John squeezed hand grips to bring back the wrists. He swam laps at the Y. He spent hours taking cuts in batting cages and playing catch with Ron's son. John pitched and Ron played second base in a New Jersey league for men over 40. By 1994 they found themselves in Florida, playing in the Roy Hobbs World Series. John won two games on the mound and singled home Ron for the run that won the national title for the New Jersey Wonderboys.

John lives in a trailer today, retired from his two jobs and separated from his wife, spending his days fixing cars for friends, playing ball with three or four teenagers whom he has taken under his wing to make sure they never give up, and learning, with Ron's help, how to read. "Symphonics," John calls their method.

Rescued? John almost thought so, but in truth, he had only reached a reef where the rescue might *begin*. One Sunday morning last March, on opening day of the 1997 over-40 season, Ron miscalculated the power of guilt. He gave John a few articles he had clipped: one about a Houston Oilers defensive lineman who killed himself with a shotgun in 1993 just moments after losing control of his car and causing a crash that killed his best friend. The other about a girl whose face was impaled by a javelin at a high school track practice.

You know what happened next. John couldn't play ball for three months, so fierce was the volcano, but then he staged another comeback on a Sunday three months ago. The oldest pitcher in the league took the hill for the Bergen Rocks and twirled a four-hitter against the Bergen Cardinals for a 14–1 win, and he was so damned excited each time he returned to the dugout, so full of hope—honest-to-God 65-year-old half-scared-to-death hope—you just wished to hell someone had been there to take a picture.

Ali and His Entourage

A round Muhammad Ali, all was decay. Mildewed tongues of insulation poked through gaps in the ceiling; flaking cankers pocked the painted walls. On the floor lay rotting scraps of carpet.

He was cloaked in black. Black street shoes, black socks, black pants, black short-sleeved shirt. He threw a punch, and in the small town's abandoned boxing gym, the rusting chain between the heavy bag and the ceiling rocked and creaked.

Slowly, at first, his feet began to dance around the bag. His left hand flicked a pair of jabs, and then a right cross and a left hook, too, recalled the ritual of butterfly and bee. The dance quickened. Black sunglasses flew from his pocket as he gathered speed, black shirttail flapped free, black heavy bag rocked and creaked. Black street shoes scuffed faster and faster across black moldering tiles: Yeah, Lawd, champ can still float, champ can still sting! He whirled, jabbed, feinted, let his feet fly into a shuffle. "How's that for a sick man?" he shouted.

He did it for a second three-minute round, then a third. "Time!" I shouted at the end of each one as the second hand swept past the 12 on the wristwatch he had handed to me. And then,

This story first appeared in 1988.

24

gradually, his shoulders began to slump, his hands to drop. The tap and thud of leather soles and leather gloves began to miss a quarter-beat . . . half-beat . . . whole. Ali stopped and sucked air. The dance was over.

He undid the gloves, tucked in the black shirt, reached reflexively for the black comb. On stiff legs he walked toward the door. Outside, under the sun, the afternoon stopped. Every movement he made now was infinitely patient and slow. Feeling . . . in . . . his . . . pocket . . . for . . . his . . . key. . . . Slipping . . . it . . . into . . . the . . . car . . . lock. . . . Bending . . . and . . . sliding . . . behind . . . the . . . wheel. . . . Turning . . . on . . . the . . . ignition . . . and . . . shifting . . . into . . . gear. . . . Three months had passed, he said, since he had last taken the medicine the doctor told him to take four times a day.

One hand lightly touched the bottom of the wheel as he drove; his clouded eyes narrowed to a squint. His head tilted back, and the warm sunlight trickled down his puffy cheeks. Ahead, trees smudged against sky and farmland; the glinting asphalt dipped and curved, a black ribbon of molasses.

He entered the long driveway of his farm, parked and left the car. He led me into a barn. On the floor, leaning against the walls, were paintings and photographs of him in his prime, eyes keen, arms thrust up in triumph, surrounded by the cluster of people he took around the world with him.

He looked closer and noticed it. Across his face in every picture were streaks of bird dung. He glanced up toward the pigeons in the rafters. No malice, no emotion at all flickered in his eyes. Silently, one by one, he turned the pictures to the wall.

Outside, he stood motionless and moved his eyes across his farm. He spoke from his throat, without moving his lips. I had to ask him to repeat it. "I had the world," he said, "and it wasn't nothin'." He paused and pointed. "Look now. . . ."

Black blobs of cows slumbering in the pasture, trees swishing slowly, as if under water rather than sky. Merry-go-rounds, sliding boards and swings near the house, but no giggles, no squeals. No children.

"What happened to the circus?" I asked.

He was staring at the slowly swishing trees, listening to the
breeze sift leaves and make a lulling sound like water running over
the rocks of a distant stream. He didn't seem to hear.

And I said again, "What happened to the circus?"

The Doctor

*A man of infinite variety. Medical doctor, jazz connoisseur,
sports figure, confidant of the great.*
            —Excerpt from Ferdie Pacheco's publicity brochure

"This is a painting of myself when I was thirty and living alone
and messing around with a German woman who loved it when there
was sweat and paint all over me . . . and this is a screenplay that
I've just cut down from a hundred eighty-five pages to a hundred
thirty-five and this one here is a seven hundred fifty–page epic
novel, a very serious look at the immigrant experience in Tampa
. . . and this is a painting I did of Sherman's March—that stream
of blue is the Union soldiers—and that one is a screenplay I just
finished about two Cubans who steal a Russian torpedo boat, and
a crazy Jewish lawyer—Jerry Lewis is going to play the part and
direct it—picks them up in a boat. . . ."

In one way, Ferdie Pacheco was just like his former patient
Muhammad Ali: He needed laughter and applause. He led people
to each of his paintings, lithographs, cartoons and manuscripts the
way Ali once led them to continents to watch him talk and fight.
Both worked on canvas: Ali, when his was not near to dance
on, used parlor magic tricks to make eyes go bright and wide;
Pacheco, when his was not near to dab on, told long tales and
jokes, dominating a dinner party, from escargots to espresso, with
his worldliness and wit.

In another way, they were not alike at all. Ali lived for the
moment and acted as he felt, with disregard for the cord between
action and consequence. This allured the doctor, whose mind
teemed with consequence before he chose his action. "In an over-
complicated society," he says, "Ali was a simple, happy man."

Twenty-five years ago Pacheco was a ghetto doctor in Miami. Today he can be found in his home, white shorts and paint-smeared white smock covering his torso, blue Civil War infantryman's cap atop his head, stereo blaring Big Band jazz, telephone ringing with calls from agents, reporters and TV executives as he barefoots back and forth, brushing blue on three different canvases and discoursing, for anyone who will listen, upon the plot twist he has just hatched for Chapter 16 of his latest novel. He receives a six-figure salary from NBC for commenting on fights, has quit medicine, has become a painter whose works sell for as much as $40,000 and has completed 600 pen-and-ink drawings converted into lithographs, six books (two of which have been published) eight screenplays (four of which have sold) and a play that may soon be performed in London. He has also formed a Florida-based film production company and appeared across the country as a speaker. "But on my tombstone," he says, "it will say 'Muhammad Ali's doctor.' It's like being gynecologist to the queen."

In our time, will we see another comet that burns so long and streaks so fast, and whose tail has room for so many riders? "The entourage," some called the unusual collection of passengers who took the ride; the traveling circus, the hangers-on, others called it. "These people are like a little town for Ali," his manager, Herbert Muhammad, once said. "He is the sheriff, the judge, the mayor and the treasurer." Most were street people, thrown together on a lonely mountaintop in Pennsylvania where Ali built his training camp, until they burst upon the big cities for his fights. They bickered with each other over who would do what task for Ali, fist-fought with each other at his instigation—two of them once even drew guns. And they hugged and danced with each other, sat for hours talking around the long wooden dinner table, played cards and made midnight raids on the refrigerator together. A family.

Because they were there for Ali, he never had to worry about dirty underwear or water bills or grocery-shopping; he could remain an innocent. Because Ali was there for them, they could be mothers and fathers to the earth's most extraordinary child.

For a decade and a half he held them together, took them to the Philippines, Malaysia, Zaire, Europe and the Orient, their lives accelerating as his did, slowing when his did, too. But among them one was different, the one who obeyed the law of consequence. Ferdie Pacheco ejected while the comet still had momentum, and made a missile of himself.

"I had an overwhelming urge to create," he says. On napkins, tablecloths, anything, anywhere. His wife cried "Help me!" when she was delivering their child. He said, "Not now"—he was busy drawing her in stirrups.

Few knew him in the early Ali days: What reason was there to consult the doctor when Ali was young, physically unflawed and all-but-unhittable? The son of Spanish immigrants, Pacheco had established a general practice in Miami's black Overtown district and become a regular at Miami Beach boxing matches, where he met corner man Angelo Dundee and began to treat Dundee's boxers for free. One day, a patient named Cassius Clay came to him. Pacheco became part of the entourage.

"It satisfied my Iberian sense of tragedy and drama," he says, "my need to be in the middle of a situation where life and death are in the balance, and part of it is in your hands. Most people go out of their way to explain that they don't need the spotlight. I see nothing wrong with it.

"Medicine—you do it so long, it's not a high-wire act without a net anymore. At big Ali fights, you got the feeling you had on a first date with a beauty queen. I'd scream like a banshee. It was like taking a vacation from life."

The first signal of decline was in Ali's hands. Pacheco began injecting them with novocaine before fights, and the ride went on. Then the reflexes slowed, the beatings began, the media started to question the doctor. And the world began to learn how much the doctor loved to talk. Style, poise and communication skills had become the weaponry in the land that Ali conquered: A member of the king's court who could verbalize—not in street verse, as several members could, but in the tongue the mass markets cried for—and foresee consequence as well, could share Ali's opportunities without sharing his fate. The slower Ali spoke, the more frequently spoke the doctor.

The doctor looked ahead and listened, heard the crowd's roar fading, the espresso conversation sobering. His recommendation that Ali quit met deaf ears. The same trait that drew him to Ali began to push him away.

He mulled his dilemma. Leave and risk being called a traitor? Or stay and chance partial responsibility for lifelong damage to a patient who ignored his advice?

Pacheco followed his logic. He wrote Ali a letter explaining that cells in Ali's kidneys were disintegrating, then parted ways with him and created laughter and applause on his own. Ali followed his feelings and walked a different path.

Today the ex-fighter turns dung-streaked canvases to the wall, the ex-doctor covers his wall with new canvases. In his studio, Pacheco shakes his head. "I feel sorry for Ali," he says, "but I'm fatalistic. If he hadn't had a chance to get out, I'd feel incredibly sad. But he had his chance. He chose to go on. When I see him at fights now, there's no grudge. He says, 'Doc, I made you famous.' And I say, 'Muhammad, you're absolutely right.'"

The Facilitator

What if a demon crept after you one day or night in your loneliest solitude and said to you: "This life, as you live it now and have lived it, you will have to live again and again, times without number; and there will be nothing new in it, but every pain and every joy and every thought and sigh and all the unspeakably small and great in your life must return to you.... The eternal hourglass of existence will be turned again and again—and you with it, you dust of dust!" Would you not throw yourself down and gnash your teeth and curse the demon who thus spoke?

—Friedrich Nietzsche

Warm Vegas night air washed through the '76 Cadillac convertible. "We had fun, mister," said the driver. "We lived, mister. Every day was history. Millionaires would've paid to do what I did. To be near *him*."

He fell silent for a few blocks. The lunacy of lightbulbs glinted off his glasses and his diamond-studded heavyweight championship ring. "When I was a little boy, I used to watch airplanes in the sky until they became a dot, and then until you couldn't even see the dot. I wanted to go everywhere, do everything. Well, I did. Europe, Africa, the Far East, I saw it all. He was pilot, I was navigating. Hell, yes. The most exciting days of my life. Every day, I think about them. We were kids together, having fun. He was my best friend. I think I might have been his."

The car stopped at an intersection. A woman, thick in the thighs and heavy with makeup, walked across the beam of his headlights. His eyes didn't flicker. Frantically, hopelessly, the blinking lightbulbs chased each other around and around the borders of the casino marquees.

"You could feel it all around you, the energy flow," he said. His foot pressed the accelerator, his shoulders rested back against the seat. "When you're with someone dynamic, goddam, it reflects on you. You felt: Let's go do it. I met presidents and emperors and kings and queens and killers, traveling with him. Super Bowls, World Series, hockey, basketball championships I saw. I was big in the discos, Xenon, Studio 54. There was myself, Wilt Chamberlain and Joe Namath: the major league of bachelors."

Quiet again. The traffic light pooled red upon the long white hood. Dead of summer, down season in Vegas. The click of the turn signal filled the car. Then the *click-click-click* of a cocktail waitress, high-heeled and late for work. He peered into the neon-shattered night. "What could I find out there tonight?" he asked. "A girl more beautiful than I've been with? A girl more caring than I've been with? What would she tell me I haven't heard before? What's left that could impress me? What's left I haven't done or seen? It burnt me out, I tell you. It burnt me out for life. . . ."

Gene Kilroy had no title. Everyone just knew: He was the Facilitator. When Ali wanted a new Rolls-Royce, Kilroy facilitated it. When he wanted to buy land to build a training camp, Kilroy facilitated it. When a pipe burst in the training camp or a hose burst in the Rolls, when Marlon Brando or Liza Minnelli wanted to meet Ali, or Ali wanted to donate $100,000 to save an old folks' home, Kilroy facilitated it.

At hotels he usually stayed in a bedroom that was part of Ali's suite. As soon as they entered a city, he collected a list of the best doctors, in case of an emergency. He reached for the ever-ringing phone, decided who was worthy of a visit to the throne room. He worried himself into a 10-Maalox-a-day habit, facilitating. "Ulcer," he said. "You love someone, you worry. Watching him get hit during the Holmes fight, I bled like a pig—I was throwing it up in the dressing room. And all the problems before a fight. It was like having a show horse you had to protect, and all the people wanted to hitch him to a buggy for a ride through Central Park."

The trouble with facilitating was that it left no mark, no KILROY WAS HERE. He has covered the walls of his rec room with 50 Ali photos. He reminisces every day. He watches videos of old Ali interviews he helped facilitate, and sometimes tears fill his eyes. "I wish I had a kid I could tell," he said. And then, his voice going from soft to gruff: "I'll get married when I find a woman who greets me at the door the way my dogs do."

The Vegas casinos, they knew what Kilroy might be worth. All those contacts around the world, all those celebrities who had slipped into the dressing room on a nod from the Facilitator: perfect qualifications for a casino host. First the Dunes hired him, then the Tropicana and now the Golden Nugget.

Each day he weaves between blackjack tables and roulette wheels, past slot machines and craps tables, nodding to dealers, smiling at bouncers, slapping regulars on the back, dispensing complimentary dinners and rooms to high rollers and "How are ya, hon?" to cocktail waitresses. He no longer gambles: All the lust for action is gone. All that remains is the love of arranging a favor, of helping other members of Ali's old "family" when they hit hard times, of facilitating someone else's wants now that his are gone.

"As you know, I was all over the world with Ali," he said, leading a multimillionaire into one of the Golden Nugget's suites.

"I got the royal gold-carpet treatment everywhere. But this"—he swept his arm across the room—"solidifies the epitome of luxury. Look. Your Jacuzzi. Your sauna." Again and again his beeper would sound, and he would be connected with another wealthy client. "Sure, I'll have our limo pick you up at the airport. . . .Your line of credit is all set, a hundred thousand dollars."

Whenever Ali comes to Vegas to see a fight, he will mix with high rollers at Kilroy's request or sign a couple of dozen boxing gloves, a stack of a hundred photographs, mementos Kilroy passes out to favored clients. In his world, Ali souvenirs are currency. "One man was so proud of the things I'd given him," he said, "that when he died, he was buried with his Ali picture and boxing gloves. I can give people their dreams."

But sometimes he feels helpless. How can he facilitate away Ali's great fatigue with life—when he, too, feels sated and weary? "I remember one day not long ago when he was signing autographs, and I was standing next to him. We heard someone say, 'Look at Ali, he's a junkie.' Muhammad's eyes get kind of glassy sometimes now, you know. I wanted to choke the guy. But Ali nudged me and kind of smiled. God, I hope he wins this last fight. . . ."

On an impulse he picked up the phone and dialed Ali's number. "Hello, it's Gene. . . . You've been out walking, huh? I wish I could walk with you. . . . I can just barely hear you. I said, I wish I could walk with you. . . . It's good you're walking; you'll feel a lot better. . . . Hey, wouldn't it be nice to have a reunion at Deer Lake? Get everybody together—Sarria, you, me, Bundini, Pat, Lana. Get Lana to cook a roast, potatoes, gravy, everything. Wouldn't it be? . . . No, not bring back old memories. Bring back *great* memories. . . . Yeah. . . . O.K., well, get some rest. See you, champ. . . ."

He hung up the phone and stared at the wall. He glanced at his watch. Another day was nearly finished, a day of facilitating rooms and meals and money for men who still had the appetite, and he knew what he would do with the night. "I could call and have three girls if I wanted," he said. Instead he would drive past the riot of blinking lights, past the ads for bare-legged showgirls and sequined singers, through the warm night air of Vegas to his home in the suburbs. His three dogs, all boxers, would jump up and lick him, and he would let them, and he would call hello to his 80-year-old mother, eat dinner and settle back for an evening of TV amid the Ali photos. "The foxhole," he said. "I'm going back to the foxhole."

The Cook

"Next! How many? Two? O.K., let's move it, please! Next! You gettin' big, honey! How come you don't stop by more to see me? Soup! Chicken noodle soup, anybody? Next! Hey, Eskimo, what you doin'? Ain't you beautiful? You want two? Gonna kill yo'self, storin' up all them fat cells. Next!"

She stood in a food-splotched apron in the basement cafeteria of a private school on East 70th Street in Manhattan, stuffing pita pockets with barbecue and rolling her hips to the music from the radio. Her hips, her soul and her name—Lana Shabazz—are those of a jazz singer, but the gaze she gave the children was that of a mother.

Hardly none of 'em down here know. That's nothin' off my teeth, no need for 'em to. I got my own life, I don't need 'em fussin' over me. Get up at five every mornin', draw me a bath, get dressed in my whites for work. Still live out of suitcases—that's from being with him. Then I go drink coffee in a deli or a restaurant. Nice to sip and socialize with folks. By seven, I'm down here workin' myself tired to the bone runnin' this kitchen, the kind of tired you got to soak out in another big hot bath at night. Ain't easy, but I'm happy, 'course I am.

"Lana," the headmaster called, "do you have some tea?"

"Lana," a teacher said, "you got any of that broiled fish?"

"Lana," said the memo on the wall, "a reminder that we will need coffee and Danish for parent tours next week."

"Mama," said the little boy. "I'm hungry. What's to eat?"

Mama, that's what the young ones call me. Three hundred and fifty kids needin' me here every day . . . but all of 'em needin'

*together can never need me like he did. He'd come in at midnight,
I'd have his dinner ready. He'd wake up at five a.m. and say,
"Lana, get me a cup o' tea," I'd get up and do it. He'd travel, I'd
pack up and cook in his hotel suite. Made sure he got all the live
enzymes. Cooked without butter to save the calories—but had to
allow for his sweet tooth. Made him cookies and cakes, then hid
'em so he wouldn't eat 'em all at once. He'd swallow what I made
so fast I'd wonder if he had teeth in his stomach. Then he'd go
back to his cabin, and I'd worry about the cold from the air-
conditionin' hittin' his chest, he kept it so high. What a beautiful
man. I'd feed his kids at camp, break up their fights—they treated
me like a mother. Nobody else couldn'ta did what I did for that
man.*

She looked up and saw the first- and second-graders fill the
cafeteria like a burst of happy swallows. They swarmed at her legs
and tugged at her white bell-bottom trousers. "Mama, do you have
cookies? Mama, can we have a cookie?" She told them she couldn't
do that, stroked their heads, then grinned and sneaked them each
a big one.

*One time, man read my cards and looked at me funny. He
said, "There's more of Ali's cards showin' than yours." That scared
me—I'd almost lost myself to him. All I thought of was Ali. But he
gave so much of himself to the world, I told myself, he needs someone to take care of him. And that was me. Veronica, his third wife,
she sat there combin' her hair while Earnie Shavers was punchin'
on him, but I couldn't bear it. I had to get up and go back to my
hotel room, where I prayed and screamed so long, God had to let
him win. Psychic told me that in another life, I was his mother.
Gets me to wanna cry, thinkin' about him. But I won't though.
No, I won't.*

She did a little samba around the butcher block, disappeared
into the pantry and reappeared bopping out a bongo beat on a shiny
ice bucket. When she leaned to dip a spoon and test the soup, her
gold earrings shook. She straightened and pushed her big eyeglasses
back up her steam-slick nose.

A teenage boy entered with a gift—a pair of stuffed grape
leaves. She laughed from her belly and thanked him. A teenage

girl said good-bye and kissed her on the cheek. "You be a nice girl," she said softly.

Even when I was fifteen, back in Bessemer, Alabama, I still kept my dolls on my bed. My first husband pushed them off and said I wouldn't need 'em now I had a real one in my belly. Guess I got that motherin' instinct—can't get rid of it. Been takin' care of people all my life. Took care of my mother 'fore she died. Raised up my two little girls. Cooked for Malcolm X, for Elijah Muhammad and then for Ali. Funny thing, people trust you when you feed 'em, and folks always seem to trust me. Sitting on buses, I end up telling strangers next to me what foods they need to eat. I read nutrition books all the time when I'm layin' alone in bed.

At four o'clock she took off her white work shoes with a sigh, slipped on her sneakers and overcoat and walked out into the chill. She wedged inside the 101 uptown bus, left the million-dollar condos of the Upper East Side behind and went home to Harlem. She stopped at the post office, then sat over coffee at the Twin Donut Shop, the way she does every evening, and read her mail. Soon she would return to her apartment—her daughters live in Chicago and Miami and she is divorced—and draw a bath. "Hey, how you doin', Lana?" someone called to her. "Doin' great," she said. "Doin' great."

'Course, maybe if you looked closer, you'd see the hurt in my eyes. Know what it feels like to think of somebody all the time, and suddenly they ain't there? Like losin' a child. Maybe he's sick because he ain't eatin' right. Maybe he ain't gettin' the right enzymes. I see other people 'round him now. Why we ain't there? We the ones made sure he was champ. Don't wanna say my life's empty ... no, but ... I have dreams about him. One where he's sick and doesn't want nothin' to do with me. Then he's all better and he's so happy to see me. Sometimes I think about that poem I wrote when he was young. Wrote that somebody like that could never live to be old.

I love him, but sometimes I get mad at him, too. People say that after workin' with him all those years, I shouldn't need for nothin' ... and I'm flat broke. If they'd only have set up a retirement fund for us, we'd have no problems now. He used to say he was gonna buy me a house when he retired. If I'd asked him, he'da done it. But I never asked for nothin'. And maybe that's best. Maybe if I had money I'd lose my love for people.

Some days, though, I just have to hear his voice. I call him, ask him what he's eatin'. People ask me all the time how he's doin'. . . . Know how that feels, when people ask you how's your child, and you don't know what to say?

The Masseur

The gate to the fence that surrounded the little yellow house in northern Miami was locked. "Sarria!" I called from the sidewalk. "Sarria!" From inside the house a dog barked, then a second dog barked, a third, a fourth. And then the whole house exploded and shook with barking, a dozen, no, two dozen different timbres and pitches, the baritone bark of big dogs, the staccato yelp of small ones, the frenzied howl of the thin and high-strung. My knuckles whitened on the chain-link fence; how many could there be? "Sarria!" I cried again—he had to be in there, people said he was a shut-in—but my shout was hopelessly lost in the din.

I swallowed hard. Such a sweet old man, everyone had told me. I began to scale the fence.

This the dogs seemed to sense and take as an insult; the whole house seemed to snap and snarl and salivate. My eyes darted, my stomach clenched. I shifted onto the balls of my feet, approached the door, reached toward it from a few feet away and knocked— my God, I could not even hear my own rapping. *Bang!* The door shuddered, but not from my knocking. *Bang-bang!* The metal meshing put up inside to protect the windows shook as the beasts hurled themselves at me.

I counted the strides it would take to flee back to the fence— how could the gentle old man live *here?*—then held my breath, reached over a bush and rapped on a bedroom window. *"Sar-riiiiiaaaaa!"* In reply came the asylum howl, the door thumping as if about to splinter, the flash of teeth and eyeballs and fur in the window. I ran back to the fence and had just jabbed a toe in the meshing when, weakly, beneath the fury, came a muffled human grunt.

Five long minutes passed. Giving up, I saw the rush of snarling black. I froze, then whirled, clawing to climb. *"Negrita!"* I heard someone call. *"Ven! Ven!"* The dog hesitated, charged again, hesitated. I looked back. The old man—thank God!—was reaching out to wave me forward.

His hands, splayed from long, long arms, were broad and black and powerful from years of hacking Cuban sugarcane. I remembered them, working endlessly up and down the smooth ripples of Ali's body, rubbing until he drifted off to sleep on the table and then rubbing some more out of love. His hands I remembered, but I could not remember *him.*

His shoulders hunched, his head poking from them, turtlelike, Luis Sarria hobbled toward the steps in front of the house. He sat, and the bottom of his puppy-chewed pant leg hitched up to show the swathes of tape that wrapped his left leg. It had been chronically ulcerated since he stepped on a sea snail while fishing as a boy, but now the wound had grown threatening. At the gym near his home, where he worked until a year ago when the leg became too painful, they wondered if the germs carried by the great pack of dogs inside his house were what kept reinfecting it, and they wondered how much longer the 76-year-old man would last.

His wife, Esther, a Jamaican with small, happy-sad eyes, came out and sat next to him. Sarria picked up the black dog and hugged it to his chest. "She is his favorite," his wife said, "because she never wants to come back in the house, and so he gets to lift her like a baby."

They are childless, she explained, and need money badly, barely making it each month on Social Security. The gentle old man can neither visit friends because of his leg nor have them in because of his dogs. "They would rip people up," his wife said. "There are twenty-five of them."

"But why keep so many?" I asked.

She shrugged. "They say Liberace left twenty-five dogs."

"How could there be room for them all in your house?"

"They live in the living room and one of the bedrooms," she said. "We live in our bedroom now. We had to move all the furniture out of the living room because they were destroying it. They broke the record player chasing rats. They dug up Sarria's garden. Dogs eat pumpkins. Did you know that?"

"How can you afford to feed them all?"

"We can't. I spend five dollars a day to buy chicken backs, turkey parts, rice. I mix it with their dog food. We spoil them. But dogs are better than people. Sarria loves to caress them."

Sarria rose gradually and hobbled to the house holding the black dog. "He is sad," she said, watching him go. "Because he cannot work, he is losing force." She glanced at the fence. "If Ali would come to that gate and say, 'Let's go to Manila,' Sarria would be young again."

I remembered how reporters used to gather in Ali's dressing room after a workout, recording every word from the champion's lips, moving then to the corner man, Angelo Dundee, or perhaps to the street poet, Bundini Brown, or to Dr. Pacheco. Never did anyone exchange a word with Ali's *real* trainer, as some insiders called Sarria. It was almost as if no one even saw him. "Even in Spanish," said Dundee, "Sarria was quiet."

He had flown to America in 1960 to train Cuban welterweight Luis Rodriguez and never returned to his homeland, yet he never learned English. He felt safer that way, his lips opening only wide enough to accommodate his pipe, and Ali seemed to like it, too. Surrounded so many days by con men, jive men, press men and yes men, Ali cherished the morning hour and the afternoon hour on the table with the man who felt no need to speak. For 16 years, the man physically closest to the most quoted talker of the '70s barely understood a word.

Sometimes Ali would babble at Sarria senselessly, pretending he spoke perfect Spanish, and then in mid–mumbo jumbo blurt out *"Maricón!"* and Sarria's eyes would bug with mock horror. Everyone loved the silent old one. They swore his fingers knew the secret—how to break up fat on the champion's body and make it disappear. "And the exercises he put Ali through each morning! Sarria was the reason Muhammad got like this,"

Dundee said, forming a V with his hands. "He added years to Ali's boxing life."

The extra years brought extra beatings. And, likely, the Parkinson's syndrome. "I used to ask God to help me introduce power into him through my hands," Sarria said in Spanish, sitting once more on the front step. He rubbed his face. "Never did I think this could happen to him. I feel like crying when I see him, but that would not be good for him to see. To tell a boxer to stop fighting is an insult. I did not have the strength to tell him, but I wish to God I had."

"Oh, Sarria," said his wife. "You have never talked."

"If I had spoken more, I might have said things I should not have. Perhaps they would have said, 'This Cuban talks too much,' and I would have been sent away. . . ." Or perhaps today he would be standing in Sarria's Health Spa on Fifth Avenue, massaging corporate lumbars for $75 an hour.

He ran his fingers across a paw print on his pants and spoke softly again of Ali. "Ambitious people . . . people who talk a lot . . . perhaps *this* is what happens to them."

Behind us, the dogs began to snarl and thump again. "Shhhhh," Sarria pleaded. "Shhhhh."

"Sarria," I said, "how did you get so many dogs?"

From his pocket he pulled three photographs. Two of them were yellowed ones of him and Ali, clipped from newspapers. The other was a color glossy of a little girl. Tears misted his eyes, then his wife's. Together they explained the story of the 25 dogs.

Fourteen years ago they had taken in the three-day-old daughter of a relative who was unable to raise her. For 11 years she gave them someone to hug and care for, to take to ballet lessons and help with homework, to fill the hole left when Ali departed their lives. And then, just like *that*, the relative reappeared and took her away. "Oh, how Sarria cried," said his wife. She turned away and clamped her lips.

"Just before she left us," she went on, "the girl brought home a stray dog. We named it Alfi, and then she brought home a second one—we named it Kelly. When she left, we couldn't give away her dogs, you see. And then they started to make babies. . . ."

The Bodyguard

Clanking and jangling with walkie-talkie, nightstick, pistol and keys, Officer Howard (Pat) Patterson swung his 220-pound body out of patrol car No. 511 on the far south side of Chicago, and the shouting match began.

"Officer, this mother's in my face."

"You reported a battery? What's your name, ma'am?" Patterson asked calmly.

"Miss Jones. I went to jail for this mother, and now. . . ."

"I didn't touch her!" hollered the man. "I called her a name!"

"I might kill him!"

"Wait a minute, both of you."

"She got my chain, officer!"

"You mother! I was locked up last summer for your honky ass."

"Did he hit you, Miss Jones?"

"No, but he was in my face!"

"She pulled the chain off my neck. I want my chain!"

"Look," said Patterson. "You assault him, miss, and I lock *you* up. You're both high. Sir, you go take a walk. Let her cool off. And you stop screaming like that, Miss Jones."

Officer Patterson stepped back into the car and shook his head. "Lot of police would put them both in jail," he said. "I know before I was Ali's bodyguard, I'd put folks in jail ten times faster than I do now. Now I just try to help them solve their problems and send them home. My attitude's different since seeing the world and rubbing shoulders with Ali."

When the comet ride with Ali began, Patterson was 31-year-old cop on the streets of Chicago. When it ended, he was a 45-year-old cop on the streets of Chicago. He had two children, a loving wife, a close-knit family, 50 scrapbooks and a couple of walls of photographs that a ghetto kid never dreamed he would have, and for all of that he was grateful.

He got the bodyguard job through a chance meeting. The day he was assigned to protect the leader of the Black Muslim movement in America, Elijah Muhammad, back in the mid-'60s, he stuck a gun into a face coming out of the darkness: Herbert

Muhammad, Elijah's son and Ali's manager. Herbert wanted just such a businesslike fellow to protect his boxer, and Patterson became the Bodyguard. He worked primarily during the weeks of fights until 1974, when he was put on permanent loan to Ali by Chicago mayor Richard Daley.

Whenever they met, Ali made a game of guessing where Patterson's gun was hidden. One time it might be the Colt Diamondback strapped to his ankle, the next time the 9-mm automatic tucked under his suit coat; then again, if it was cold enough for an overcoat, the Colt *and* a 3X would be buried in his pockets. Upon reaching Ali's hotel suite, the Bodyguard would hide the pistols in a flower vase or beneath a sofa cushion, so he would always have one near, along with the shotgun he kept in a closet or under the bed. In a briefcase he carried as much as $50,000 in cash—spending money for the champ.

His protective instinct was fierce. At Yankee Stadium on the night of the fight against Ken Norton in 1976, he had a $400 leather suit ripped to shreds while fighting off a mob from the fender of Ali's limo. He turned down four-figure bribes from people desperate to get past his checkpoint in hotel hallways and see Ali. When Ali entered a public bathroom, Patterson went, too. "If anything at all happened to Muhammad," he said, "I figured it would be my fault."

During fights, he always kept his hand clamped over the water bottle so no one could sabotage Ali. But the Bodyguard had to sit on the corner stool and watch helplessly when his man needed protection most, in the ring when the end was near. "Watching him get hit was like watching someone stick my mama with a knife," Patterson said. "Ali fights stopped being a party. I tried to tell him to quit. . . ."

He drove the patrol car through the streets as he reminisced, head continually swiveling, eyes sweeping, ears listening for his number on the radio. The recruit he was training listened to the stories silently. Now and then a wino or a pimp called from the sidewalk, "Hey, Patty, how's Muhammad?"

"Traveling with Ali opened up the whole world for me," said the Bodyguard. "I'll admit it, I was afraid of flying before I got on that first airplane to meet him in Toronto. I never thought of going to other countries. Now I feel like there's nothing I can't do; my wife and I travel all the time.

"With him I saw that people all over are the same: trying to educate their kids and get enough to eat—just like us. Only most of them don't have as much as we do. That changed me, too. I used to worry about being a success, getting a promotion. Now that's not important. Seeing how somebody as powerful as Ali never used force to get things done, I learned from that. I'm not a police officer anymore, I'm a *peace* officer. I'd rather drive a drunk home or give somebody five dollars to solve an argument than stick them in jail. People need help, not jail."

Not long ago, he was in London with a tour group when a disheveled, unbathed man approached and asked for money. The others averted their eyes and edged away. "There's a sucker," some said when Patterson gave the beggar a bill and talked with him, but they didn't understand. He wasn't safeguarding a man anymore. He was safeguarding an idea.

"Whenever he saw someone old or sick or in trouble," said the Bodyguard, "Ali always wanted to help them. He'd say, 'Who knows? Someday I might be that way.'"

The Manager

The last man to enter the Chicago mosque was short and round and rumpled. His sport coat was two sizes too baggy, his shirttail spilled across the seat of his pants. His shoes were unbuckled, his face stubbled with whiskers. He looked not at all like the man who had reached into his pocket for a million dollars to buy the land and build the mosque he stood in.

The others at prayer stood near the front. He slipped off his shoes, padded to the back and dropped to his knees behind a pillar. Few were aware of it, but he remembered well a passage in Muslim scripture advising worshippers to pray behind an object, an obstruction for the devil.

All his life Herbert Muhammad has hidden behind pillars. As a young man he was the quiet, respectful houseman and chauffeur for his powerful father, Elijah Muhammad. Then he became the manager of Muhammad Ali, taking 33 percent of Ali's multi-million-dollar purses but remaining so obscure that bouncers at Ali workouts sometimes barred his entry to the gym. "I never wanted to be a leader," he said. "I never wanted to be a target. My role is to support those in the lead."

Now he was 58, and he had trouble. His pillar was crumbling, his point man fading away. His dream of building 49 more mosques like this first one, using the money Ali and he could generate, was drifting further and further from his reach. Ali slurred words and shook and didn't want to be seen on television. Ali didn't care about making money anymore.

Herbert remained Ali's manager. He wasn't going to give up his dream without a fight. Beneath the untucked shirt, unshaven face and tufts of black hair was a man burning with determination not to be forgotten when the Muslim history in America is written. Perhaps not equal to his father, nor to his younger brother Wallace, whom Elijah anointed as successor, but close. "Fifty mosques," said Herbert. "Allah said if you build him a mosque in this life, he'll build you a paradise in the next life. My father established two hundred mosques, my brother two hundred and fifty. But they didn't *pay* for them. I want to *pay* for fifty. That would make my father proud. Every day my wife tells me to relax. How can I? I want to go till I drop. If I can't do something meaningful, take me now."

He sighed. The Muslim movement had changed since Elijah died in 1975; it had dropped the black separatist thrust and become rounder, softer—more *Herbert*. Big-name athletes weren't changing their names to Abdul and Rashad as they did in the '60s and '70s. The glamour years were gone, and now it would take the quiet, behind-the-scenes work—the kind Herbert was cut out for—to keep the movement growing.

"Seemed like we were always doing something back when Muhammad was fighting," he said. "Building buildings, schools, starting mosques, buying buses, helping people. Now everything has quieted down with Ali, but I still got the taste of it in my mouth."

The irony was pungent. For years the Manager tried to restrain Ali. Now Ali was restraining the Manager. "I'd beg him not to be so proud, not to mess around with women, not to say, 'I am the greatest,'" Herbert said. "'I am the greatest' was an insult to God—in our prayers, we say, '*Allâhu akbar*,' *God is* the greatest. That was when I was trying to make him more meek and religious. Back then I had to run to keep up with him when he *walked*. But this sickness stopped him dead in his tracks. Now everything's in slow motion. Now he's a hundred times more religious and meek than I ever thought he'd be. His whole life is his prayers. But he doesn't seem to care about anything. . . ."

The Manager had ushered in the era of million-dollar sports contracts, brilliantly playing promoters Don King and Bob Arum off against each other. Now he has an agreement for 25 percent of the cut if he negotiates a product deal with Ali. "If he wanted it and he wasn't sick, he could be making twenty million to thirty million dollars a year in endorsements," said Herbert. "He's probably making a couple of hundred thousand. Last year I made five hundred dollars from him."

Now and then the fighter would leave his farm in Berrien Springs, Michigan, and drive two hours to meet Herbert at a coffee shop in Chicago. He would listen with blank eyes as the Manager hatched plans, as the Manager tried everything to wake him. If Ali were dead, could Herbert feel alive?

"I tell him, 'Joe Frazier ain't sitting around,'" he said. "'If you lost some weight and took your medicine, you could make a whole lot of money. You could even fight.' I know he can't fight, but I say it just to motivate him. He won't take his medicine, he hates to depend on anything. I think his problem is getting worse. He's shaking more. Sometimes it's hard to be in his presence, like someone sick in your family. I love that man. He is quicker to help a stranger, he has more inner compassion than any human being I've ever met. But I'm afraid he's losing the values of this earth. Allah said to do everything in your power to seek an afterlife, but not to neglect your share on this earth. Ali gave away that big house of his in Los Angeles, he gave away cars. He's giving up things *too* easy. I don't want to push him, but I have got to make him realistic. His mother, his father, his eight children, what will he do about their expenses, the kids' college educations? And he shouldn't dress the way I dress. He should have a suit and a tie, and he should have his hair groomed, because he represents something to people.

"He says. 'I don't need no car, I'll just ride a bike.' One night when he stayed over in Chicago, he slept on the floor of the mosque instead of getting a hotel. I told him, 'People are going to think you've lost all your marbles or your money—and neither one is good.' The whole world rallied around Islam as a universal religion because of Muhammad Ali. But if he doesn't watch it, he's going to become a monk."

One day last summer the Manager received a call from Mexico City. It was Ali, seeking counsel: Should he chance a new form of brain surgery that might cure his illness? Two of the 18 patients who had undergone the operation—in which adrenal cells are placed inside the brain to help make dopamine, a brain chemical essential to controlling voluntary body movement—had died shortly thereafter, but others had shown marked improvement. Ali might be Ali again!

Ali's fourth wife, Yolanda, cried on the telephone and begged him not to risk it. Herbert Muhammad closed his eyes and thought. He so hated to see Ali hurt, he used to keep his head down and pray during fights.

"I felt if he put his trust totally in God, the operation would be a success," said Herbert. He looked down at his hands. "But I didn't tell him that. If he turned out like a vegetable, it would be seen as my decision. People would think I said yes just because I wanted more paychecks from Ali. So I told him to listen to everybody but to make up his own mind."

Ali decided against the surgery. Part of him, it seemed, was afraid to be again what he was, filled with an energy that needed lights and action and other people's eyes. And so the Manager, nearly 60, was left like Ali toward the end of his career, still able to visualize himself doing what he wanted to do, but unable to do it.

"Not just fifty mosques," said Herbert Muhammad. "But fifty mosques with day-care centers and schools and old folks' homes attached to them. I keep telling Ali, 'Let's get back in the race.' How could I have ever dreamed I'd have to beg Muhammad Ali to *go*?"

The Motivator

*The scene: a small motel room in downtown Los Angeles that costs, at monthly rates, $5.83 a night. A finger of afternoon light makes it through the curtains, falling on a tablecloth etched with the words god—*MOTHER*—son. On top of the television stands a small statue of Buddha, its head hidden by a man's cap. Four packs of playing cards and a Bible lie on the head of the bed, tin dinner plates are set on a small table. Affixed to a mirror are a photograph of a young Muhammad Ali and a leaflet for a play entitled* Muhammad Ali Forever.

On the bed, propped against a pillow, is a 57-year-old black man, slightly chubby, with black woolly hair on the sides of his head and, on the top, a big bald spot with a tiny tuft of hair grow- ing at the very front. As he talks his eyes go wide and wild . . . then far away . . . then wet with tears.

His name is Drew (Bundini) Brown—the ghetto poet who motivated Ali and maddened him, who invented the phrase "Float like a butterfly, sting like a bee" and who played bit parts in The Color Purple *and* Shaft; *who licked Ali's mouthpiece before slid- ing it in but never said a yes to him he didn't mean; who could engage the champion in long discussions of nature and God and man, then lie in the hotel pool before a fight and have his white woman, Easy, drop cherries into his mouth; who, when he felt good, charged two $300 bottles of wine at dinner to Ali's expense ac- count and then made Ali laugh it off; and who, when he felt bad, drank rum and shot bullets into the night sky at the mountain train- ing camp in Pennsylvania—a man stretched taut and twanging between the fact that he was an animal . . . and a spirit.*

Oh yes. A visitor sits in a chair near the window of the motel room but often Bundini Brown talks as if he is ranting to a crowd on a street corner—or as if he is completely alone.

The old master painter from the faraway hills
Who painted the violets and the daffodils
Said the next champ gonna come from Louisville.

I made that up 'fore we was even champion. Things just exploded in my head back then. Guess that's why Ali loved me. I could help him create new things. See, he never did talk that much. People didn't know that about him, 'less'n they slept overnight and caught him wakin' up. All that talkin' was just for the cameras and writers, to build a crowd. He was quiet as can be, same as now. But now people think he's not talkin' 'cause of the Parkinson's, which is a lie.

I remember when he fought Jerry Quarry, after that long layoff. Going from the locker room to the ring, my feet wasn't even touchin' the ground. I looked down and tried to touch, but I couldn't get 'em to. Like I was walkin' into my past. Me and the champ was so close, I'd think, Get off the ropes—and he'd get off the ropes! Man, it made chill bumps run up my legs. We were in Manila, fightin' Frazier. The champ came back to the corner crossin' his legs. Tenth or eleventh round. I forget. Angelo said, "Our boy is through." I said, "You're goddam wrong, my baby ain't through!" I was deeply in love with him. Ali tried to fire me every day, but how he gonna fire me when God gave me my job? So I stood on the apron of the ring, and I said out loud, "God! If Joe Frazier wins, his mother wins, his father wins, his kids win. Nobody else! But if Muhammad lose—God!—we *all* lose. Little boys, men, women, black and white. Muhammad lose, the world lose!"

And you know what? The nigger got up fresh as a daisy. Everybody seen it! Got up fresh, man *fresh!* And beat up on Frazier so bad Frazier couldn't come out after the fourteenth round! God put us together for a reason, and we shook up the world!

(*He picks at a thread on the bedspread.*) People'd see us back then and say, "It's so nice seein' y'all together." We made a lot of people happy. I was a soldier. (*His hands are shaking. He reaches down to the floor, pours a glass of rum as his eyes begin to fill with tears.*) I was happy then. It'd be good for Muhammad if I could be with him again. Be good for me, too. Then I wouldn't drink as much. By me being alone I drink a lot. Always did say I could motivate him out of this sickness, if me and the champ was together. He needs the medical thing, too, but he needs someone who truly loves him. If we were together again, more of the God would come out of me. (*His voice is almost inaudible.*) Things used to explode in my head. . . . I'm kind of runnin' out now. . . .

He asked me to go stay on the farm with him. (*His eyes flare, he starts to shout.*) What you goin' to do, put me to pasture? I ain't no horse! I don't want no handouts! I got plans! Big things gonna happen for me! I gotta get me a job, make some money, take care of my own family 'fore I go with him. If I don't love my own babies, how in hell I gonna love somebody else's?

First thing I'd do if I had some money, I'd go to the Bahamas and see my baby. King Solomon Brown's his name. Made him at Ali's last fight, with a woman I met down there. He was born on the seventh day of the seventh month. There's seven archangels and seven colors in the rainbow, you know.

I brought him to America and lived with him until he was one. Then he went back to the Bahamas with his mother. Didn't see him for a year and a half, then I went back. Wanted to see if he'd remember me. I said, "A-B-C-D-E-F-G; *dock-dock*" (*he makes a sound with his tongue and the roof of his mouth*)—that's what I always used to teach him—*and* he *remembered!* He ran and leaped into my arms—I mean, jumped!—and we hugged, and it wasn't like I was huggin' somebody else, we was one body, we was one! (*He wraps his arms around himself and closes his eyes.*) I'll never forget that hug. Couldn't bring him back to America, I had no house for him to come back to. Stayed eight weeks and went broke. Came back and after that I'd see kids on the street and think of my kid and I'd start to cry. . . . Why don't you get up and leave now. Put two eggs in your shoes and beat it. You stirrin' up things, you know. (*The visitor starts to stand.*)

I'll make some money. I'll get a home he can come to, and put him in school. Got two grandchildren, too, and I wanna be near 'em. They're by my son Drew; he's a jet pilot in the Persian Gulf. And I have another son, Ronnie, here in Los Angeles. One son black, one son white, born a day apart. And then Solomon. I'm a boy-maker. Don't see my kids like I want to. Can't go back to my babies till I got somethin' to give 'em. Right now, I'm broke. I said *broke*, not poor—there's a difference. (*He glances across the room and speaks softly.*) I know one thing: You get used to good food and a clean bed, hard to get used to somethin' else. Why don't you leave now. Please?

(*He rises and goes to the door, shredding a piece of bread and tossing it outside to the pigeons.*) People don't know it, but feedin' the birds is like paintin' a picture. . . . Some people think Muhammad's broke, too. He ain't broke. He's brokenhearted. He hasn't found himself in what he really want to do. Maybe he just be in the freezer for a few years. Maybe he's going through this so he has time to think. Last time I was with him, his fifteen-year-old son said to him, "Daddy, Bundini is your only friend, the only one that doesn't give up on you." Muhammad looked at me, and we started cryin'. But this is not the end for Ali. Somethin' good gonna happen for him. Maybe not while he's still alive on this earth, but Ali gonna *live* for a long time, if you know what I mean. Like my kids, even when I'm gone, I'm gonna be livin' in 'em . . . if I can be around 'em enough to put my spirit into 'em. Go fishin' with 'em. There you go again, you got me talkin' about it. Didn't I ask you to leave? (*The visitor reaches for his shoulder bag.*)

It ain't nothin' for me to get up and walk down the street and have fifteen people yell, "Hey, Bundini, where's the champ?" That one reason I stay in my room. (*He pauses and looks at the visitor.*) You think I'm alone, don't you? Soon as you leave, God's gonna sit in that chair. I call him Shorty. Ha-ha, you like that, don't you? By callin' him that, means I ain't got no prejudice about religions. I was born on a doorstep with a note 'cross my chest. It

read, "Do the best you can for him, world." I had to suck the first
nipple come along. I didn't run away from home—I been runnin'
to home. I'm runnin' to God. And the nearest I can find to God is
people. And all around me people are fightin' for money. And I'm
tryin' to find out what makes apples and peaches and lemons, what
makes the sun shine. What is the act of life? We all just trancin'
through? Why can't we care for one another? There's a lady that
come out of church the other day and got shot in the head. I want
to know what the hell is goin' on. God, take me home if you ain't
gonna give me no answer. Take me home now. If you're ready to
die, you're ready to live. Best thing you can do is live every day
like it's the last day. Kiss your family each day like you're not
comin' back. I want to keep my dimples deep as long as I'm here.
I want to see people smile like you just did.

(*His lips smile, but his eyes are wet and shining.*) The smarter
you get, the lonelier you get. Why is it? When you learn how to
live, it's time to die. That's kind of peculiar. When you learn how
to drive, they take away the car. I've finally realized you need to
be near your kids, that you need to help 'em live better'n you did,
that you can live on by feedin' your spirit into your babies. But
now I ain't got no money and I can't be near 'em. Back when I
was with the champ, I could fly to 'em anytime. See, I was in the
Navy when I was thirteen and the Merchant Marine when I was
fifteen, and they was the happiest days of my life, 'cause I was alone
and didn't have no one to worry about. But now I'm alone and it
brings me misery. . . . C'mon now, get on up and leave. Talkin' to
you is like talkin' to myself. . . .

See this bald spot on my head? Looks like a footprint, don't
it? That come from me walkin' on my head. Don't you think I know
I'm my own worst enemy? I suffer a lot. If my kids only knew how
I hurt. But I can't let 'em know, it might come out in anger. And
'fore I see 'em, I gotta have somethin' to give to 'em. I owe nine
thousand dollars 'fore I can get my stuff out of storage. (*He bites
his lip and looks away.*) One storage place already done auctioned
off all the pictures of Ali an' me, all my trophies and memories
from back then. Strangers have 'em all. . . . (*A long silence passes.*)
Now the other storage place, the one that has all Ali's robes from

every fight we ever fought, every pair of trunks we fought in, lot of jockstraps, too, enough stuff to fill a museum—I owe that place nine thousand dollars, and I'm talkin' to 'em nice so they won't auction that off, too, but I don't think they'll wait much longer. Sure I know how much that stuff's worth, but I can't sell it. That's not right. I want that stuff to be in my babies' dens someday. That's what I'm gonna give my babies. I can't just sell it. . . . (*His head drops, and he looks up from under his brow.*) You know some-body'll pay now?

(*He rubs his face and stares at the TV set.*) You stirrin' it up again. Go on, now. You know if you just keep sittin' there, I'll keep talkin'. Pretty please? (*He gets to his feet.*) You can come back and visit me. We friends now. I can't go out. I gotta stay by the phone. I'm waitin' on somethin' real big, and I ain't gonna get caught off-guard. Somethin' big gonna happen. You wait and see. . . .

A few days later, Bundini Brown fell in his motel room and was found paralyzed from the neck down by a cleaning woman. And then he died.

Seven years ago, when the group broke camp at Deer Lake for the final time, everyone contributed money for a plaque that would include all their names. They left the task to Bundini Brown and departed.

Today the camp is a home for unwed mothers. In front of the log-cabin gym, where babies squeal and crawl, stands a tall slab of gray granite, chiseled with 16 names and surrounded by flowers. Bundini Brown had bought a tombstone.

Home Run Fever

You're out of it, pal. You're hungry, and the kitchen's closed. You don't live in St. Louis or Seattle or Chicago, where *the* story of this American summer of 1998 is cooking, nor in the other big cities where the dailies bring it piping hot to the breakfast table every dawn. You live a five-and-a-half-hour drive from the nearest big league ballpark, and your newspaper's serving it up like bulletins from the front in World War I—GRIFFEY HITS 39th; SOSA'S 36th LEADS CUBS; McGWIRE MASHES 2 MORE—followed by a bare-bones sentence or two, and cripes, there's not even *SportsCenter* to fill your belly because your wife bears a deep grudge against TV and sneers whenever you creep down the stairs at 7 a.m. to turn it on.

But you're a sportswriter, and people assume you know. "What do ya think?" they ask. "Is Maris's record gonna fall? Which one's gonna do it? What kind of guy's McGwire? Who do you like?" You don't know who you like. Never met any of the three men in your life. It's scary, not being able to answer the water-cooler question.

This story first appeared in 1998.

So you get this idea. It's too good to be true, but you ask your boss anyway. How about letting you chase the chase? Three cities, three nights, three men—go on a long-ball bender, a four-bag jag. Enter the bubble to feel what it's like to be one of them right now, belting homers and stalking legends. Then become one of the mob up in the seats, rising to snag history. Big Mac in San Diego on Monday, Junior in St. Petersburg on Tuesday, Slammin' Sammy in Chicago on Wednesday, back-to-back-to-back . . . pretty please?

Sure, says your boss. Why not?

Hot damn! You're going . . . going . . . *gone!*

It's only when you're up in the air at dawn, a week ago Monday, blinking on four hours' sleep and staring at the travel schedule you've scribbled out, that you start thinking, Man, this is lunacy, and what are the odds you'll actually see any of the big boys launch? Two flights, 2,500 miles and 14 hours later you're sitting in a football locker room next to the visitors' clubhouse at Qualcomm Stadium, waiting for the press conference that Mark McGwire holds on his first day in each city when he's on the road. You remember reading about the media horde that swallowed Roger Maris in 1961. Ten to 15 reporters would converge on him before and after each game. That was in September, when Maris had 55, 56, 57. Today is July 20. McGwire has 42. There are 30 of us. There were 50 on the last road trip, in Cincinnati, a writer tells you.

McGwire walks in, St. Louis Cardinals cap tugged low on his head, dressed for battle. He sees the four cameras aimed at a chair and a table holding a half-dozen microphones. He shakes his head in disgust. "I'm not gonna sit down," he says. "This is informal stuff, so. . . ." He leans against one of the lockers, his green eyes blinking like those of a cornered ox as the humans and their hardware close in. Someone takes pity on him, lobs him a lollipop about his team instead of about what everyone's here for. He shakes his head grimly again. "This is for Mark McGwire home run questions," he says. "That's the only reason I'm doing this. I talk about the team after the game."

Haltingly, the questions come. You have this feeling that if you ask the wrong question, he might chomp your head off, and you would absolutely deserve it, so you wait for someone else to ask it. "I don't know how anybody can get used to this," McGwire says. "I don't play the game for this. I'm sick of seeing my mug. I've always believed that the more people know about you, the more they get sick of you. The media sets this up like it's going to happen . . . so how are they going to write it if it doesn't happen? I assume people want this record to be broken. So let's use some sense. Why not wait until somebody gets close to breaking the record? If people want to see something done, it makes sense to do this in a way that won't wear the person down."

Is he having any fun? "Between the lines, I have a lot of fun," he says.

What does he think of Mexican pitchers? He rolls his eyes.

The cameras and microphones reap the 20-second snips they need and begin peeling away, the crowd dwindles to a dozen men with notepads. McGwire's stiff, mammoth body loosens—the cornered ox is gone. He looks every questioner in the eye and answers earnestly. He wraps an arm around the divider between two locker stalls, lets it have some of his 250 pounds and smiles. "I wish every player could feel what I've felt in visiting ballparks," he says. "The receptions I've received. . . . It's blown me away. It's absolutely remarkable."

After the All-Star break, he says, he pulled the shutters over the looking glass. No more *SportsCenter*—his finger clicks right past it on the remote control. No more sports pages—he extracts that section from newspapers, folds it and drops it in the trash. No more reading the mail.

You follow him into the Cardinals clubhouse, feeling bad because now you like him, and your eyes feel like cameras. There it is, blaring from the television that hangs from the ceiling and faces all the lockers—an ESPN segment on the home-run-swinging styles of McGwire, Ken Griffey Jr. and Sammy Sosa, the crack of McGwire's bat and the bark of his name coming over and over. You watch how swiftly he walks past the screen to retrieve something from his stall and then strides back to remain on the TV's dark side until it's time for batting practice, ferrying his bat to the trainer's room, to the manager's office, to the corridor outside, the look in his eye that of a man on his way to do something very important, so no one will stop him with more questions. You can't help feeling that here's a guy who wishes to hell he could do this without expectations, without the dread of letting people down.

A teammate, pitcher Todd Stottlemyre, watches him hurry by. "It's like a starting pitcher in the seventh inning of a no-hitter," Stottlemyre says. "We don't say anything to him anymore about home runs. We can tell he doesn't want us to talk about it, and nobody's gonna question him, because it's too damn big."

You're startled, as you follow McGwire down the tunnel to the dugout, to hear the cries begin even before he emerges. "McGwire! *McGwire!*" He walks past the bleating fans, never looks up. Every head, every camera is on him. His face is a mask, eyes gripping a nothingness before him. He lifts his arms overhead to stretch. A woman with a tiny camera taps his armpit with her fingernail, asking him to turn and pose. He never looks at her. She doesn't exist.

Two hours before game time, the leftfield stands are choked with people wearing mitts. The air crackles. Foul territory is thick with writers and photographers and special guests—a hundred, easy. Every few minutes McGwire's eyes meet those of someone he knows. Immediately the mask vanishes, the eyes and lips become animated; you see how grateful he is to be human again. There's Scott LaRose, his comedian buddy who tells you that McGwire cackles so loud at comedy clubs that he brings a towel with him to bite on rather than draw attention to himself. There's George Will and his two sons. "It's not about the pennant races anymore," Will tells you. "It's about the home run race. You'd think I'd want Sosa, because I grew up a Cubs fan, but I'm rooting for McGwire. The base of achievement is there—he's earned this. He's got the swing down, it never varies, so he won't have any long periods of mechanical trouble. But all three of them seem to be nice human beings. There's not a Sprewell in the house."

Three of them? Or is it four now? You look up, and there's San Diego Padres outfielder Greg Vaughn standing 10 feet away. His 34th home run, yesterday, has brought him within two of Sosa, to the lip of the volcano, and since you're here, hell, why not nudge him in too? He gives you a big, warm, no-way-in-hell grin and says, "I won't even think about it. I don't want to hear or see anybody blowin' smoke up my butt. It's so far-fetched, so unrealistic, it hasn't even entered my mind. Man, McGwire's a monster. He's got *Nintendo* numbers! Junior, he was born to play baseball and be a superstar, and Sammy, he's like a little kid having fun. I love to watch those guys go over the top."

As if to prove he doesn't belong, he goes homerless his first four rounds of batting practice and exits the cage with a sorrowful shake of his head. "Got the worst BP swing in baseball," Vaughn laments. Then, looking over your shoulder, he cracks up. "McGwire just called over to me. Says he wants to rub me, I'm so hot. Imagine that!"

Vaughn trots to McGwire's side, spilling laughter. Nobody back home has ever even asked you about Vaughn, but for pure warmth alone, maybe he's the dark horse you should pull for.

Big Mac walks toward the dugout. He reaches above it to sign a few autographs, looking at no one as he signs, his face a blank. The crush of people mashes a redheaded little boy against the railing atop the dugout. The boy breaks into sobs. His father and a security guard shove and shout to set him free.

McGwire strides to the plate for BP. You park yourself right at the rope that keeps noncombatants back from the cage. Everyone's on his feet. A couple of grounders, *ohhhh*, a couple of fly balls, *ahhhh*, and then the thunder, *whoooooah!* Twenty-two compact swings in all, seven bullets into the sea of begging bare and leathered hands. Just before McGwire finishes, a boy runs out to the cage in a Cardinals uniform with McGwire's name and number on the back—Mark's son, Matthew, reporting for duty as batboy and Nation's Luckiest Child. Big Mac grins, slaps five and hugs the boy, then heads back to the clubhouse.

You go up into the stands, buy a soda and a hot dog and grab an empty seat near the Cardinals' dugout. Along the way, in three conversations, you hear men explaining to their women about Ruth's 60 and Maris's 61 and the history afoot here tonight. Big Mac approaches the plate in the top of the first to a standing O. He's not a Cardinal anymore. He's on everyone's team.

Lord, those thighs. In McGwire's knock-kneed stance, they scream to burst out of his pants, and as he takes those swift little warm-up swipes, his 33 ounces of northern white ash becomes a toothpick. With distance, up here in the crowd, you can see the appetite for legend that he's feeding. He's the caricature that a children's artist would draw of a home run slugger; he's Bunyan swinging an ax, the gentle giant whose charity for abused children everybody you'll meet tonight is amazingly quick to point out. Camera flashes pop all around the concrete bowl. McGwire lashes a white-blur single to left, Little Mac gallops out grinning to collect his daddy's shin guard, and you're thinking, Damn, wouldn't it be nice if your son could be beside you to see this, and how can you not root for this guy?

Bottom of the second. Vaughn launches number 35, which goes 433 feet to dead left. Look out, people tell you. Here comes Vaughny. Sitting on the third-base side, watching that home run descend, you know where you need to go—on the double.

Up in the leftfield seats, everybody wants McGwire to take the record and snap it in half over one of those thighs. Junior? "Great player, the best, but . . . a little arrogant . . . kinda smug." That's what you're hearing. Sammy? "He won't last." Big Mac is their choice because of the sexually-abused kids he's helping. Because of his humility and respect for the game. And most of all: "Because he's so extravagant, so monstrous," says Daria Zanoi, a 24-year-old nurse who examines sexual-assault victims, of all things, and who's giving McGwire the I'm-not-worthy bow as he steps in and singles once more. "It's like he should be on his own team because he doesn't match anyone else. I just want him to break the record, nobody else. That would make it even more special."

Second deck, that's too obvious. For Mac's third at-bat, in the fifth, you guess first row, lower deck, pure rope, and man your battle station. Fool! There she goes—good God, they really *are* as long as you've read!—a 458-foot bomb into the second tier in left center, the second-deepest one since distances were first recorded in this ballpark. You jump to your feet with everyone else, jam your notepad under your arm and pound your hands together, hardly believing your good luck. You've got to find who snagged that baby, but when you get up there, it looks like a hospital tent at Shiloh. A silver-haired man is holding a wet folded paper towel to an ugly red welt high on his forehead. A seat away, a man with a Padres hat tugged over unruly blond hair is wincing and fingering a humdinger of his own on his left cheek. "We're victims of McGwire!" cries Bob Colwell, a 46-year-old machine operator from Ocean Beach, California.

"McGwire did this?" you ask. "To both of you?"

"To both of us!" shouts Colwell. "Can you believe it? I'm up here during batting practice explaining to her"—he jabs a thumb at his girlfriend, Dawn Mariani, a dispatcher for the San Diego police—"about Roger and the Babe, and she's barely listening, she's reading *Sphere* by Michael Crichton. All of a sudden I see McGwire hit one that's coming straight for me, and it's like a scene from *The Natural*, it's surreal, and I'm wearing a glove, which I haven't worn in twenty years, thinking, I've got a chance! I reach up, but everybody bumps me, and it hits the top of my glove and then hits my cheek, and there I am bumming out, bleeding profusely, when I turn and . . . there's my honey holding the ball! Thank God, thank God! Then what happens? Lightning strikes twice! The home run McGwire just hit? It comes right up here again! And this guy, who I didn't know before tonight"—the factory worker reaches across Dawn to thump attorney James Conway on the back—"this time he gets nailed! Do a story on us! Victims of McGwire!"

So who got number 43? you ask. They point to the row behind, where a thick 49-year-old high school football coach named Robert Byers Jr., from Moreno Valley, California, took it on the ricochet off Conway's noggin. "As I watched it coming, I just kept telling myself what I always tell my receivers," Byers says. "*Soft hands, soft hands.* I just turned down an offer of seven hundred dollars for this ball."

Big Mac goes 4 for 4, with a walk. Cards win 13–1. What you want to do right now is go get a cold one with James and Robert and Bob, but there's no time for that. Junior's waiting back on the other side of the country. The only way to get there in time for batting practice tomorrow in Florida is to take the red-eye, but it's 11 p.m., too late to catch the last flight to the East Coast out of San Diego, so you've got to drive two hours up I-5 to catch the 1:55 a.m. out of L.A. and change planes in Dallas.

You can die in the dinger wringer. This occurs to you an hour north of San Diego, after your second Coca-Cola's gone and the rumble of the lane dividers has just snapped your eyes open for the third time and your body realizes it's gone 24 hours without sleep. You roll down the windows, crank up the radio, scream with The Who and Jethro Tull at the top of your lungs for the next 45 minutes—that's how you reel into L.A. International and live to see Griffey swing his black bat.

Only nine of your kind surround Junior in the clubhouse when he looks up, stick of red licorice poking out of his mouth, eyes cool, voice distant. You can touch the tension again, glimpse the cliff edge these three sluggers must walk. If they play along with your questions, if they ignore teammates' glances in a clubhouse where code dictates that no player steps above the other 24, if they reveal their deepest cravings for immortality, they're inviting free fall and ridicule from within and without should they fall short of 61. If they don't play along, if they ask to be left alone when they hear the same question for the 23rd straight day, or if they give the *Dogpatch Gazette* reporter's question the glare and bark it deserves, they risk ruining their reputation forever even as they lay claim to the most acclaimed individual sports record in America. How's Junior going to play this game before the game?

"I don't like to talk about myself," he says. "Hard to believe, isn't it? I'm not going to talk about home runs. I just want to win. I'm not going to talk about McGwire and Sosa. They don't help this team win. It's hard for people to believe that Roger Maris's record isn't important to me, but it's not." Nine of you clutch empty notepads, all your questions about McGwire, Sosa, Maris, home runs and Griffey himself just blown away in the top of the first, so now what do you do? Play cat and mouse, of course. Ask Junior 20 questions about why he *won't* talk about McGwire, Sosa, Maris, home runs or himself. In no time Junior's sitting on an equipment chest, feet propped up, grinning and spinning the nine of you wherever he wants, in no hurry at all to leave. He's the cat, you're the mice, and as long as that's clear, he enjoys the attention.

A journalist uses the word *chase.* Junior won't have it. "Only thing I wanna chase is my kids," he says. Nobody's going to pigeonhole him as a home run hitter when he's clearly the finest all-around player in the game. Nobody's going to make him pant after a goal that 270 million *others* have set for him.

"That's all people want to talk about," he says, "but fifty home runs will probably win you only twelve games a season. I think more about the little things, like playing defense, getting guys over—that might win you forty games. I think about wanting to be the last guy on the field at the end of the season, spraying free champagne all over my teammates. I just wasn't brought up to talk about myself. Growing up, my dad [former Cincinnati Reds star Ken Griffey] would probably bop me on the head if I bragged. He's got three rings, and I want a couple for myself. If someone doesn't like me because I don't want to talk about myself or home runs, that's their problem."

Strikes you as odd, then, Junior's answer to one of the last questions: Which of the Reds, whose clubhouse he rattled around in as a boy, impressed him most as a player? "George Foster," he says.

"That surprises me," says the questioner, obviously expecting Junior to say Pete Rose, Joe Morgan or Johnny Bench. "Why Foster?"

"Fifty-two home runs," Junior replies.

"But with all their great players. . . ."

"None of the others hit fifty-two home runs in a season," says Junior. Hmmm.

There's no BP buzz at domed Tropicana Field. Maybe it's because everything, from the grass under your feet to the canopy overhead, is artificial. Maybe it's because the Tampa Bay Devil Rays are going down the toilet without a gurgle, and maybe it's because an appearance at the ballpark here is just an outing, not a subpoena from the heart. A half-dozen signs and the loudest applause are for Junior, but it's just polite, backside-buried-in-the-seat clapping from the 30,298 in the house.

Still, everyone you approach is thrilled when you raise the question. Yessir, here's your tip for the awkward and lonely of this land, those whose every pickup line has failed. Sidle up to any stranger and ask, "Who you pullin' for? Big Mac, Junior or Sammy?" Everyone wants to chime in, even when your press credential's in your pocket and your notepad's stashed away. Everyone, when he finds out what you're doing, howls, "Oh, man! Can you take me?" Everyone's dying to get into the clubhouse to meet the mashers, not realizing how much better it is out here. Everyone's mainlining *SportsCenter.* Everyone knows all the ins and outs, can't wait to point out that of the three, Junior's surrounded by the most dangerous hitters, making him the least likely to be pitched around, while Big Mac's got the least cover and a history of second-half declines and Sammy sits at the mercy of the wind direction at Wrigley Field. Everyone wants to know who *you're* pulling for, but you say you're not going to decide until your escapade's done.

Now you've got another tip, for those who haven't decided yet whom to lay their money on. If Maris's record is going to fall to the man whose muscle tissue stays loosest before he walks to the plate in the dry-mouth months of August and September, then it's going to fall to Junior. That's what you know after you catch his first at-bat from field level. Griffey gazes into the crowd from the on-deck circle, makes eye contact with people shouting to him and then rags on a photographer: "I know you got a better camera than that." Then he sweet-swings a run-scoring double down the leftfield line.

Whew, you almost blow it. Just before the fourth, you grab a slice of pizza and rush back in when you realize Junior's fixing to hit. *Crack!* Number 40 goes screaming over the 407 sign in center, and the fans finally come off their cans to scream too. You drop your pizza box and almost pinch yourself—counting Vaughn you're 3 for 3!—and head to the rightfield seats with five innings left because when you're on a roll, you never know.

You plunk yourself down next to a 32-year-old man wearing glasses, a blue cap and a glove, who is flanked by an eight-year-old nephew and a nine-year-old son at his first big league game. The man is an Air Force staff sergeant named Ralph Thomas who pored over seating charts for this game as if he were preparing for war. Had to be seats where Griffey's natural swing would most likely send a ball, he tells you, but also seats near enough to Junior's centerfield position to make the thing he had been telling his son R. J. for weeks come true: that when you sit near the great ones, some of their greatness jumps out and comes into you. It took them nine hours to drive here from Panama City, Florida, through torrential rains and frightening funneling clouds, but nothing was going to stand between them and Junior's siege of Maris, and when they finally arrived, too late for batting practice, dammit, the boy sat there in his Griffey hat and Griffey shirt staring wordlessly at his man in centerfield for 10 long minutes, letting the spiritual transfer occur.

"See how Junior's smiling?" Sergeant Thomas points out to his son. "See how he throws everything on a line, even when he's just playing catch before the inning starts? Remember Rule 1 and Rule 2?"

"Have fun and always try your best," replies the boy.

"That's right!" says the father. "Junior *never* forgets those two things!"

Maybe it's as simple as that, you're thinking. Maybe you should root for Junior because of Rule 1 and Rule 2.

Sergeant Thomas sure is smiling, too, because nine hours of coming and nine more of going back are nothing compared with the impending joy of ramming his eyewitness account of number 40 down the gullet of his boss, Capt. Roger Scott—Cardinals fan extraordinaire, Big Mac lover and namesake of Roger Maris himself, a former Cardinal!

"Can't wait, can't wait," Sergeant Thomas keeps crowing as the Mariners lock up an 8–3 breezer. "Cap'n's always sticking McGwire articles and pictures on my desk, and I do the same to him with Griffey stuff—but now I got *this*. I *told* him Junior would catch McGwire by the end of July! McGwire can't take the media and the pressure. And like I told Cap'n, doesn't matter if the ball goes one inch over the fence or three miles over—you can't add that extra distance to the next hit. *Love* telling Cap'n that—nothing he can say!"

The five ladies at poolside must think you're daft the next morning, Day 3, swimming those 46 laps in that little L-shaped hotel pool before you hightail it to the airport to fly to Chicago. It's the only way you know to knife through the fatigue, now that you're too juiced and jet-lagged to sleep. Slammin' Sammy's next. The wild card in the deck. Holding at 36, he has jacked just one in the last 11 days, but just might hit 20 in the next month, as he did in June.

As your plane wings toward O'Hare and everyone around you is reading about the home run chase, you're wondering: Could you possibly go 4 for 4? Then you land, and the dark skies start spitting rain on your rental-car windshield, and a flutter runs through your belly. No, God, please. What if you and Sammy get washed out?

You enter the clubhouse three and a half hours before the Cubs–Montreal Expos game and find Sosa swaying to Latin music. "I'll take care of you," he tells you. "Just wait?" You take a stool at a table five feet from his locker, back turned to him, delighted that you're going to speak to him alone and that this all seems so easy, just like the p.r. man promised . . . till Sammy shoos you away, tells you to go camp somewhere else. Over an hour you wait, and when you finally get the nod, Sammy opens a magazine of local real-estate listings. Uh-oh. . . .

Even for Sammy, who's never been a household name, the novelty's gone. He'll light up when he has an audience, but one-on-one with you and other reporters who follow, he answers questions lifelessly, eyes rarely lifting from photographs of houses with circular driveways and swimming pools. He says the media don't bother him. He admits it's nice to be part of the big story. He admits he's been overswinging again lately, his evil habit of old. He admits he doesn't know what position Roger Maris played. He says 18 minutes is enough. You resist recommending the brick colonial. What right do you have to be miffed? Jeez, isn't each one of these guys entitled to his own little way of hiding right in front of everyone's eyes?

When you exit the clubhouse, the sky's clear, the temperature's perfect, the sun's showering pinks and golds on the earth's most beautiful ballpark, and you decide, what the hell. It's the final night of your tater tear, so why not go drink a few cold ones with those bare-chested kids in the first row of the rightfield bleachers?

They're a whole different herd from the people you've met in San Diego and St. Petersburg. Everybody up here's got wit, everybody's got beer, everybody's got a desperate clear-eyed love for his team and an astonishing intimacy with it. Everybody's trying to decide whether he'll betray rightfield—family—and sneak over to left when Big Mac comes to town next month, and mulling how to stash an extra ball somewhere so that if Mac sends one into his palms, God willing, he'll have something to hurl back on the field when the mob chants, as it always does for visitors' home runs, "Throw it back! Throw it back!"

Nobody, *nobody*, thinks Sammy's got a prayer to bust Maris's record, not even the Sosa Boys, each of whom wears a letter of Sammy's surname in dripping blue paint across his bare chest. "Wore Sammy's number in high school," says Jake Abel, who's a letter S. "Got two dogs, named Wrigley and Sammy. But Griffey's gonna do it."

"Sammy won't even break Hack Wilson's team record of fifty-six," declares Chris Ramirez, a bartender and rightfield diehard. "Sammy thinks about it a little too much."

"That's exactly why he's never hit a grand slam," chimes in Linda Eisenberg, a 48-year-old rightfield regular for 20 years. "Not one. He can't resist swinging for the fences. He's better about it this year, but still. . . . See that bare spot he dug out with his spikes? That's so he'll remember where to stand. He and [shortstop] Manny Alexander share a brain. That's why we're always asking Sammy how many outs there are. We're doing it to make sure *he* knows."

"Aw, don't ask *them*," says Ramirez. "That's the anti-Sammy faction. Let's talk about *you*. Man, is it true? Did you *really* see McGwire and Vaughn hit one on Monday and Griffey hit one last night? And they *pay* you for that job? Don't worry, Sammy's gonna hit one for you, too. How 'bout a beer?"

Here comes Sammy to take his position, bolting out of the dugout like a pitchforked bull, veering sharply at the warning track and acknowledging the bleacher bums' *Sam-my! Sam-my!* chant with a fist thump on his heart and a kiss to his fingers. It's been 16 days since the second-place Cubs have been home, and when Ramirez cries, "Ahhhh, it's good to be home, Sammy!" the rightfielder turns immediately, nods and flashes him a clenched fist.

Amazing, how everything changes up here. With words out of the way, Sammy's pure heart comes shining through—he's the faithful mute using hand and body language to keep up a steady patter of appreciation for the legions behind him. Clenched fists, heart thumps, peace signs, finger kisses and hip wiggles come in relentless sequences, conveying a message after each event on the field that everyone around you understands, and always, the big forefinger stabbing up or the pinkie and the thumb when the mob cries, "How many outs, Sammy?" Shouldn't *he* be the one you pull for?

In the fifth Sammy singles home the run that knots the game at 2–2, and George Shields, a grad student sitting one row down and two seats over, turns and tells you, with embers in his eyes, that he would cut off his finger, honest to God, if it meant these Cubs would get into the '98 World Series. You buy rounds for the Sosa Boys, along with Ramirez and his two pals, union laborer Marty Crowley and air-conditioning mechanic Jeff Cline. "Don't worry," Ramirez keeps telling you as the sixth and seventh innings pass. "Sammy's gonna wait till his last at-bat to give you your homer."

Sammy steps to the plate for his last poke in the home eighth, Cubs up 5–3. You look across the stadium to the poor guys sitting on their hands up in the press box and ask yourself why—if you ever cover a ball game again—you would do it from there. It's nuts here tonight, fans heaving balls at Expos players, fans racing on the field and dodging the diving tackles of security guards, fans raining beer cups on the field. Now there are runners on the corners, wind blowing to right, fans waving fishnets and thumping HIT IT HERE, SAMMY T-shirts, packed house on its feet, and you right there with them, thinking, No, these sluggers have already given you three homers and a combined 9 for 14—you can't ask for more.

Then more comes. Across the night sky it comes—impossibly, Sammy's 37th, straight at you. You're watching it, feeling the beer splash across your neck and the regulars closing around you like a fist. George Shields throws up his hand in front of you—

there's the finger he swore he'd trade for a shot at the Series—and the ball smacks off the heel of his palm and bounces into the green mesh basket along the lip of the wall. Now it's a dogpile of flesh at your feet, everybody you've been drinking beer with diving and clawing and grunting. Crowley, the union laborer, wants it most. He goes headfirst into the basket, legs flying up before you, wrenches it from the Sosa Boys and comes up whooping.

You? You just stand there like a happy idiot as Ramirez pounds you on the back and bellows, "You did it! Three nights in a row! This is incredible! You sure you're not coming back tomorrow?"

No . . . no, you're not. You're on an 8 a.m. flight home the next morning, looking like something the cat dragged in, wondering who it is you finally want to break the record. Your eyelids begin to sag, and a smile comes to your lips as it dawns on you.

You've got the record. Nobody on the planet's ever going to see all four of the men assaulting history hit home runs on three straight nights—just let 'em try. Go to sleep, you tell yourself. . . . You've got it. . . . You've got it in the bag.

Tyson the Timid,
Tyson the Terrible

Just now he rang up Robin. He's sprawled out with the phone cradled against his ear, hungry to hear her voice and the smile in it, but all the phone does is ring and ring and ring. Where is she? God, he doesn't need this; *Robin, pick up the phone.* Just now Mike heard it on the news, about the girl pinned down by six men in the woods, raped, sodomized, found trembling four days later in a trash bag with NIGGER and KKK scrawled in charcoal across her flesh. This world is sick, this world is evil; *Robin, pick up the phone!* Of course, this is silly, she's fine, she lives 2,800 miles away, she's just not home—but this world is sick, this world is evil, *Robin, please pick up the phone. . . .*

The first to be hanged was Mike Tyson's friend. The little boy screamed and kicked, but he was nothing against the anger of the men. They knotted the rope around his neck and heaved him over the edge of the tenement fire escape; the rope played out, then jerked. Urine flooded the little boy's pants.

This story first appeared in 1988, two years after Mike Tyson became heavyweight champion, four years before he was convicted of rape.

In a moment they would reel the boy in, slip the noose over the other boy's head—Mike Tyson's head—and throw him over, too. His body froze, his mouth hung slack and mute. A neighbor noticed, shouted a threat. The boys' captors panicked and fled. Barely, Mike avoided death. Death for trying to steal a man's pigeons.

In the winter, when the earth has grown hard and the food scarce, the hawk flies circles in the sky. Its black eyes angle back and forth, from the big white house in the country where the heavyweight champion lives to the small brown one behind it where he keeps his pigeons.

For weeks now the two have been marking each other. When the man lets the pigeons fly free, the hawk drops from the sky, seizes one by the shoulders and wings off to devour it. The man mourns and plots his revenge.

Now only two of his hundred pigeons remain. The hawk must not die one death, but 98 deaths; how else will evil be balanced, how else can life make sense?

The heavyweight champion is well versed in cruelty, knows its nuances in a way that only one who has suffered it can. He lies in bed and pictures how he will catch the hawk, file its beak and claws to nubs, clip its wings, send it hobbling off to know the same helplessness and humiliation as the pigeon. And slowly, slowly die.

One morning he comes out to check his birds. For a moment their eyes meet, the hawk with its talons caught in the wire mesh of the pigeon coop, the man rigid with surprise. He reaches out, grabs its neck, tears its leg free of the mesh. At last he can mutilate it, cripple it, teach it *justice*.

Instead his hands part. The hawk bursts into the sky.

Last night he broke Larry Holmes. Left him twitching on the floor, the ring doctor rushing in to secure Holmes's tongue before Holmes could swallow it. That was nice. That was justice. The only thing nicer would have been for Holmes to end up sitting on the canvas, staring up at Mike Tyson, able to stand, but deciding not to, his will broken instead of just his body. But this was quite acceptable.

None of these fistfights for money ever brings Tyson happiness. They only bring him relief. Now it's morning and the wealthy white people in the East Side Manhattan apartment building where he has recently rented are approaching him, one after the next, to shake his hand for breaking Holmes. "I'm going crazy," he says under his breath.

He gazes at the young woman on his arm, a beautiful TV actress named Robin Givens, who has grown up in private schools and upper-middle-class suburbs, just like most of the well-wishers congratulating him. She wears a short black-and-white pin-striped skirt with matching vest, her hair falling in perfect curls across her shoulders. He wears unlaced sneakers, a sweat suit and a wool hat tugged low over his round, rough head. "You want to go to my old neighborhood?" he asks her. He cocks his head and grins. "You afraid?"

They choose the silver Lincoln stretch limousine over the black Mercedes-Benz stretch limousine waiting for them outside. In just a few minutes, they are riding through the holocaust. He stares out through the black-tinted window at empty lots full of broken glass and rubble, rusting cars, washing machines toppled on their sides, windowless and doorless houses, burned out, staring through black sockets—skulls. Brownsville, in Brooklyn. "My neighborhood," he says. His face is shining. "I grew up here. It's *mine!*"

He presses a button, the window slides down. "Rockaway Avenue. . . . All up and down this road, I robbed people. Who? Anybody who was a victim. And right here, by the train station, women would get on the bus, we'd reach in the windows, rip off their necklaces."

"Oh, Mike," says Robin.

"If a kid knew his mom was going out with money and didn't want to steal it himself, he'd tell me where she was going, what time. I'd wait for her and rob her, then we'd split it."

"*Mike.* . . ."

"And we'd rub drunks' fingers in the snow so we could pull off their rings. There's the grocery store. See those women coming out? We'd wait outside and offer to help them carry their bags to their cars, then, while we were handing them back their bags, we'd reach into their pocketbooks and steal their wallets."

"Mike, I can't picture you doing that. Look at all the barbed wire. This place is freaking me out."

"Can you see Robin walking these streets? Look at these people, look at their faces. Tough faces. These are *my* people. These are the people I represent when I fight. Slow down here. See the building with the boards over the windows? That's where we lived." Gleefully he says it: "Condemned!"

"Turn right at the corner. Look at this place. This is why I have the desire to win dramatically and brutally. That's Bristol Park. I saw people shot here, stabbed, beaten with baseball bats. That building over there—I ran inside it and hid, the cops were chasing me. Sure I used a gun. I'd walk in a store with a .22 and hold it in front of the man's face."

"Oh my God. . . ."

"The last time I robbed someone I was fifteen. They were a couple, they had on those big sheepskin coats and hats like Russians wear. We tore them off."

"Mike, that wasn't long ago. You lived *here* not long ago. . . ."

"But I don't feel the urge to steal anymore. I don't need to, I'm established. God, I hate that word, *established.* People who call themselves established—put them on these streets for five minutes, let's see how established they are. There's Lincoln Terrace Park. We'd see dead whores there in the morning. What memories. Good memories. Beautiful memories. I was happier then. I had pure fun here. Every day I was living on the edge. I was wild and free. I love coming back. Do you understand? When I'm here, I feel like a *warrior.*"

He enters the ring with no socks, no robe, no dancing, no music, just the black shoes and trunks, the hard, massive body, the refrigerated anger in his eyes. There was never any choice, the violence about to occur had to be—this is what his face and body say. The bell rings, and the photographs of him in the next morning's papers will show that same terrible lust in his face, the same wrinkled-up nose and drawn-back lips, the same urgency to *hit something.*

People say he is an instinctive fighter. People are wrong. His first instinct was to run. Driver, slow down: Yes, in front of that gutted building—up there, on the roof—that's where Mike Tyson stopped running and finally fought back. Yes, it was 12 years ago. No, it was *just now.*

Can you see him? He's shorter than the other boys his age. His left eye crosses when he's nervous. His face is one of those big, round ones old women like to squeeze. He lisps and talks softly, like a little girl. Other kids recognize him immediately—a victim. Everyone beats him up, even girls. They make fun of him, take his money and clothes; they hit him and laugh and hit him again as he runs home in tears.

Home is not always better. His older brother beats him up when his mother's not there. He cowers behind the refrigerator, sometimes even eats meals there. His father—he left when Mike was inside his mother's belly. Lorna Tyson and her three children survive on public assistance. She bounces Mike on her knee when he comes home crying, until, at last, the funny sound of his own jiggling sobs makes him stop.

She is one of the sweet innocents of Brownsville, one of the generation of big, round women whose families migrated from the South believing in God, the ones who still look to the sky for justice. Her children have never seen a cornstalk ripen or watched a newborn calf grow old; they can't see what she sees in the sky. All around them are those empty lots, those abandoned houses, those skulls. The last tenement they lived in had no water or heat. They slept with their clothes on and their eyes open. Neighbors, hoping the city would move them to a public shelter, kept torching the place.

When Lorna's youngest son lifts his eyes to the heavens, he sees birds, not justice. In his mind's eye he's looking down from inside one of their little heads, winging his way free of all the rubble, fear and death. Birds are freedom. If there is justice in the sky, a man can accept limits on his freedom. But if there isn't. . . .

He keeps his pigeons on the roof of an abandoned building, depending on its ghosts and rats to fend off intruders. When his birds are sick or newly hatched, he stays all night on the roof, listening to the sirens scream, the pigeons coo. When it is cold, he brings them inside the apartment. My babies, he murmurs as he strokes them.

Just now, Killer smelled them. It's cold, and Mike has moved them inside the vacated apartment next door. Killer is the Tysons' Labrador retriever. He noses open the lids on their boxes, crushing 25 pigeons, one by one, between his jaws, and arranges them in a pile. He has no desire to eat them; no, he does it simply because he can. Mike walks in, screams out in grief, runs sobbing to his room. He hates that dog; why can't he be more like him?

Please put it down. A teenager, five years older and bigger, has one of Mike's baby pigeons, shakes it in Mike's face. For no reason other than Mike's weakness—no reason different than the dog's—the teenager's hands jerk, the pigeon's head is gone. Blood pumps out and the bird still walks; its feet don't know it's dead.

All at once Mike's hands and feet are kicking and gouging and punching—he's fighting back for the first time ever, he's making the teenager bleed. *He* is justice! Instincts haven't made him fight. Outraged innocence has.

For the first time, when the beating of the teenager is done, Mike feels peace. Once a man stops running, once he allows the frenzy and chaos out there to come inside him, he and the world are in harmony. It seems so simple; how has it eluded him?

"It became fun for him to beat up kids," says his sister, Denise. "Everyone was afraid of him. His name stopped being 'Mike.' It became 'Mike Tyson.' Boys would come to the door and say, 'Mrs. Tyson, is Mike Tyson home?' He was very mean. And he was the sweetest, most compassionate boy you ever saw. My mother lived in fear that he would do one of two things: kill someone, or get killed.

"He became the best pickpocket in Brownsville. He'd shake your hand, and your watch, ring and wallet would be gone. Little kids, adults, anybody. He was good. Real good. Very, very good. We all dressed up as witches and ghosts for Halloween. Mike dressed up as a thief."

What a discovery! Anything the world inflicted on you, you could inflict on the world. If, *if* you could bring yourself to do it.

There, on the couch, his older brother slumbers. Mike takes a razor blade and makes an incision on his arm so fine that Rodney doesn't stir. "Nurse," he whispers to his sister, "alcohol." He pours it on the cut and dances away as Rodney jumps up howling.

He demands that a little girl give him her lunch. She refuses. He snatches her eyeglasses and lays them on the bumper of a truck heading out of state. His mother pays for the glasses and cries. *Look at me, Michael. Explain to me.* He can beat and rob a man twice his size, pass the night inside the skulls with the ghosts and rats, but he can't look his mother in the eye.

"I did evil things," he says. "But my heart was always pure."

Just now, in the middle of the night, a hand touched his shoulder. A dream with cold fingers. His eyes open. No dream—a big, round, white face in the dark just above him. "Do you remember everything I told you today?" the lips whisper. "Mike, you have to remember. . . ."

The old man is dying, he can feel it. A world champion will keep him alive. What a strange dream life is: it has brought a black juvenile delinquent and an old Italian man together in a Victorian house on the Hudson River, each looking for a reason to live.

They had put Lorna Tyson's son in a series of juvenile detention centers in Brooklyn, then moved him to a reform school upstate. He was 12. His body and anger were a man's. Sometimes it took three men to subdue him. One of the counselors at the school was a former boxer, and Mike began learning to be brutal in a scientific way. The counselor brought him to the attention of the old boxing man in Catskill, New York, named Cus D'Amato.

Now Cus is Mike's legal guardian. "A job delivering newspapers?" the old man roars when the 14-year-old wants to make some pocket money. "You don't need a job, you're going to be the heavyweight champion of the world!"

For hours and hours Cus talks, driving home the lesson Mike had begun to grasp in Brownsville. Control your fear and you are free. He who has the strongest will, who best controls his fear—he is freest of all. Night after night Mike watches films of former champions' fights, leafs through scrapbooks of their clippings, stares up at pictures of them that he has taped to the ceiling and the headboard of his bed, installs them in his empty sky as gods. He falls asleep mumbling, "I'm going to be great, I'm going to be a champion." Then he feels the old man touch his shoulder in the night, review the lesson, press the commandment deeper, deeper into his subconscious.

The first 13 years of his life, when he saw white people, they were usually in blue uniforms or in courtrooms. Now he's living in the same house with them. Now they're telling him to get up and run, go to school, respect the teacher, study. To be free, you have to be a slave? Sometimes he'll suddenly disappear, turn up back on the streets of Brownsville, mug or beat someone just to remember how it feels. "Whenever he was hurt, he *ran,*" Camille Ewald, the woman who owns the house where he and Cus live, will recall years later. A week amid skulls always makes him run back to the house upstate. The freedom of Brownsville smells too much like death.

Sometimes, at the public school he now attends in Catskill, the other kids slur him. Sometimes he only thinks they do. He goes crazy when it happens. The file of incidents becomes too thick, the school expels him. Now he's scared. He's a 16-year-old lying in bed staring up at the pictures of his gods on the ceiling, the ladder he is building toward them about to collapse into the rubble of his past. He gets up and goes to the gym.

Teddy Atlas, the young man Cus depends on to do the physical training, orders Mike out of the gym for two weeks as punishment for being expelled. The old man flinches. "This boy," Cus growls, "is a special case." He gets him a tutor, takes him right back to the gym. Eventually Atlas will depart. "As far as guidance in the ring, everything was perfect," Atlas will say years later. "We had him in a time capsule up there in Catskill, we stacked the deck for him to become a champion without any outside influences. But I thought there were compromises being made as far as his guidance as a human being. Put up a house too fast, it can come back to haunt you when a strong wind comes along."

* * *

Just now word has come: His mother is dead. The guilt from
the grief he has caused her is so sharp he wants to roll up in a ball
on the ground and scream. Where can he do that—in front of the
gruff old man in his new home, in front of the pigeon decapitators
in his old? He looks so cool and powerful on the outside—sometimes three-quarters of his weight class at amateur tournaments
withdraw the moment they lay eyes on him—but inside, the self-
hatred is chopping him up.

Like that thing with Duran. He loves Roberto, he can almost
picture him as an older brother walking beside him down Rockaway Avenue to kick some ass and steal some birds. "So mean,
so—*mean!*" he revels. "An intelligent animal!" He goes to Albany
to watch Duran's second fight against Sugar Ray Leonard, on
closed-circuit TV. What's this, the killer surrendering to the pretty
boy, the animal whimpering *"No más"*? Back in his room, Mike
cries. It's me! All those years Duran was champion before I started
liking him. . . . I ruined him. I ruin everything. He fell apart because of me.

And then: Don't I fight like Duran, don't I bully people in the
ring? If Duran can cry "No more," can't *I*? Where's the old man
right now? Is he sleeping? He kicks off the sheets, the air cold
against his sweating skin. Cus, where are you? Is this it: Fear is a
beast you must keep feeding fresh kills to keep quiet, in the ring,
outside the ring, it's all a ring, the beast must have new conquests
to stay silent. . . . Is that how it works? Suddenly the old cherry
floorboards are thumping, the old man—who sleeps a floor below
him—is awake; Mike is up there, dodging a jab, ripping the dark
with uppercuts and hooks, flattening someone, giving the beast a
snack to hold it until daylight.

What is it with girls? Funny, he never wants it to last. It's
almost like in the ring: He only wants to break down their resis-
tance, bend their will to his, conquer them and move on to the next.
A girl says something that hurts his feelings, brings all his old fears
about himself rushing back. Watch this, he tells a friend. For days
he buries the hurt, pretends to flirt, makes her fall in love with
him. Very good, now she's ready. He sneers at her and walks away.

His first four amateur fights, they have all said yes very quickly, tumbled to their backs, arms open, at his feet. The old man has dozed through the night, not a thump, not a single thump through the ceiling. Now comes the fifth one, in Scranton, Pennsylvania. Mike punches, the guy falls—no, wait, the guy is getting up, throwing punches! Mike knocks him down again, the guy gets up again. *My God, I cannot dominate him!* His arms forget how to strike a man, his legs forget how to sidestep and spring. The bell rings, he sags onto the stool. "My hand is broke," he says. Atlas, who was still his corner man then, squeezes his hand to check; he doesn't flinch. "You're letting yourself fall apart," hisses Atlas. "You have to control your feelings!" Mike wades back into the ring, throws a punch; the guy topples again, the guy gets up again! To everybody in the crowd Tyson is winning easily, but he clinches and holds, the whole world whirls before his eyes. "I can't go on," he says, panting, before the third round. "Get out there!" shouts Atlas. Suddenly Atlas senses it—he might go down! Atlas ignores the rules, leaps onto the apron, screams, "Don't you do it, don't you *dare* do it!" Tyson hangs on, wins the decision, closes his eyes, hugs his trainer and pants, "Thank you, thank you, thank you."

Oh, God, will it be a whole life like this? Feed the beast, feed the beast, miss a single feeding and the beast eats you.

Someone's killing little boys in Atlanta. Someone's putting cyanide in Tylenol. Months pass and everyone else forgets it, but it eats inside Mike, burrows into the soft place that never had a chance to toughen, so young was it paved over.

Today he's in one of those moods that people who haven't lived his 16 years can't understand. He stayed out late last night, past curfew. Cus barks at him. He mutters back. Cus shouts. Tears fill Mike's eyes. Cus wraps his thick arms around him and hugs him; oh, it feels so warm, so good. Mike begins to stay out late on purpose, so Cus will scream at him, so he will cry, so Cus will hug him once more.

Then Cus dies. Fights it with every ounce of his will, sweats like a horse and arches off the bed. It takes three men to subdue him. But he dies.

This world is sick, this world is evil. Mike is 19. Now he can stop fooling himself. He has always been happiest alone.

"He's ready to die," his assistant manager, Steve Lott, is saying. "That's what makes him the best fighter in the world. He's like a Roman gladiator: He's ready to die."

Roman gladiators were slaves. Seven decades before Christ, a gladiator named Spartacus rebelled. Seventy other gladiator slaves, as outraged by the world as he, followed his lead; together they brought their masters down. The insurrection swelled to an army of 70,000 that marched to the outskirts of Rome, that was poised to topple the empire, to bring all the old laws and institutions down, down, down. . . .

Spartacus hesitated. Rebellion here wasn't personal. He found himself retreating to the place where his heart first cried out, back to what was purest in his life, to the land where it was easy and right to rebel, to fight, even to die.

Midnight in Brownsville. Through the shadows, past the rubble and skulls, walking wide and nonchalant, moves Mike Tyson. He comes here after every fight, sometimes breaks training to come before. Beneath a streetlight, something gleams. Take off the $80,000 diamond-studded wristwatch when you go there, his friends have begged him. Take off the 30 grand worth of rings. Man, you're crazy, get yourself a bodyguard.

They don't understand.

"He'll just start staring at things when he's there, in a daze," says his friend Rory Holloway. "It's like he has to get something out of his system."

Or, perhaps, back into it.

Mess with me. Right here, in the rubble. Somebody. Anybody. Here it will be right to hit, here it will be pure.

An old woman, crazy with poverty, shambles up the sidewalk. He folds three $100 bills into a tight roll, tucks it so nimbly into her hand that she barely feels it. Can people understand? A chairman of an organized charity calls, he might mumble an excuse and hang up. But when no one's watching he will slip hundreds inside palms and pocketbooks of poor people—

reverse-pickpocket them—or bolt out of a car to help someone
old hobble across the street. This way it's right to give. This way
it is pure.

Can't people see, that's all he really wants. It's easy to mis-
understand him when his fists are wrapped around the rafters of
the world and he's pulling down with all his might, but that's what
he actually seeks—a philosophy, a religion, something to make it
all feel whole and pure.

He takes a deep inhalation of Brownsville and tries not to let
go—God, when you walk into Manhattan and they slap you on the
back, it's so hard to hold it in. How else, if he lets his past recede,
can he preserve the hurt and outrage that made him rebel, the anger
that compels him to hit a man? Everyone is trying to dilute it, every
request for an interview or a photo or an autograph threatens to
weaken it, every multimillion-dollar offer, every fan that sidles up
to him on the boardwalk in Atlantic City and says, "You're going
to kill Holmes, he's an old man," every reminder that he has become the favored one, that he now is society's champion. Don't
they see what they're doing to him? They're making him master,
but to succeed he must be the rebel. He is driven to conquer; to do
it, he must feel oppressed. How can he keep fighting with his lips
curled back if they rob him of that? Why does the way he satisfies
himself have to satisfy them; how can he take the paycheck and
keep the cry of the self pure?

"What am I going to do with all that money?" he groans.
*Twenty-one years old, 60 million dollars this year, six-sevenths
of what Ali earned in his entire ring career.* He buys a Mercedes,
a Jaguar, a Rolls-Royce, a Corvette, but a week later every one of
them bores him. "Real freedom is having nothing," he says. "I was
freer when I didn't have a cent. Do you know what I do sometimes?
Put on a ski mask and dress in old clothes, go out on the streets
and beg quarters."

It's late December in Atlantic City, four weeks before the
fight with Holmes. Soon, as they are a month before each bout,
20 black-and-white photos of former champions will be taped
to the walls of the condominium he stays in. Videos of their epic
battles will play again and again on his screen; he, with each

squeeze of his remote control, pumps life back into their flickering spirits and fights away the question: Who one day will do that for him?

He doesn't measure himself against his contemporaries, but against *them*—the gods. He wears the same bulky sweaters, long overcoats, cuffed trousers and caps that they did; squints and tries to see his own life in grainy black and white, bathed on a screen with the same soft white light as theirs; why, *why* doesn't his life ever seem quite as magical?

Sometimes, wrapped in knee-length white mink, he'll go 72 straight hours prowling the nightclubs, streets and hotels of New York. Then come days of listlessness and boredom in his apartment, staring at videos of movies in which people's heads get split open and their eyes are gouged out. One day, he'll eat 15 chicken wings and a gallon of ice cream. The next, he won't eat a thing. Life must be devoured, to prove that there are no limits to his freedom. Life must be shoved away, to prove that he remains in control.

He walks into the wind on the boardwalk, distant, moody. Too many backslaps since that last night in Brownsville, his lungs can't hold it anymore, that deep breath at midnight has escaped him. Everything's compromised, it's all drudgery, four weeks of killing himself in training, all for another staged social event. He looks up at the Trump Plaza marquee advertising the fight, sees the big picture of him with one title belt around his waist and two crisscrossed like bandoliers across his chest—suddenly he recaptures the snapshot of himself that he needs. "Look!" he cries. "Look at me! Like a f—— bandit!" He hop-steps like a little boy. "It's going to be great! I can't wait, it's going to be great!"

Please, don't ask him to explain. Confusion is his gunpowder. Every explanation lets a little of it leak. O.K., listen well; he won't do this often. He is pacing in a dingy locker room above the police station in Catskill, where he trains, night crowding all around a single naked lightbulb. One moment he is in the shadows at the far end of the room, fingering a boxing glove, a wad of tape, anything his restless hands can find. The next he looms above you, touching your shoulder, an intelligent man trying to press into you a feeling for which he never learned words. His voice, it's soprano, a bird trapped inside a tenement.

"In my mind, everyone is against me," he says. "Some people may act like they respect me, but they don't. I'm in a business of phonies. I want to believe the whole world is against me. I love the smell of danger. I love living on the edge. In my mind I'm not a man who has made twenty-five million dollars. I'm still the wild kid on the streets.

"I believe in taking chances. There's nothing I won't try, as far as my social life. Small stakes don't interest me. Only big. I never stole for the money, I stole for the excitement. No one will ever tell me what to do. I refuse to have anyone dictate to me.

"When I say I'm the best fighter on the planet, I don't say it because I want to prove something. No one knows I'm a jerk more than me—I screw up all the time, I'm somewhat immature. I just say it because I want to get under people's skin. I want people to boo me when I walk in the ring. The chip on my shoulder is my security. I'm the bad guy, I want to be the bad guy . . . *but I'm not the bad guy.*

"What society gives me doesn't mean anything to me, because I know when I go it will be like I never existed. I don't want celebrity. It's disrespectful, coming up and asking me for autographs while I'm eating. What does a seventy-year-old white person have in common with a twenty-one-year-old black man? Nothing. Nobody is going to come up to me and say they love me now, when he has no reason to love me. Where was he when I needed someone to love me?

"Five years before I was born, black people had no rights. If you were twenty, five years before I was born, your ways were set. It's hard for me to believe that someone who was twenty in 1961 could change his mind about blacks. It's still inside them. People don't want to see a twenty-one-year-old black man making sixty million dollars a year, owning four, five cars. But I don't need them to love me. I don't need anyone but myself.

"Tell me, how do people expect me to react: Give the nigger a little money and he's satisfied? Why is my friend Rory a great guy when he's with me, but not when he's not? I'm a commodity, I'm supposed to entertain them. You know in the old days, how slaves sang and danced for their masters? Then they had to go home and mop the floors. Think about it. I'm supposed to be a role model. What kind of role model would I be if I forgot where I came from?

"I know that basically I'm not wanted here. Americans aren't civilized people. I love the freedom of speech and opportunity here . . . but sometimes, I'm embarrassed by America. We should be a great enough country to take care of the weak. If there wasn't poor, there couldn't be rich. If there wasn't sickness, there wouldn't be health. Suffering is the only way we don't take life for granted, it makes us realize how good we have it. I love retarded people, animals, kids—they're innocent. But people take affection for weakness. When people do that, I get very upset, I don't know what I might do.

"If a man hit me outside of the ring, I'd kill him and not think anything of it. I refuse to take s——. I took enough of it when I was a kid. I ran away—I don't ever want to do that again. If somebody smacks me, it's reason to fight to the death. Then I will take responsibility for what happens. Be a man.

"I love to hit people. I *love* to. Most celebrities are afraid someone's going to attack them. I want someone to attack me. No weapons. Just me and him. I like to beat men and beat them bad.

"I'll break Spinks. None of them have a chance, I'll break them all. When I fight someone, I want to break his will. I want to take his manhood. I want to rip out his heart and show it to him. My manager, Jimmy [Jacobs], tells me not to say those things. But that's how I feel. People say that's primitive, that I'm an animal. But then they pay five hundred dollars to see it. There's so much hypocrisy in the world. The world is so f—— up."

His listener asks about the letter Tyson's old social worker, Ernestine Coleman, wrote to him in 1986 after his devastating sixth-round knockout of Jesse Ferguson, when he told the media, "I wanted to drive his nose bone into his brain."

"Be an athlete," Coleman wrote. "Not an animal."

Tyson's face darkens, he shakes his head no. His explanation has spilled out of the locker room and into a restaurant. "I'm not an athlete, don't call me an athlete. How can you compare me with Billie Jean King or Magic Johnson? They're athletes. Athletes have careers. Athletes have to prepare. At any moment, I'm ready. I never liked sports. Sports are only social events. I'm a warrior, a missionary. What I do is an obsession. If I wasn't in boxing, I'd be breaking laws, that's my nature."

Abruptly, his face turns, shines as it must have before he knew that a human being could behead a bird, and to the waiter in a restaurant that serves half a dozen Gulf Shrimp Garibaldi for $24.75, he asks, "Do you have ice cream on a stick?"

"Once I was supposed to meet a girl," he says, "but on the way I saw an ice-cream store. I knew if I went in, I'd miss the girl. I didn't know what to do. I went into the store, and while I was eating the ice cream, I was very happy, I didn't care at all about the girl. It was only when I was done that I wished I'd met the girl."

He laughs and grabs his listener's shoulder. His head nuzzles against it, almost like a puppy's.

In the big white house where Mike still sometimes stays, 83-year-old Camille often looks down from the TV and finds his round rough head lying in her lap. "He's almost purring like a kitten," she says. "He's begging to be stroked. He needs affection very much. Oh, I worry. I worry about the people he goes out with, that only care about having a good time. I worry what could happen if he gets angry in public—I've seen him angry, and I know. He has ring discipline but not life discipline; Cus died before he had time to teach him that. He still can't sit in one place. He'll be sitting here with one girl and go to the phone and call another. But after all, he's still a child. . . ." She pulls out a recent Mother's Day card. "For someone I love," it says, "and wish you was my mother. Happy Mother's Day and I love you. By Michael, your black son."

She puts away the card. The house is quiet; it's the night before a snowfall. Somewhere out there, his Rolls-Royce prowls the streets. There's one other way to hush the beast, people say. But perhaps it's even more frightening, more dangerous, the biggest risk of all.

On February 7, 1988, he walks up the aisle of a Catholic church in Chicago. The scores of women who said yes to him are nowhere to be seen. The TV actress who turned back his engagement ring, the one he had to conquer, is the one who, on the spur of the moment, he marries.

The room is silent. His new wife falls asleep, he stares into the darkness. Please, Cus, just one more question, the one he never had a chance to ask: What becomes of him if the beast ever goes away?

An hour before midnight on June 15, 1976, George Foreman's right foot twitched. Nearby lay Joe Frazier, victim of a fifth-round knockdown. Arms raised, Foreman stood above him, aching to consummate his conquest by planting that foot on Frazier's chest.

At that stage in his life, Foreman often went through two women a day; his need to have flesh beneath him had become desperate. This urge made him the heavyweight champion of the world. It also made him ripe to be dismantled. He who needs to dominate most, most fears being dominated. Consider Sonny Liston and Foreman, one the 1960s' most glowering intimidator, the other the 1970s'. Who could picture either of them lying on the floor until they were there—both having been undone by Muhammad Ali.

Six months ago George Benton, Tyrell Biggs's trainer, had a warm afternoon's dream. He thought perhaps his fighter could do that to Mike Tyson. Instead Tyson broke Biggs in seven rounds, made him issue whimpering sounds, as Tyson exulted later, "kind of like a woman." Benton didn't change his mind about Tyson's vulnerability. "It's Katie-bar-the-door when that kind of mind-set gets frustrated," he says. "It doesn't bend. It just breaks."

But who can break the breaker?

"It won't be easy—Tyson's far more polished than he's given credit for," says Atlas. "There are people talented enough, it just hasn't been urgent enough for them to do what it takes."

Which is . . .?

"Someone who, when Tyson hits after the bell, hits him back until they have to pull them apart. Someone who, when Tyson hits him with an elbow, hits him back with his elbow, his head, the stool. Someone who makes Tyson think, My God, this guy will do things even *I* wouldn't do. Someone not just trying to survive—someone trying to win."

Does that man exist on the heavyweight landscape? Michael Spinks? Evander Holyfield? "Sixty to seventy percent of what he's done in the ring is because of intimidation," says Holyfield. "His reputation has his opponents halfway down before they get in the ring. I met him once, at the Red Parrot in New York. He grabbed my bicep when we were introduced and tried to crush it. Everywhere I walked, he wouldn't take his eye off me."

That is fear. Great fear, tightly controlled, is great strength, a cold, hard wrecking ball deep inside a fighter. One flicker of doubt, and the cold ball turns molten, rages through the rib cage, incinerates him.

Men who have fought with violent imperative, constant aggressors in the ring, rarely have endured as champions. Jack Dempsey defended his title only five times before losing it. Rocky Marciano did it six and retired. Joe Frazier lasted for nine title defenses, four if you don't count his New York State Athletic Commission title. The flame that consumes their opponents consumes them, too. "It requires such a tremendous amount of physical and mental and emotional energy to fight that way that very few men can sustain it," says HBO analyst Larry Merchant. "Unlike Ali or Holmes, they must put their whole selves into every moment in the ring. Usually they are people who live fast and die young."

Just now, a dream awoke him. *I've lost!* These dreams come all the time—*I've lost the fight, I've lost!* He kicks the sheets away, scrambles to his feet, dodges a jab, rips the darkness with uppercuts and hooks.

The fight draws nearer. Please make it come soon, it's like a scream stuck inside, please let it come out. He drops to the floor—push-ups, sit-ups—lies back in bed huffing and snaps on the TV. Without a human voice in the room, he can't fall asleep.

An hour passes. At 4 a.m., without an alarm clock, he awakes, laces on his sneakers and heads outside. It is darker and colder and earlier than when the other fighter, his opponent, runs— another small fresh kill, a little nibble for the beast.

Please make it come soon, please let it come out. Daylight arrives. Outside again, he dips into a shop, buys a piece of bread and shreds it. The pigeons come to him to feed, his hand snaps out, grabs one, brandishes it, flings it over his shoulder high into the sky.

He let go of the hawk because it was so beautiful, says one friend.

He let go of the hawk because he felt sorry for it, says another.

I let go of the hawk because it was so powerful, says Tyson. I let go of it because I was scared.

Two days to go, please make it come soon; can't they schedule these fistfights any closer? His eyes catch the newspaper. *What? I've lost the fight, I've lost!* Look right there, on the back page of the *New York Post*, a large photograph of him dropping to the floor, Larry Holmes standing above him as he falls. *I've lost, I've lost, I don't remember it, but I've heard that happens to fighters, I've lost!*

It never happened, it's a photographer's trick, Mike's trainer, Kevin Rooney, assures him. Mike seizes the picture, rips it into tiny pieces.

Was it six years ago that he stepped outside the arena, just before the U.S. Junior Olympic finals, and broke into sobs—"If I lose, I'll lose all the people who like me, I'll lose everything I have. . . ." Or was it just now; dear God, why does everything in his life seem like *just now*? Dear, gruff Cus, on whose grave he poured a bottle of champagne when he won the title, and his dear dead mother, and all the grainy black-and-white gods and all the ghosts inside all the skulls of Brownsville—who's he fighting for? For them. Why? They're gone!

And now they say it's time to fight. He sits in his black trunks and black shoes, the past circling over him like the hawk; he can

feel it there, smell it there, hear its wings beating the air—or could
that be his heart? This world is sick, this world is evil, *Robin, please
pick up the phone.* The hawk is circling, the noose is dropping, the
pigeons are cooing, it's midnight in Brownsville, the holocaust's just
minutes away by limo, *Robin, please pick up the phone.* This world
is sick, this world is evil, they rip heads off birds, they put poison in
aspirin, they murder little boys, they pin down girls in the woods,
scrawl NIGGER on their bellies. Somebody's got to stop it, nobody will
stop it, I will stop it, I will be justice, *I* will repay them all.

The bell rings. The people gape. Look, they cry. Look at Larry
Holmes's face—why, he's scared!

Someone to Lean On

We begin way over there, out on the margin. We begin with a dirty, disheveled 18-year-old boy roaring down a hill on a grocery cart, screaming like a banshee, holding a transistor radio to his ear. No one ever plays with him, for he can barely speak and never understands the rules. He can't read or write a word. He needs to be put away in some kind of institution, people keep telling his mother, because anything, anything at all, can happen out there on the margin. There's already a gully over his left eye from the time he stepped in front of a car as a five-year-old and nearly died from the impact. There are teeth missing from the day he swerved in front of a car while riding his grocery cart, and there's a scar on his thigh from the day he was playing with a packet of tiny sticks and suddenly everything around him was ablaze. There is something, as well, that you can't see, except sometimes in his eyes: It's fear. Of people. Once some kids told him to pull the lever on the fire-alarm box and then watched him being led away to jail. Another time he was seized by a group of boys who yanked down his pants and painted his buttocks with paint thinner, burning him nearly as badly as the blazing sticks had.

This story first appeared in 1996.

All of which might explain why his grocery cart keeps taking him to a football field at McCants Junior High in Anderson, South Carolina. It's autumn 1964. Everything on that grid is so different from life out on the margin. All the boys wear the same neat, clean clothing and move to assigned places at the bark of a one-word command. There are units and sub-units, and everyone knows precisely where he belongs. From a safe distance, the boy watches. T.L. Hanna High School's junior varsity team practice on the McCants field and mutely absorbs it all.

One day the players hear noises and look over. The boy on the margin is commanding his own team, one that only he can see, through a series of calisthenics and drills, doing his best to mimic the coaches' body language, signals and commands. The players giggle; it's a distraction, to be sure. The young coach, whose future hinges on his ability to maintain discipline and precision on that grid, turns and looks too.

The choices that make or unmake a life are so small. "Come over here, boy," calls the coach.

When we speak of the power of sports today, it's always in terms of their grip on the national marketplace, their headlock on the American psyche. It's so easy to forget all about their other power. . . .

Radio turned 50 two months ago, but you might not have read about it. He bounded through the corridors of T.L. Hanna High collecting his birthday gifts, waving and slapping fives and hugging kids and wiggling his rear end as the students chanted, "Go, Radio, you got it!" It took the whole bed of head football coach Harold Jones's pickup truck to get all the gifts home, just as it has on the other birthdays and the Christmases that Radio has celebrated at the school for the last 32 years.

No, he never made it to an institution. He became one instead. Just before his last birthday, folks in Anderson were remarking on all the speckles of white on his head and in his whiskers. "When Radio dies, it'll be the biggest funeral in the history of Anderson," said Herb Phillips, an assistant football coach at Hanna. "It'll be like a senator's or a governor's funeral."

"Gonna be *sad* sad, like losing a family member," said Terry Honeycutt, another football assistant.

"He's the best-known figure in high school football in upstate South Carolina," said former Hanna coach Jim Fraser.

"He *is* T.L. Hanna—it's that simple," said Coach Jones, who for three decades has kept Radio under his wing.

In many countries where towns have plazas and cafés and bars and butcher shops all within a few blocks of people's homes, there is no margin. There are places for those with defects, impediments and afflictions to mingle with their neighbors, to be taken care of and teased, to feel part of something larger. They become local characters, not freaks. Somehow in our country those places have vanished or never existed, and people like Radio end up in homes behind walls, living with strangers who are just like them, or mumbling, ragged and gaunt, through the streets of large cities.

But there remains one rarely noticed place where they can still belong, a niche no sociologist figured on—after all, isn't sports where people turn to watch the strong chew up and spit out the weak? But something about high school athletics is still human enough to accommodate people whose minds work at different speeds and angles from minds in the mainstream, and so you can find these people on the sidelines or in the bleachers all across the U.S., lighting up as they exchange greetings with the regulars. Why, in just the small circle of schools against which Hanna competes, there is one-eyed and slow-witted Lonnie McGee racing onto the field with the football team at Greer High each Friday night, and before him there was Housecat, whose mission in life, until he died not so long ago, was to chase down every foul ball and home run hit at Greer baseball games, even if he had to barge into someone's home to do so, and hurry that ball right back to the umpire. There is Marlee Gambrell, born with heart and hearing and vision defects, hooting "Don't worry 'bout it!" in the darkest moments at Belton–Honea Path High. And up until recently, there was wild-eyed Doris, taking care of the water bottles and ringing that half-ton bell on the sidelines at Easley High. Thrilled, every one of them, to take on the title—team manager—that most teenagers smirk at.

But none of them has been more loved, or more legendary, than Radio. He holds more high school varsity letters than any other man in history, having received one each from the Hanna football, basketball and track teams every year for the past three decades and filed them all carefully between his box spring and his mattress. Who else can lay claim to having missed just one week of high school in the past 10 years? Only once, and long ago, did Radio make the mistake of saying he was in the 12th grade, and then he was consumed by terror when the coaches told him that meant he would be graduating soon. Ever since then he has nodded wisely and declaimed loudly to one and all, *"I be in 'lebenf grade,"* always reaching out a hand to touch his listener when he speaks, always seeking assurance that he still belongs and that everything is O.K.

He awakens each morning before six and, being unable to tell time, has to be restrained by his older brother or by his brother's wife from making an immediate beeline for the bus stop. Radio is the first of the 15 kids at the stop to bound onto bus No. 9 and the first to bound off it in front of T.L. Hanna High. He bops in and out of classes all day, taking copious notes—an unrelenting series of loops—and glowing at the end of each marking period when he receives his report card just like everyone else. A mesh sack full of footballs slung over his shoulder, he bounds onto the practice field after school, and the players, like their fathers before them, rub his head as if he were a pet retriever and laugh as he commences his gibber-jabber commands, gobbledygook pep talks and flapdoodle defensive signals.

"Dat yo' man, boy! Don' you unnerstan' dat? Dat yo' man! Don' you worry 'bout yo' man! You got to git dat kwahback! Ain' dat right?"

"Right, Radio."

"Huh?"

"You're right, Radio."

"What? Huh?"

Oh, yes, sometimes Radio can drive them up a wall and across the ceiling. But it's all worth it, every maddening and bewildering moment of it, when practice ends and all the coaches sit in a circle around Radio in their office, competing to see who can recount the latest or most vintage Radio anecdote, knowing that he will bark out some four-word proclamation that will make the moment even richer. Each sentence Radio speaks is a victory for them, because they know it is the love and attention they have been showering on him for decades that has given the mute boy a voice. Maybe Coach Jones will tell the story about the time back in the mid-'80s, when he was also T.L. Hanna's track coach, that he took Radio to the all-day Trojan Relays at Northwestern High in Rock Hill, South Carolina, and wondered for hours what had become of Radio . . . finally finding out upon returning to the team bus at the end of the meet. There lay Radio in the front seat, doubled up in pain, sweating bullets . . . and there lay the cooler, bereft of all 30 roast-beef sandwiches, not to mention a dozen sodas, that Jones had packed for the kids. *"Dem sammiches good!"* Radio still yelps a decade later. Which no doubt leads into the tale of the time Radio lifted the entire canister of cheese at a school cafeteria salad bar and dumped a foot-high pile of grated cheddar on his lettuce (*"Cheese go good wid salad!"*). Which brings up the time Radio was so fixated on the hot dog he was carrying before a game at Greenwood High that when he slipped on the wet grass, rather than release his cargo and use his hand to break the fall, he salvaged the frankfurter and landed on his wrist, fracturing it. Radio sat in the mud, polished off his hot dog and *then* burst into tears.

No name for Radio's defect has ever been pronounced, as far as anyone knows. It is no doubt genetic, because he shares it with his father, whom he has rarely seen since his first few years of life, and with Cool Rock, the brother two years his junior who shares Radio's bedroom. Cool Rock still can't be understood when he tries to speak. But then, Cool Rock was never adopted by a team.

Even when James Robert Kennedy was a little boy, everywhere he went, his radio went too, until folks finally had no choice but to make Radio his name. From the radio came a human voice, the only one he could count on to speak to him when his mother, Janie Mae Greenlee, left for long hours to clean and cook at the local hospital or schools. Now and then the boy would even lift his radio to his lips and talk back to it.

He attended a school for the learning disabled for a few months one year, but it didn't take. Back then he couldn't use a fork or pedal a bike, and because cruelty runs downhill, it wasn't a good idea for a cat or a dog to annoy him. "What's my name?" Coach Jones asked as he and his fellow jayvee coach, Dennis Patterson, began luring Radio closer and closer with bottles of soda that autumn of '64. "Do you remember what I told you yesterday?"

"*Woomifflcojowu.*"

"Try again. You can have this whole bottle if you can say it. *Coach . . . Jones.*"

What made Jones invite the wild boy with the missing teeth to come to a game, to help carry the watercoolers and then hop into Jones's pickup truck for a ride home? Why would a coach work so hard at discipline and deployment and then let loose a pinball on his chessboard? After all, everyone knew Coach Jones to be a strict and quiet man who virtually never showed emotion or affection. No one knew that when he was a kid growing up in Anderson, he was the one who would fight anyone who picked on the delicate boy who lived across the street, that he was the one who, when working at his grandfather's theater, would slip a retarded man in the door for free and put a box of popcorn in his hands.

And so, before you knew it, Radio was going everywhere Coach Jones and his jayvee team went, and Radio's halftime show was gaining renown. Radio would charge onto the field and bend down like a center, screeching those preposterous signals, hike the ball to himself and dipsy-doodle all around. Finding no one open except himself, Radio would flip the ball to Radio and then, to the crowd's roar, boogie-woogie all the way to pay dirt.

In no time, Coach Jones was inviting Radio to school on game days, handing him sneakers, a T-shirt and shorts so he could take gym class with the other kids. Soon Radio was following the kids into health class, history and social studies. Sure, it probably broke some law, and no doubt it exposed the school to all manner of liability. But one glare from Coach Jones was all it took to keep Radio in line, one threat that he would be banished from the team if he misbehaved. The principal had little choice but to accept Radio as part of the school. "The kids would *kill* me if I ever got rid of him,"" says current principal Mike Sams. They loved the frantic hip-hop way he ran in phys-ed class until that sorry day four years ago when he tore a hamstring and scrabbled around the gym floor like a crab, sobbing, *"I wan' my mama!"* They loved the way he rubbed his furrowed face and sighed *"Whoooo!"* as he took history tests, as if in deep consternation over the complexity of the questions, and then painstakingly filled in each blank with the same set of loops.

Soon Radio was wolfing down breakfast and two lunches a day in the cafeteria, then cleaning up the tables in his long yellow rubber gloves and running errands for teachers all over the school. Soon he was jump-starting dull assemblies and sluggish pep rallies, erupting out of his seat to do one of those shimmy-shuffle-shakedowns that got the whole student body to bopping and bellowing. It only got better when Radio was inducted into Hanna's Naval Junior ROTC unit, and he began wearing a full military uniform each Wednesday. What a sight he was in crisp dress whites and blues and merit ribbons, racing into special-ed class and pulling out his Crayolas for 10 or 15 minutes of coloring, then bolting out the door and up a stairway, two steps at a time, to monitor the halls—*"Where you goin', boy? Don' wun! No wunnin' in da hall! Hi, honey! I like you!"* All at once, standing fully erect and with his eyes open, he would fall dead asleep. Of course, if his schedule simply didn't permit a snooze, he could always—in the midst of a violent six-on-six drill later that day at football practice—sprawl out on a tackling dummy and doze like a baby.

It was all too wonderful to confine to autumn, and soon Radio was the manager of the basketball and track teams as well. How could Coach Jones resist when Radio put on that basset-hound face at track meets and begged to run too? And so, even though Coach Jones was in charge of a juggernaut, a team that would win 10 state titles between 1970 and '92, he would take the opposing coach aside and ask if Radio could enter the slow heats of the 100-, 200- and 400-meter dashes. Wearing spikes and shorts and a singlet just like everyone else, Radio would blast out of the starting blocks, blazing when he was in front of the stands and then slowing to a walk, or stopping altogether to pull up his socks, once he reached the curve and there was no attention to bask in. "What happened on that curve, Radio?" the coaches would kid him later. "Did the gorilla jump on your back?" It was at times such as those—when Radio's eyes might suddenly cloud with fear, and he would ask, *"Where dat go-wi-wa hide? Behind dem trees?"*—that everyone would be reminded of how frightening a place the world could be for Radio, and how close an eye they would have to keep on him.

Coach Jones took Radio to the doctor every year, monitored Radio's diet when his blood-pressure readings and cholesterol count went through the roof and made sure his medical and dental bills were paid. "Radio," says assistant coach Honeycutt, "would be dead by now if not for Coach Jones." The players who lived in Radio's neighborhood kept at bay the bullies who used to target him, and a half-dozen players might each deliver a hamburger and an order of fries to Radio on game day, each unaware that Radio was squirreling the food away in his backpack, each proudly believing that his offering was the only one. One day when Radio's invariably empty billfold was stolen at school, the players all but formed vigilante squads, and the coaches hastily bought Radio a new wallet for fear that a student might be found dangling from a ventilation duct. Even in the fourth quarter of a tense game, when a player was bent-in-half tired and cringing from a coach's screams for blowing a coverage, and Radio would get right in his face and reenact the entire tirade, or demand out of the clear blue to know his shoe size, the player's tolerance would hold. "O.K., Radio, O.K.," the Hanna kids would say, and a few seconds later, Radio would have them giggling.

Just once, 22 years ago, did Radio miss a game. It was not long after Coach Jones and Radio had gotten their promotions to the varsity, but being only an assistant coach then, Jones could only swallow his Adam's apple when Fraser, the head coach, decided the bus was too crowded for Radio to make the road trip to Northwestern High. Fraser slipped Radio a five to ease his conscience, but the sight of that slump-shouldered man standing alone in the school parking lot, tears rolling down his cheeks, would haunt the coach forever, as would the 27–20 loss that followed. "He'll be the first one on the bus from here on out," Fraser vowed that night, and when the T.L. Hanna Yellow Jackets, with Radio leading them onto the field, rolled all the way to the state final that year, Radio's position was forever secure.

From then on rain was the only thing that Radio had to fear on game day. Each wet Friday he would scramble out the school's back door every few minutes, mournfully holding out his palm to feel the air, then rushing back to Coach Jones to confirm, for the 28th time, *"Gonna 'top wainin', wight, Co' Jone'?"* And when God smiled, and the rain clouds ran away, Radio bloomed.

Imagine, just for a moment, that you could go to a football game one day and play every role, be *everyone* in the whole stadium. That's what Radio did *every* game. Gumming and gnawing another freshly mooched fried-chicken drumstick, he would start out as the official greeter, holding open the Hanna program to make sure all arriving fans saw his photograph and hoisting up his pants legs to make sure everyone got a gander at his new pair of shoes—*"Wook at my Weeboks!"*—along with his socks, one white and one black. Then, dropping one drumstick and seizing another, he would commandeer the bass drum as the Hanna band made its knee-pumping entrance, quickly double back to wolf down a free hot dog and then scurry up to the press box to become the radio color commentator, barking over the WAIM airwaves, *"We gon' beat dey butt!"* All at once it would occur to Radio that he was also Hanna's coach, and he'd bolt down onto the field to yelp stretching instructions to the team during warm-ups—*"You roll dat neck, boy!"*—and then rush back to the bleachers to scarf some free popcorn and sign his autograph, loop-de-loop.

For the next two hours, to the ricochet of impulse, he would be the band director leading the touchdown celebration tune, the pom-pom-shaking cheerleader, the team trainer kneading cramps from players' calves, the 15-year-old flirt tossing popcorn at the cheerleaders' bare legs, the drum majorette in the halftime show, the fanatic racing up and down the sidelines with a giant Hanna flag, the water boy rushing squeeze bottles— empty, as often as not—onto the field during timeouts, and the coach arm-waggling defensive signals at the offensive line . . . all to the steady background bleating, from white-haired alumni and kids alike, of "Raaaa-dioooooo! Hey, Raaaadiooooooo, come over here!"

His legend radiated from the school throughout the town. At the annual Anderson Christmas parade, the local cable television crew could not get enough of Radio marching the loosey-goosiest goose step in martial history, wearing his Santa Claus hat and shaking a fistful of sleigh bells—especially that Yule when his beltless pants slid to his ankles. He no longer had to pay to eat anything or walk to go anywhere in Anderson—there was always a free meal or a free ride. In the history of long shots, was there ever one longer than the possibility that a man such as he would be known and loved wherever he went? And if there was room in the program for Radio, then who *couldn't* be included, who *wasn't* welcome to join the community at its largest weekly gatherings? That was the message that Radio's presence sent to all those who felt a little odd, a little different.

The fans from the surrounding towns also embraced him over the years, and one day when an assistant coach took him to a Clemson football game, it finally became clear what Hanna High had wrought. Honking and waving and cries of "Radio!" accompanied the two men the entire bumper-to-bumper trip, and no man has ever tailgated upon as many tails as Radio did that day.

But when darkness fell on Christmas Eve each year, just one car crunched onto the gravel in front of Radio's house. The curtain on the front window would rustle, for that's where Radio always awaited Coach Jones. The coach would hand Radio the wrapped gifts he had bought or collected from donors: shoes, socks, shirts, belts and, of course, another radio, for each year Radio's curiosity about who spoke to him from inside the little black box was more than the little black box could bear.

Fierce was Radio's loyalty in return. Fists pummeling, he would leap on the back of an assistant coach who pretended to sneak cases of soda from Coach Jones's truck, and he would materialize like a bad dream before the eyes of any referee who argued with Coach Jones. The one time in his career Coach Jones was ejected from a game, Radio screamed *"You ass!"* at the ejecting referee so often, and with such precise diction, that he too got the heave-ho.

Coach Jones was wonderful at hiding his exasperation with Radio, which might have been why he had to sip buttermilk during games to soothe his burning stomach. Who knew how many times a poignant silence during one of his pregame orations had been blown to smithereens by a shriek from Radio, and yet all Coach Jones would do was throw an arm around Radio's shoulder and roll his eyes toward heaven. Maybe that explained something. There was no one, outside of his five grandchildren or his wife, whom the coach would touch like that. He was the no-nonsense guy with bare gray cinder-block office walls, but unlike most people, he hadn't completely done away with his other self, the loose and long-buried child. It was always right there at his elbow, rocking from foot to foot.

One August day two years ago, a few weeks before school opened, Coach Jones got a phone call. Radio's mother had died of heart failure in the middle of the night, and Radio was out of his head with grief. He had smashed two holes in a wall of his house, and the police had been called to restrain him. Surely, now that his mama was gone, he would finally have to go into a home.

Coach Jones had always worried about what would happen to Radio the day he retired or the day Radio's mother died. He knew his assistants loved Radio as much as he did, but still. . . . He marshaled his staff and collected a big tray of food that day and headed to Radio's house. One by one the coaches hugged Radio and cried with him. If he could just hold on until football practice started again, and if Radio's older brother, Walter Turner—the only one of Janie Mae Greenlee's three sons who wasn't born with the defect—and Walter's wife, Pat, could take care of Radio in the evenings, when the school day was done, then Hanna and Coach Jones and his staff would handle the rest. And that's just what has happened.

Summers, though, are still the most difficult time for Radio. Should a traveler ever get lost in upstate South Carolina some July or August day and find himself wandering near the railroad tracks in Anderson and happen to notice an old boarded-up school with a FOR SALE sign planted in the weeds out front, he ought to take a little look at the abandoned McCants Junior High football field just behind it. He might just see a man with sprinkles of white hair gesturing wildly at thin air, screaming, *"All wight, tomowwow's Thuhsday, dat's a light day! You wear yo' shorts an' T-shirts, no pads, an' be on da fiel' at four o'cwock on da nose, you got dat, boys?"*

Just smile and wave. It's only Radio, living the dream.

True Lies

When the sunlight and the angle are right, you can see your face on the screen of your computer. Staring back at you through the words of the story you've already half written on Earvin (Magic) Johnson's contented life in retirement. How could this have happened to you?

You *believed* him. You, who surely should have learned your lesson a dozen years ago, listening to a fat, happy minister named George Foreman swear to you he could never close his hands into fists and strike a man again.

You, who wrote about the whiplash Muhammad Ali and Sugar Ray Leonard felt each time they tried to retire from the sport at which they were geniuses. You, with white already in your whiskers, sitting there just two weeks before word leaked of Magic's return to the Los Angeles Lakers, nodding and scribbling down every word as he told you the exact moment he knew he would never again play in the NBA.

This story first appeared in 1995, days after Magic Johnson's surprise announcement that he would end a four-year retirement due to the HIV virus and return to the Los Angeles Lakers.

His eyes were wide with the telling of his story, and all its sweetness shone upon his face. It was the night last summer, he said, when he opened Magic Theatres, a state-of-the-art 12-screen cineplex in South Central Los Angeles, just a few miles from where the Rodney King riots had erupted, and everyone from the neighborhood—the grandmas and gangbangers, the housewives and housepainters, the businessmen and busboys—came at him with hugs and with tears, thanking him for erecting this glorious house of fantasy so near the rubble and the ruins.

"I came out of there that night covered with lipstick," Earvin was saying. "People telling me, 'I've been in this community for forty years, and nothing ever happened like this.' Wives crying, thanking me for creating jobs, for changing their husbands' lives. Me crying, too, the happiest day of my life. I felt God was taking me and saying, 'This is what I want you to do.' It was a different love than I got on the court. It wasn't attached to winning. This love's forever. It hit me right then: This is it. I'm not ever going back to the NBA."

So now you're leafing through a pile of notepads, retracing your route, noticing all the little right and left turns you might have taken. Reminding yourself that this story wasn't like all the other ones of athletes who had retired in their prime. That death hung over this one. Odd, how vaporlike death is in this story: there one moment, like the morning mists of Los Angeles in winter, and gone the next. Magic Johnson could do that to death. Make it evaporate, like the sun.

Where is the horror? you kept wondering on your way to visit him. *Where is the dread?* There was never a trace of them in all the photographs, the videotape, the quotes. All you kept seeing was sunshine, the world's most wondrous smile, and all you kept reading was "I'm not scared of death. I'm not worried. Everyone else cried for me. I've never cried over HIV. I'm going to beat it." And all you kept hearing about was not the gradual diminishing of a life readying itself for its conclusion, but about extension, enlargement, expansion. The 30 pounds of muscle he had added to his chest and upper arms since the day the infection was discovered.

The daughter, Elisa, whom he and his wife, Cookie, adopted a year ago. His new theater complex, which astonished the film industry by regularly ranking among the 10 top-grossing movie houses in America. The plans to build more theaters, in largely black communities in Atlanta, Detroit, Houston, New York City and Washington, splitting the investment 50–50 with Sony. The mall he was helping to finance in Las Vegas. The new line of athletic shoes he was unveiling. The 5 percent ownership he had purchased of a Lakers franchise worth roughly $200 million. The Magic Johnson All-Stars he was taking around the world for exhibition games against national basketball teams, drawing standing-room-only crowds, amassing a 55–0 record and netting more money per game for Earvin—as much as $365,000 when corporate sponsorship fees for local appearances were included—than any NBA millionaire earns. The sports-apparel company he was running, the corporate speeches he was giving at as much as 100 grand a pop, the AIDS foundation he had established, which raised $6 million. Profits up, bench press up, helper T-cell count up. *Death?*

And so, four years and three months past the day when a lab technician spotted the telltale marker—the thin black antigen bands confirming that HIV had entered Magic Johnson's bloodstream—you went looking for the other indicators of a man marked to die. For the eye flicker and the dry mouth and the shadows between words, for the soul grottoes which cameramen and microphone holders frequently miss. For the soot and cinders of a blazing self-deception.

What you found was a man running his life as if it were the Lakers' fast break. Up at 6:30, scouring the sports and business sections with a giant cup of herbal tea and a breakfast of grains and fruits. Working the phones, calling Magic Theatres to learn the previous day's take, buzzing Lakers general manager Mitch Kupchak to evaluate personnel and blow off steam about another ho-hum team performance. Leaving his Beverly Hills mansion in his limousine to pump iron at the Sports Club/L.A., then going directly to the club's basketball court and shooting 10 times from each of 15 different spots on the floor, matching shot for shot with a friend named Marchell Henry, always barking the names of Henry's former girlfriends whenever the poor fellow was about to launch a shot that could swing the outcome, always insisting that the loser (guess who?) place an imaginary title belt around the waist of the winner (how did you know?) while he crowed, "And *still* heavyweight champion of the WORRRRRRRLD!!!" Then back into the limo, where Earvin, forever the point guard, directs his driver into swifter-moving lanes as he skims the sheaf of documents on his lap and sizzles the cellular phone, heading for another meeting with one of L.A.'s power brokers and then on to a two-hour practice with his touring team. Then home to tease Cookie for a few minutes, to grab a bite and a nap and a little time with three-year-old Earvin III and fourteen-month-old Elisa, and then back into the car to catch the Lakers' game at the Forum, where he sits in the front row a few feet from the bench, smiling and squirming and standing to flash hand signals to players—*Slow it down, little fella* or *Take him low, big man* or *How in God's name did you miss the cutter on the right baseline, fool?*—and the players look to him and nod in midaction.

You listened to Denise Villanueva, executive director of the Magic Johnson Foundation, which raises funds for the fight against AIDS, saying, "I can't imagine how he could've gone through this and not changed, but he hasn't. It's like he had this little bump in the road, went over it and just kept going. Everything he does keeps being so successful that it just keeps that adrenaline going." A little bump? But his friends, his wife, his mother all agree: They have never seen him, even for a few minutes on a gray Monday morning, in sadness or anger over his infection. "Like nothing ever happened," said his father, Earvin Sr., shaking his head.

And you wondered if this was just another life in which everything painful and true vanished in the vortex of meetings and marketing and motion, another triumph of adrenaline over angst, another man who never slowed down enough to let the word sift through him: *death, death, death.* And yet those closest to him said he was more relaxed than before, more spiritual, more patient, and there he sat in front of you, calm and smiling and looking you flush in the eye, the easiest stranger in the world to talk with. Telling you, just a few weeks ago, "I don't think about HIV. I just live. I just go. Everyone thinks I should be down, brooding. Everyone thinks I'm in denial. It's not denial. If I were in denial, I'd be on the court for the Los Angeles Lakers."

What *were* you thinking? The sheer ferocity of his daily work-outs should have set off a signal flare. The 700 sit-ups he some-times did in a day. The hour and a half he spent each morning in the weight room, driving his bench-press capacity from 135 to 300 pounds in less than three years. The weights and treadmill he hauled onto the yacht he rented for two weeks on the Mediterra-nean each summer, so he wouldn't miss a single day's workout. "He's gone nuts," said Cookie. "He's busting through his shirts and suits, and he thinks that's cool." His two or three hours a day on basketball courts, which he even rented on the road when his craving grew too strong. This was not a man gently letting go of his athletic life.

Every three months a few dozen cubic centimeters of Earvin Johnson's blood would be drawn from his arm and sealed in glass tubes. The tubes would be flown to New York City, where a flow cytometer at the Aaron Diamond AIDS Research Center would tally the number of helper T-cells—the ones that fight viral infection—per cubic millimeter of blood, and a branch DNA test would be conducted to count the number of viral particles.

"Right now," said Dr. David Ho of Aaron Diamond, "his virus is under very good control through the use of a combination of drugs and his routine and his attitude. He's sure he'll beat it, and who knows? If it continues at this rate, it may be true. He may hold out long enough to benefit from some medical treatment that could come along. We've learned that in rare cases, there are defective strains of this virus, and that some people are still living fifteen years after being infected. There's no evidence that he has the defective vari-ety—his virus *does* replicate in a test tube. But his isn't the overly aggressive type. Looking through the retroscope, he probably didn't need to retire, but we just didn't know that then. Earvin has the advantage right now. But that's not to say it will remain that way.

"The biggest unknown is what we call Time Zero—when he became infected. If Time Zero was just a few months before he tested positive, then what we've seen with him isn't that unexpected. There are many HIV patients showing no symptoms after four years; the average time before onset of AIDS is about ten years. If Time Zero was fifteen years ago, however, then what we're seeing with him would be extraordinary."

That was how doctors scored his battle. But Earvin had his own HIV test. Each day he sought out a group of former NBA players in L.A. to play pickup ball. Four or five times a game he would take the inbounds pass after his opponents had scored and race the ball upcourt, throwing off head fakes and shoulder shakes like sparks when the other players tried to stop him, spinning 360s and throwing his 6' 9" body into the seam between defenders, going coast-to-coast to score. "I'd ram it down their throats," he said. "That's how I'd know that nothing was wrong with me."

He turned the infection into a contest, because a contest was something he could never see himself losing. "It's like a big game," he said. "A big series. That's how I approach it. I've always loved a challenge. My whole life has been a challenge, and this is just another one. I love to shock people. To beat the odds. They said I was too tall to play guard. They said I couldn't shoot. Each time I said, 'O.K., I'm just gonna show you.' And this is just another one of those things."

Gary Vitti, the Lakers' trainer, couldn't look at Magic after the announcement of the infection without feeling his heart break. "I'm having a tough time with this, Earv," Vitti finally admitted one day in the Lakers' weight room.

"Don't worry about me," said Earvin. "God gave this to the right person when he gave it to me. I can handle this. I'm gonna take care of this for him."

This interpretation—Earvin as God's messenger—created an odd contradiction in his war with the disease. In public, he discussed HIV with ease. By warning the nation's youth about AIDS with shocking honesty, he opened himself to criticism for his promiscuity, but he also evaporated his guilt. He was not being punished by God; he was not the tainted one. "He was the chosen one," said Cookie. Earvin explained, "God has said, 'I want you to be the messenger.' He was trying to get the message through before, but nobody, including myself, was listening. It was hush-hush, then I got it. Now you talk openly about it."

In his private life, however, he rarely mentioned HIV. His family and friends, sensing this, virtually never brought it up either, never came much closer to it than "How you feeling, Earv?" The Earvin who was locked in a life-and-death struggle with HIV was the elite athlete, the one whose friends all knew, on the day of a playoff game, not to discuss the impending battle; the one feeding HIV silently into the jaws of his enormous will. Any emotions spent agonizing over it, any energy spent mentioning it, only siphoned emotion and energy from him and funneled it to the enemy. Even when he awoke one morning and read in the newspaper that his mentor, Elisabeth Glaser—the AIDS activist who addressed the 1992 Democratic Convention and educated Earvin for his public fight against the disease—had died of AIDS, he said nothing. "It broke my heart, because she was my hope," said Cookie, "but when I brought it up, he changed the subject."

"That's not hiding from it," Earvin told you. "I never hid from this. I never went undercover. But I don't let out pain. I choke up when something sad happens in a movie, but I can't cry about HIV. I never want to let it out, because it might take away something from my competitive edge. How am I going to defeat it, and how am I going to help people? That's the only thing I concentrated on. Everything must be poured into meeting the challenge and winning."

And somehow, for him, for the moment, it was working. "I see a sparkle in his eyes," said Lakers assistant coach Michael Cooper. "He's finally living the way he played basketball. He's much more at peace now."

He has blown right past all the normal stages of grieving, and you wondered if there would be hell to pay down the road for that. Or if none of the rules apply here; if the virus has never bumped into anyone quite like this. When he coached the Lakers for 16 games in 1994, Earvin would get a couple of assistant coaches and bench warmers and take on the Lakers' starting five. He would tell the man guarding him exactly what he planned to do. *All right.*

I'm gonna post you up, take two dribbles to the right, fake left and go right. He would do just that—and score anyway. He would beat the starting five, just to let them know who was still king. He quit coaching as soon as the season ended, because his players' will to win seemed so puny next to his own.

As a player he would change his telephone number each year at playoff time and enter a tunnel that ran from the basketball floor to his bedroom. The man who loved crowds and noise would want only silence and solitude. He wouldn't marry Cookie until more than a decade after they started dating, in part because he couldn't imagine allowing anyone inside the tunnel. During the playoffs he wouldn't sleep. "Imagine it," he said. "Weeks, just living on adrenaline." He would barely eat. His complexion would pale. He would snap at people. It was his favorite time of the year.

Nothing changed when he quit. Shouldn't *that* have set off your smoke detector? Look, it's right there in your notebook, a dozen different people rolling their eyes and telling you how monstrous Earvin's need to win—at *anything*—remained. Picture Earvin, afloat in the middle of the Mediterranean last summer, having teamed up with his buddy Lester Conner, a former NBA player, to demolish Cookie and one of her friends in 10 consecutive card games, shrieking when he notices Conner showing compassion in Game 11: "No, no, no, Lester, never let them win! Never! We're going for the sweep!" He would cheat at any game he was losing, reverse the score in a volleyball match, rule every opponent's shot wide. He forbade wives to play in holiday picnic softball games—they would dilute the competition. He threatened to send all the members of his touring team home from Argentina when they got silly during a shoot-around in 1994, and every player was on notice: The first time Magic Johnson's All-Stars lost, Earvin was going to dissolve the team and assemble a new roster.

So along came that Friday evening last September when Earvin and Cookie had a date to see a movie. For weeks, on a basketball court that had been assembled inside a tent to accommodate Michael Jordan during the filming of the movie *Space Jam*, the best players living in or visiting L.A. had been gathering to play each evening. Jordan, Reggie Miller, Grant Hill, Dennis Rodman, Cedric Ceballos, Pooh Richardson, Juwan Howard—it was a veritable nightly NBA All-Star Game, but poor Earvin couldn't play, thanks to the league rule forbidding owners, even five-percenters, to fraternize with players during the ongoing collective bargaining impasse. Now it was Jordan's final day of filming, the last night of ball at the tent, and the impasse had just ended. "You playing?" asked Conner on the phone. "Can't," said Earvin. "Cookie and I are going out." Then came a long pause.

Everything you needed to know about Earvin and the NBA, you had time to figure out during that pause. In no time, he wrangled a rain check from Cookie, slipped into his sweats and sneakers and slid out into the night. He entered Jordan's tent. The joint went silent. All the NBA studs, all the Warner Bros. producers and directors, just stared.

Rodman, on the NBA all-defense team five times, covered Magic. Magic spooned it all out that night—all the no-look passes and junior skyhooks and post-up power moves; the sorcerer come back to life with a blacksmith's body. When Jordan had watched enough, he playfully motioned Rodman aside and elected himself to cover Magic. "MJ," said Magic, "I'm not the regular guy I used to be. I'm six-nine, two hundred fifty pounds. Why don't you cover one of the guards and send a big man over to me?"

Grinning, Michael regarded Earvin for a moment and then said, "Guess you're right." And then Earvin, having had a little more fun, having won again, grabbed his sweats to head home, shining like a Sunday morning and shrugging it off as the players kept asking, "Damn, why aren't you still playing?"

"Nah," Earvin told you. "It didn't tempt me. See, I was past it by then. I like my life now. I have time to enjoy the sunsets with Cookie. Time to enjoy being with my kids. Time to just think and reflect on all the great moments."

Moments. Surely that was the word that should have set off alarm bells. Quiet moments, sunsets, hand-holding—lovely now and then, but *come on*. Has there ever been a lover of the large moment who outranked Magic Johnson?

This is the man who longed for Indiana State to advance to the 1979 NCAA final against Michigan State so that he could go down as the cat who stopped Larry Bird. The rookie who announced, as he strolled onto the Lakers' plane for their flight to Philadelphia for Game 6 of the 1980 NBA Finals—the game Kareem Abdul-Jabbar would watch at home with a sprained ankle—"Never fear, EJ's here," and then, in case anyone misconstrued the message, lowered himself into Kareem's seat, 1B. Earvin played center, forward and guard in that game, scored 42 points, grabbed 15 rebounds and dished out 7 assists, and Los Angeles won the title-clinching game by 16.

Sunsets with Cookie? This is the man who, three months after retiring, walked back onto the court for the 1992 All-Star Game and won the MVP award, drilling three straight three-pointers in the final minutes and finishing the game in the midcourt embrace of both teams. Who appeared at the opening ceremonies of the 1992 Summer Olympics while some of the Dream Team remained in the hotel, and brought anarchy to the parade on the stadium floor as the world's best athletes scrambled toward him for photos and autographs. Large moments? How about the one he told Oprah Winfrey about, when he assembled six women on his bed? Large. Very large. Or that moment he mentioned in his autobiography, the one with the woman atop her office desk while a business meeting took place on the other side of the door?

Yes, there it is, right there in the notes: the way he kept appearing in the aureoles of large moments. Kept going to Super Bowls and big fights in Vegas, kept renting nightclubs, hiring deejays and bands, hosting big parties once a month.

Yes, that was the trouble with HIV. He would always have it. There would never be a dramatic, satisfying showdown. He would try to apply to it all the psychological tools he once applied to playoff and All-Star Games, when he used to sit alone before tip-offs and visualize his passes, his shots, his steals as clearly as if he were watching a movie. But the only picture he could conjure for his triumph over AIDS was one of Cookie and him, wrinkled and white-haired, rocking on a porch. There would never come a day when he could raise his arms as the title belt was wrapped around

his waist and crow, "The *first* man *ever* to beat the human immu-
nodeficiency VIIIIIIRUS!!!" There would only be another day to
live. There would never be any *moments*.

"No," Earvin told you a couple weeks ago. "No reason to come
back. What I'm doing right now is working. I don't want to dis-
rupt that."

Perhaps it was his charisma that disarmed you. Beheaded you.
Gelded you. You wouldn't have been the first, you know. Consider
what occurred last summer at one of UCLA's gyms. It had always
been Magic's summer house, even after he retired. His rules determined who played first among the two or three dozen college,
pro and ex-pro players who invariably appeared each day at 3 p.m.:
seniority over youth, NBA over overseas pros, regulars over occasional guests. Nobody argued when Magic was magistrating, but
then suddenly, because of that dang rule against owners fraternizing with NBA players during the bargaining breakdown, he
couldn't play with the boys anymore.

So he decided to play at 9 a.m., to avoid contact with any
league players. But what happened a few days later? A couple of
NBA players appeared at the earlier hour—now the word was out.
He looked up the next morning, and there were a dozen NBA players. He called the league office and said, "What can I do? I'm not
fraternizing with them, *they're* fraternizing with *me*." He looked
up the next day and there was Hakeem Olajuwon, there was Reggie
Miller, there were all those Lakers and the Clippers, there were a
hundred fans—it was 3 p.m. at 9 a.m. "Oh, man," said Magic.
"Ooooeeee!"

Yes, maybe the truth about his return resides here, in the
interchange of love between Earvin and people. Other performers
inhaled an audience's love, but Earvin, he exhaled it right back.
It was like breathing for him—couldn't you see that? Yes, the grand
opening of Magic Theatres was a remarkable night for Earvin's
respiration, but a theater could open only once. The NBA is three
nights a week.

His purpose on earth, he once said, was to make people happy.
Didn't his sister Kim tell you about his vast hunger to please, to

keep re-winning love? Ten minutes after a spanking from his
mother, Earvin would return to kiss and hug her.

Awakening on that Mediterranean yacht he hired each summer, allegedly to get away from it all, Earvin would gaze across the
blue, blue sea, the white beaches, the skyline, the vineyards, the birds
. . . and the hundreds of people waiting for him everywhere he
docked. And Earvin would smile. And Earvin would wave. And
Earvin would lead the people in their incessant chant—*Ma-JEEK!*
Ma-JEEK!—and then on a jog through the cobblestone streets. Even
when he had no time to sign autographs, he usually leaned close to
each fan, looked him in the eye, shook his hand or touched his shoulder, exchanged a few words and a laugh. "It's like he's running for
office," said Dale Beard, a longtime friend of Magic's, "and he has
to go around to make sure all the voters are for him."

Perhaps, in the end, it was the popcorn that threw you off
the trail. That story Earvin told you about the day not long ago
when *Waiting to Exhale* opened at his theater, and eight lines, each
nearly a hundred yards long, formed outside. On the run came
Earvin, bouncing behind the concession counter to serve popcorn
to the customers surging in. Earvin never said the story meant a
damn thing. It was just you, wanting to believe that a multimillionaire megacelebrity with HIV who would grin and pop popcorn
at his movie house no longer needed the big arena with the TV
cameras and the 17,000 fans.

"I just wanted to call you and tell you not to worry about the
rumors," said his agent, Lon Rosen, when Earvin began practicing with the Lakers a few days later. "He's just trying to light a
fire under the team. He likes his life too much now. He'll never go
back."

"O.K.," you said.

The popcorn. The popcorn. . . .

Forget the damn popcorn. Maybe it all had to do with the spirit
that kept coming to Earvin in his dreams. It was such a funda-
mental blunder—paying too much attention to what Earvin was
saying when he was awake and not enough to what he was hearing in his sleep. He's a man, after all. Just as afraid of dying as

you, way down deep. He's a man petrified of going into water above his waist in a swimming pool, has been ever since he was nine and a lifeguard pulled him unconscious from a pool. He's a man who endured his sister's and grandmother's wakes but couldn't witness their funerals.

At night, in his dreams, his oldest friend would arise from the car wreck that killed him when Earvin was 16. Mutt and Jeff, people had called them back in Lansing. Reggie Chastine was a year older than Magic, a little guy with a big Afro, toughest little s.o.b. on the courts of Lansing. He was the one who saw Earvin's greatness before Earvin did, who wouldn't permit Earvin to back away, not an inch, from anyone or anything. "I doubted myself back then," said Earvin. "He was who I *should* have been." Earvin should have been in Reggie's car that night, because he always was. But for some reason he had begged off, and when the news came by telephone, Earvin screamed "No, no, no!" and ran out the door of his house, ran blindly for hours, tears streaming down his cheeks.

In the dream that kept returning after Earvin's infection was discovered, Earvin and Reggie would be playing one-on-one at sunrise in St. Joe Park, just as they used to, and Reggie would see the look in Earvin's eyes, the question: *Am I going to have to join you, Reggie? Am I going to have to come . . . over there?* Reggie would stop and stick the ball under his arm. "Man, what's wrong with you, Earv?" he would howl. "Don't take that crap! You can't quit! You can't back down! You beat all the odds! You'll beat this too!" And Earvin would wake up, heart pumping too hard for sleep, and he would leave his bed and go to the big television screen. He would play the videotape of him leading Michigan State over Indiana State in the NCAA title game or that game against Philly in the 1980 NBA Finals, sit there in the darkness watching himself do rare things, feeling the slow return of the strength he would need to face the dawn. He had played those tapes so often, the images began to shudder on the screen. NBC and the NBA sent him new ones, and he had a dozen copies made of each.

By the time the sun rose, Earvin would be in control once more. Control meant everything to him. It was why he became the tallest point guard in history, of course. As a teenager, even when Earvin was the biggest player on the court, he couldn't bear to relinquish the ball—and the outcome of the game—to a smaller, lesser player, so he kept control of it. Years later, when Cookie was in the throes of childbirth, Earvin screamed "Hold it!" when the baby's head appeared. "My baby has to come out to Luther!" He had Cookie's sister run to the stereo and insert a tape by Luther Vandross, then he said to his wife, "O.K., honey, push him out!"

His rareness arose from this paradox: that big, loose, unbuttoned spirit fused with that necktie-taut need to control. How could you have expected such a man to live with the psychological silt of having been pushed into quitting—not just once, at the urging of his doctors in 1991, but a second time, in '92, after the fear of an HIV carrier's playing in the NBA crested when one of his arms was cut during a preseason game? How could he not help but hear the echoes of Reggie's voice: "Don't take that crap! You can't quit!" How could he resist the chance to return and do it over, to control how he would leave the game he loved?

You *knew* he had wavered before. You *knew* that he wanted to return two seasons ago, when his old Lakers coach, Pat Riley, asked him to play for Riley's new team, the New York Knicks; *knew* that he went to Lakers management and asked if his playing rights were still locked up—which they were.

"But I'm settled now," said Earvin last month. "I'm settled, mind and body."

Now the magazine is calling for the story behind Magic Johnson's decision to return, and Magic's not taking any phone calls, and a cool sweat's breaking on your brow. And you're looking high and low, between the lines and under the rug, forgetting completely about Mama Johnson. Maybe the answer to everything had been right there, on that face right across the kitchen table that afternoon a few weeks ago in Lansing. The 60 years she had lived, the brother and sister she had raised after her mother had died, the eight children of her own she had raised, the full-time job as a custodian at a middle school that kept her up until 2 a.m.

at home doing the cleaning and the next day's cooking, the evenings when her head sagged onto the dinner table and she fell asleep. . . . Where was the toll on that smooth, happy face? Gone. Just like Earvin's HIV, it seemed. Gone.

"Don't dwell," Christine Johnson had told you. "Dwellin' makes you sick. You have to *live*, not sit and cry and worry. That's when you die fast."

Go back to the day she learned her son had HIV. That autumn Saturday, near noon, when she returned from church and was surprised to find her industrious husband still in bed, looking stunned. She asked twice if he was sick. "Sort of," he finally said. "Talked to Earvin on the phone. He's . . . he's got HIV." Christine's legs wanted to give, but she went to the phone, begged Earvin to let her fly to him and hold him, but he said no, not now, not until he figured out what to do. So she left her bedroom, never said a word to her two adult daughters in the kitchen, got in the car and drove, crying alone, no idea where she was going. Then a name came to her, the name of an 80-year-old woman she knew whose sister had died recently, and Christine dried her eyes and went there. "Lord must've sent you, because I've been down in the dumps lately," the old woman said. And so Christine spent two hours comforting the old woman, never mentioning the sledgehammer that had just hit her, and then drove home. She didn't tell her daughters the news about Earvin until later that night and her sons until the next day.

It ran like a cast-iron chain through Earvin's family, this reflex of closing one's mouth when life caved in, of going right back to work, believing God would make something good come out of it. Christine and her mom, both turned into mothers as teenagers by their own mothers' deaths. Christine's dad, smiling right up to the end, even through the cancer that killed him at 84. And Earvin Sr., working the night shift in a hail of sparks as a spot welder in a General Motors plant, hurrying from there to a car dealership to clean it at 2 a.m. and then home to catch a few hours of sleep, and then jumping into his truck to collect garbage from midmorning till midafternoon. Ignoring the searing pain in his side until his appendix nearly burst 25 years ago. Ignoring, eight years ago, the

28 pounds he lost in two weeks and the blurry vision and the pressure to urinate every 15 minutes, so that he could keep working until Christmas and collect the year-end bonus before going to the doctor with a dangerously high blood-sugar count and being told he had diabetes. And Earvin's dad's dad, still cooking at a junior college cafeteria at age 84.

"You got a choice," Earvin Sr. told you. "You either root and be a hog, or you die a pig."

When it came time to die, Earvin had a plan all ready. "I'll tell them to give me a basketball," he told you, "and roll me onto a basketball court. That's how I want to go." And you, like a fool, didn't make the little leap, didn't gather that if he was determined to be rolled there *then*, how could he resist running there *now*? "A basketball court," he said, "that's the comfort zone. That's where I forget everything."

If there was one rectangle on earth you could step into and forget you were ever going to die, who among us wouldn't take that step? When Michael Jordan was coming at Earvin with the ball on a fast break, no one could ask Earvin, as the European reporter did a few years ago, how it felt to know he wouldn't see his children grow up. When Michael was coming at him, there would be no reminder of anything. There wouldn't be a single thought.

"Just one thing I regret," he told you. "That's that my three-year-old son will never see me in a Lakers uniform."

"The whole time I was away, right up until I signed my contract this morning, I knew I should be playing. I've just been kicking myself for walking away. This is like a release from my own mind. Not playing ball, that's what was killing me."

It's Tuesday morning, January 30. The newspapers are out, the big photographs, the thick headlines, the quotes. It's official. You blew it. To smithereens.

By evening, when you're tired of pulling out your hair, when you've given up waiting for Magic to return your phone call and explain the difference between the quotes in your notepads and the quotes in the morning paper, you find yourself leafing through a book of photographs on the life of Louis Armstrong. Magic and Satchmo. The two best smiles of the 20th century. And just before Earvin comes on to your TV screen in Lakers purple and gold, comes out smiling just as he smiled through the championships and the HIV, you're looking at Louis busting that heart-melting smile through everything, through poverty and the Colored Waif's Home for Boys, through the lean and fat years and the heart disease at the end. And you're thinking that it's crazy to ask Magic to explain and just as crazy to try it yourself. Thinking that perhaps every now and then, maybe once in a generation, these great forces of nature, these large, happy mammals, arise from the gene puddle and lay big footprints across the land. And that they can never explain the force, because they *are* the force.

The night after his return, the phone rings at 10:36 p.m. It's Magic. His laugh is deep and rich. "Maybe I was kidding you," he says, "and maybe I was kidding myself, too."

And you know what? You believe him. Absolutely.

Three months after this story appeared, Magic Johnson's NBA playing career ended for good . . . we think.

Shadow of a Nation

*I have not told you half that happened when I was young. I
can think back and tell you much more of war and horse stealing. But when the buffalo went away the hearts of my people
fell to the ground, and they could not lift them up again. After
this nothing happened. There was little singing anywhere.*

—Plenty Coups
Chief of the Crows, 1930

Singing. Did you hear it? There was singing in the land once
more that day. How could you not call the Crows a still-mighty
tribe if you saw them on the move that afternoon? How could your
heart not leave the ground if you were one of those Indian boys
leading them across the Valley of the Big Horn?

It was March 24, 1983, a day of thin clouds and pale sun in
southern Montana. A bus slowed as it reached the crest of a hill,
and from there, for the first time, the boys inside it could see everything. Fender to fender stretched the caravan of cars behind them,

This story first appeared in 1991.

116

seven miles, eight—they had made the asphalt go away! Through the sage and the buffalo grass they swept, over buttes and boulder-filled gullies, as in the long-ago days when their scouts had spotted buffalo and their village had packed up its lodge poles and tepee skins, lashed them to the dogs and migrated in pursuit of the herd.

But what they pursued now was a high school basketball team, 12 teenagers on their way to Billings to play in a state tournament. The boys stared through their windows at the caravan. There was bone quiet in the bus. It was as if, all at once, the boys had sensed the size of this moment . . . and what awaited each of them once this moment was done.

In one seat, his nose pressed to the window, was one of Hardin High's starting guards, Everette Walks, a boy with unnaturally large hands who had never known his father. In a few weeks he would drop out of school, then cirrhosis would begin to lay waste his mother. He would wind up pushing a mop at 2 a.m. in a restaurant on the Crow reservation.

In another seat sat the starting forward, an astounding leaper named Miles Fighter. He too had grown up with no father, and recently his mother had died of cirrhosis. In just a few years, he would be unemployed and drinking heavily.

Not far away sat the other starting guard, Jo Jo Pretty Paint, a brilliant long-range shooter, a dedicated kid—just a few minutes before a game at Miles City, his coach had found him alone, crouched, shuffling, covering an invisible opponent in the locker room shower. In two years Pretty Paint would go out drinking one evening, get into a car and careen over an embankment. He would go to his grave with a photograph of himself in his uniform, clutching a basketball.

Hunched nearby, all knees and elbows and shoulders, was Darren Big Medicine, the easygoing center. Sixteen months after Pretty Paint's death, he would leave a party after a night of drinking, fall asleep as he sped along a reservation road, drive into a ditch and die.

And then there was Takes Enemy. . . .

Weeping. Did you hear it? There was weeping in the land that day. Sobs for those missing from that glorious caravan, those decaying in the reservation dust, for Dale Spotted and Star Not Afraid and Darrell Hill and Tim Falls Down, Crow stars of the past dead of cirrhosis and suicide and knife-stabbing and a liquor-fogged car wreck. Sobs for the slow deaths occurring every night a mile from Jonathan Takes Enemy's high school, where an entire squad of jump shooters and dunkers and power forwards from the past could be found huddling against the chill and sprawled upon the sidewalks outside the bars on the south side of Hardin. Jonathan's predecessors. Jonathan's path-beaters. "Good Lord!" cries Mickey Kern, the computer-science teacher and former basketball scorekeeper at Hardin High. "How many have we lost? How *many*?"

But Takes Enemy—he would be the one who escaped, wouldn't he? That was what the white coaches and teachers and administrators at his school kept telling him. His mind was sharp, his skill immense; the destiny of all those others needn't be his. Brigham Young wanted him. Oregon State and Arizona State had sent letters. O. J. Simpson would shake his hand in New York City and present him with a crystal cup for being named Montana's Outstanding Athlete of 1984. He was 6' 2", he could twirl 360 degrees in the air and dunk the ball, he could shoot from distance. He loved to take a rebound with one hand and bring it to his other palm with a resounding *slap*, make a right-angle cut on the dribble at a velocity that ripped the court wide open, then thread it with a blind running pass, an orange blur straight from the unconscious. "Watching him play," says Janine Pease-Windy Boy, the president of Little Big Horn College, the junior college on the Crow reservation, "was like watching clean water flow across rocks."

Young Indian boys formed trails behind him, wearing big buttons with his picture on their little chests. They ran onto the court and formed a corridor for him and his teammates to trot through during pregame introductions, they touched his hands and arms, they pretended to *be* him. The coaches had to lock the gym doors to start practice. Girls lifted their pens to the bathroom walls: "I was with Jonathan Takes Enemy last night," they wrote. "I'm going to have Jonathan Takes Enemy's baby." He was a junior in high school. Already he was the father of two. Already he drank too much. Already his sister Sharolyn was dead of cirrhosis. Sometimes he walked alone in the night, shaking and sobbing. He was the newest hero of the tribe that loved basketball too much.

Takes Enemy felt the bus wheels rolling beneath him. The sun arced through the Montana sky. The circle was the symbol of never-ending life to the Crows—they saw it revealed in the shape and movement of the sun and moon, in the path of the eagle, in the contours of their tepees and the whorl of their dances. As long as the people kept faith with the circle, they believed, their tribe would endure. Jonathan settled back in his seat. Sometimes it seemed as if his life were handcuffed to a wheel, fated to take him up . . . and over . . . and down.

Somewhere behind him on the highway, his first cousin would soon be getting off his job on the reservation's road crew and joining the exodus to the ball game in Billings—*the* legendary Crow player, some people said; the best player, *period*, in Montana high school history, said others; the one who ignited his tribe's passion for high school basketball back in the 1950s and seemed to start this dark cycle of great players arising and vanishing: Larry Pretty Weasel. The one whose drinking helped drive him out of Rocky Mountain College in Billings and back to the reservation in 1958, just a few days before the NAIA's weekly bulletin arrived proclaiming him the best field goal percentage shooter in the country.

Horns honked in the caravan behind Takes Enemy, passengers waved. In the long-ago days before white men had brought their horses or guns or cars or liquor, his people had chased buffalo in this same direction, across these same valleys, stampeding them over cliffs near the land where Billings would one day arise. This same creature whose skull the Crows would mount on a pole and make the centerpiece of their religious Sun Dance . . . they would drive over the edge of the cliff and then scramble down to devour.

The bus ascended another hill. Takes Enemy looked back at his people once more.

One winter night in 1989, the custodian at Lodge Grass High on the Crow reservation forgot to flick off a switch. When the team bus pulled into the parking lot after a road game nearly four hours away, the lights above six of the seventeen outdoor baskets that surround the school were still burning. It was 2 a.m. It was snowing. Two games of five-on-five were being played.

Somehow, in the mindless way that rivers sculpt valleys and shame shapes history, the Montana Indians' purest howl against a hundred years of repression and pain had become . . . high school basketball. Yes, the Crows' 8,300 people were racked by alcoholism and poverty, 75 percent of them were unemployed, the attrition rate for those who went to college was 95 percent, and their homeland, through cheating, broken treaties and sellouts, had dwindled from the 38.8 million acres guaranteed them by the U.S. government in 1851 to the present-day 1.1 million—but just let them lace on sneakers and lay their hands on a basketball. Though Indians constituted but 7 percent of Montana's population, their schools would win 10 Class A, B and C state high school basketball titles between 1980 and '90.

To the north and northwest of the Crow reservation lay the reservations of the Blackfeet, Sioux, Flathead, Assiniboine, Gros Ventre, Chippewa, Cree, Salish, Kootenai and Pen D'Oreilles; to the east lay the Cheyenne. These tribes too loved to run and shoot and jump. At tournament time in Montana, Indian teams were known to streak onto the floor for layup drills in war headdress, their fans to shake arenas with chants and war cries and pounding drums as their boys raced up and down the floor at speeds few white teams could sustain. Old women wrapped in blankets were known to pound the bleachers in unison with their canes, to lose their cool and swing the canes at the calves of enemy players; a few, back in the 1940s, even jabbed opponents with hat pins as the boys ran up the sidelines.

Their children spent their days shooting at crooked rims and rotting wooden backboards. Their young men drove for days to reach Indian tournaments all across America and came home to strut the dusty streets in the sheeny jackets they had won there.

Of all the perplexing games that the white man had brought with him—frantic races for diplomas and dollar bills and development—here was the one that the lean, quick men on the reservations could instinctively play. Here was a way to bring pride back to their hollow chests and vacant eyes, some physical means, at last, for poor and undereducated men to reattain the status they once had gained through hunting and battle. Crow men had never taken up the craftwork, weaving or metallurgy that males in other tribes had. They were warriors, meat eaters, nomads whose prestige and self-esteem had come almost entirely from fulfilling an intricate set of requirements—called "counting coup"—while capturing enemy horses or waging battle. A man could count coup by touching an enemy, by seizing a bow or a gun in a hand-to-hand encounter, by capturing a horse in a hostile camp or by being the pipe carrier (which signified leadership) on a successful raid. Only by counting coup, some say, could a man marry before the age of 25; only by counting coup in all four categories could he become a chief. Children were named after the exploits of warriors; men starved themselves for days and slept alone in the mountains to invite dreams that would guide them on raids; a woman attained honor by the number of scalps and the war booty captured by her man, tokens of which she brandished when she danced.

And then the white men hunted the buffalo nearly to extinction and banned intertribal warfare. "It castrated the Crow male," says Ben Pease, a tribal elder who played basketball for Hardin High in the 1940s. "It created a vacuum. During World War I we still weren't citizens, so our men couldn't gain prestige from that war. People began living off the war deeds of their ancestors, depending on them for their status. Some Crows fought in World War II, and for a while these men, especially those who came back with wounds or proof of bravery, became our leaders, and our ceremonies often revolved around them. But time passed, and there weren't enough wars or war heroes; there was a void that needed to be filled. In the late fifties Larry Pretty Weasel emerged at Hardin High, and our basketball players began to be noticed in the newspapers. That continued through the sixties and seventies; more and more of our children began to play. Something had to take war's place, some way had to be found to count coups. It was basketball."

Old Crow rituals had warm blood and fresh drama again. Some players tucked tiny medicine bundles—little pouches that might contain tobacco seeds or small pieces of bone or feather—inside their

socks or tied them to their jerseys, the way warriors once had tied
them to their braids before entering battle. Some burned cedar and
prayed before big games. The same drum cadence and honor songs
used 200 years ago to celebrate the seizing of a dozen horses or the
killing of three Sioux now reverberated through gymnasiums and
community halls at the capture of a basketball trophy.

But no Indian had ever played in the NBA. Only one, Don
Wetzel of the Blackfeet, ever came off a Montana reservation to
play for an NCAA Division I team (the University of Montana,
1967–71). Trophy cases in the lobbies of Indian schools throughout the state are filled with gleaming silver . . . and with black-
bordered dedications to the dead.

Every now and then, a lesser player left the Crow reservation
and quietly, with no scholarship or fanfare, got his degree. But as
best as anyone can figure, since 1970 only one prominent Crow
player, Luke Spotted Bear, had received a college scholarship and
graduated (from Mary College in Bismarck, North Dakota)—and
Spotted Bear often felt that his people held this *against* him. "Some
of them say I'm too good for them now," he says. "If possible, they
don't want to be around me."

College recruiters stopped coming to the reservation. The
game that was a highway into mainstream America for black men
. . . was a cul-de-sac for red ones. Something happened to their
heroes when the drumbeats died, when the war whoops faded,
when the faces in the audience were not like theirs. Something in
the Crows' love for basketball was toxic.

And along came a nice, shy boy who was asked to change all
that. Along came a Jonathan Takes Enemy.

His people understood his significance. They sent him off to
do battle with all the spiritual might they could muster. Before big
games a medicine man would receive a cigarette from the Takes
Enemy family, take it outside their house just in front of the Little
Big Horn River in the town of Crow Agency, light it and pray to
the Great Spirit for Jonathan.

Once, the medicine man wafted cedar smoke and an eagle
feather over the gold chain that Takes Enemy carried with him to

games for good luck. He warned Takes Enemy not to shake his opponents' hands before a game, so they could not drain away his power. All these steps were meant to protect Jonathan from harm, but he couldn't quite trust them. How could he escape the reservation and take up the solitary quest for success in the white world if he let himself think in the old way? How could he escape the dark fate of Spotted and Not Afraid and Falls Down if he believed that a man's destiny hung upon a puff of smoke in the wind?

When members of the tribe invited players on Jonathan's team to join them in sweat baths before the division and state tournaments, in order to purify their bodies and spirits in the ritual way their ancestors had before battle, Jonathan had refused; it was simply too hot in the sweat lodge. Jonathan's coach at Hardin, George Pfeifer—in his first year of coaching Indians and curious about their rituals—consented to do it. On a 20-degree day on the banks of the Little Big Horn, a powdery snow falling from the sky, the short, stout white man followed the example of eight Crow men and stripped off his clothes. "Go in, Brother George," directed one of them. Brother George got on his knees and crawled behind them into a low, dome-shaped shelter made of bent willows and covered by blankets. Inside, it was so dark that Brother George could not see the hand he held up in front of his face.

Someone poured a dipper of water over sandstones that had been heated in a bonfire for hours. Steam erupted from the rocks, hissed up and filled the sweat lodge with heat more intense than any sauna's. Sitting cheek to cheek, the men put a switch in Brother George's hand, expecting him to beat himself upon the back and legs to make it even hotter. In the darkness, he heard the others thwacking themselves, groaning and praying for his team in the Crow tongue. He gave up all pretense, flopped onto the floor and cupped his hands around his mouth to find a gulp of cooler air.

A half hour passed like this. A couple of dozen more dippers of water were poured onto the scalded rocks. At last the sweat-soaked men crawled out into the frigid daylight and promptly leapt into the icy river. Brother George's legs refused. He stood there, trembling with cold, about to be sick for three days.

"You're not going to dive in the river, Brother George?" one
cried.

"No way."

"That's all right, Brother George. No goddam magic in that."

But here was the difference: In a few weeks Pfeifer would
laugh and tell anecdotes about the day that he left his world and
entered another. Jonathan could not. Sometimes he felt the suspicious eyes of whites upon him, felt his tongue turn to stone, his
English jumble, when he tried to express to them his feelings. He
had but to utter that name to white ears—Takes Enemy—to feel
his own ears begin to turn red.

All day and night as he grew up, the television had been on
in his home, floating images into his head of white men who drove
long cars and lived in wide houses, of Indians who were slow-witted
and savage and usually, by the movie's end, dead. One day, when
he was in junior high, he saw a movie about Custer's Last Stand.
He couldn't help himself; in his stomach he felt thrilled when the
Indians rolled over the hills and slaughtered every white man. It
bewildered him, a few years later, to learn that it was the Sioux
and Cheyenne who had slain Custer's troops—that several Crow
scouts had ridden *with* Custer. Everything was muddy, nothing
ran clean. It was whites who made him speak English most of the
day when he entered first grade, rather than the Crow language
he had grown up speaking; whites who hung a dead coyote from
the outside mirror of Plenty Coups High School's team bus; whites
who sang "One little, two little, three little Indians" at his brothers
when they played away games in high school. And yet it was
Hardin's white athletic director and assistant principal, Kim Anderson, who sometimes drove far out of his way to make sure Jonathan
made it to school in the morning; white teachers who offered him
encouragement and hope when he passed them in the halls.

Sometimes he would bicycle up the steep incline to the Custer
Battlefield, a mile and a half from his home, to sit alone near the
markers that showed where each of the white men had fallen, and
to stare off into the distance. From here the world stretched out
and waited for him to touch it; from here he could see land and a

life beyond the reservation. In the daydream he often had here, it would be *he* who was walking from the wide house to the long car, *he* waving a cheery good-bye to his wife and kids, *he* driving off down the well-paved road to the well-paid job, *he* acting out the clichéd American dream he saw on the TV screen. What choice had he? There no longer existed an Indian success cliché to dream of.

An hour or two later he would fly back down the hillside from the battlefield, barely needing to touch his pedals, determined to make the dream come true. It was only when the long hill ran out, when he labored back into his town, that the heaviness returned to his legs.

One evening a few months after his senior season—in which he averaged 28 points a game and shattered a Montana record by scoring 123 points in three state tournament games—his mother, Dorothy, held a "giveaway" in his honor. She was suffering from diabetes, which in a few years would force the amputation of her right leg below the knee and lash her to a kidney dialysis machine three days each week, yet she was determined to thank God and her tribe for the greatness of her son. Jonathan, her seventh surviving child (two had died shortly after birth), had been born with a crooked face and a too-large nose, and so in her hospital bed Dorothy had lifted the infant above her eyes and turned all her fears for him over to God. "Here, Lord," she whispered, "raise him up, he's all yours." The Lord's day-care center turned out to be a basketball court; from the age of three, all Jonathan did was dribble and shoot. On dry, frigid days he would play for so long that the ball would chafe away his skin, and he would come home at dusk with bloody fingers for his mother to bandage. Dorothy's eyes still shone when she stared at the Mother's Day card he had drawn in crayon for her in second grade: three yellow flowers in a blue vase, a snowcapped mountain beneath the sun—and a man slam-dunking a basketball. And just look how the boy had turned out, with a face straight and well proportioned, a body long and strong, a name that the wind had carried across the Big Horn and Wolf mountains, had whispered into the ears of the Cheyenne and Sioux, even laid upon the tongues of the pale skins. If only the boy's eyes would leave his shoes. If only

the boy would stop stumbling home at 4 a.m. with the same stink
on his breath as her husband, Lacey. . . .

In the giveaway ceremony, Jonathan's exploits were to be
celebrated in the same manner in which Crows once commemo-
rated a successful raid. Besides all the cousins and uncles and aunts
and nephews and nieces who gathered, Jonathan's other "family,"
his clan, was there. There were 10 clans in the Crow tribe, some
consisting of as many as a thousand members; at birth one auto-
matically became a member of the same clan as one's mother. First
Jonathan was to dance in a circle as singers sang his honor song,
then he was to stand to the side as an "announcer" gave an account of his deeds, and finally he was to give away packages that
consisted of four gifts to his clan uncles and aunts. It is a lovely
ritual, one in which the hero, in a reversal of the white man's cus-
tom, showers his community with gifts in gratitude for the support and prayers that enabled him to succeed. Jonathan's family,
just barely getting by on his father's meager salary as a custodian
in the reservation hospital, couldn't possibly afford all these gifts,
but in keeping with tradition his relatives had contributed so that
the giveaway could take place.

Jonathan dreaded the stares that would be drawn to him if
he wore the ritual Indian clothing, but he couldn't bear to disappoint his people. Slowly he pulled on the ribbon shirt, the buck-
skin vest, the colorful beaded armband and the war bonnet. They
felt so odd upon him; he felt like no warrior at all. The first horse
he had ever ridden had flung him from its back; the first bullet he
had ever fired at an animal had slain a dirt clod far from its target. One of his great-great-grandfathers, known simply as Fly, had
been a powerful warrior, a possessor of six wives. Another, Red
Bear, had been a medicine man so potent that he simply had to
fill his peace pipe and hold it toward the sun and all the tobacco
in it would burn. Their home had been the river-fed valleys and
shimmering plains, their roof the sky, their walls the snow-topped
mountains a week's walk away. Jonathan? His home was a
cramped three-bedroom box in which as many as 15 siblings and
cousins often vied for sleeping space, sometimes on the floor beneath the kitchen table or even in the driveway, in the backseat of

a car. Jonathan's bed, until he was seven, was a mattress jammed between the beds of his mom and dad.

With his family and his clan trailing behind him, he lowered his eyes and led them into the Little Big Horn College building for the giveaway. Rather than tokens of scalps or war booty captured from the enemy, Dorothy wore a huge orange shawl with large black letters stitched upon it that listed his coups: JONATHAN TAKES ENEMY, STATE CLASS A MVP, ALL-STATE 1ST TEAM, ALL-CONFERENCE 1984, CONVERSE BASKETBALL ALL-AMERICA HONORABLE MENTION, HERTZ AWARD, ATHLETE OF THE YEAR. Beneath were sewn four white stars; four is the Crows' sacred number. Jonathan was supposed to lead the assembly in a dance, but his feet could not quite bring themselves to do it. Almost imperceptibly he shifted his weight from one foot to the other, leading everyone around the room again and again in a plodding circle as the big drum pounded and the 11 singers in the center lifted their voices to his glory—and reminded him of his obligation to those around him.

Outstanding man
Look all around you
Nothing lasts forever
Look all around you
Share your talent and knowledge

Share what? All he had to divvy up, it sometimes seemed, were self-doubt and pain. One day in ninth grade, at the end of basketball practice, his family had come to the school and told him that his sister had died at the age of 24, after years of hard drinking. He turned to the wall and broke down. Just a few weeks later his girlfriend told him she was pregnant. Terrified, he dropped out of school for the rest of the year, hid from his teachers on the streets, sometimes even hid from his own family—and reached for the same poison as his sister had.

He knew the danger he was wooing. The night he learned he had made the varsity, a rare honor for a freshman, he and a few friends went out in a pickup truck to drink beer. A tribal police car pulled up to the truck. Alcohol was banned on the reservation, but Crow policemen sometimes looked the other way. "Go home," this cop ordered the teenagers, but the kid at the wheel panicked, jammed the accelerator and roared away. Suddenly, Takes Enemy, a boy who was afraid even on a sled, found himself hurtling down a curving country road at 100 mph, four police cars with flashing lights and howling sirens just behind him. One came screaming up beside the truck, trying to slip by and box the teenagers in. Instead of letting it pass, Jonathan's friend lurched into the other lane to cut the car off. The pickup truck skidded off the road, toppled onto its roof and into a ditch. Takes Enemy limped out, somehow with just a badly bruised hip.

He vowed not to drink again. He remembered how uneasy he had been as a child, awakening on the mattress between his parents' beds to see the silhouette of his father stagger into the room. Even in an alcoholic haze, his father was a gentle man, but, still, that silhouette was not Dad—it was a *stranger.* Then, too, there was what alcohol had done to his cousin the legend, Pretty Weasel. So many fans thronged gymnasiums to watch Pretty Weasel play for Hardin High that his team had to crawl through windows to get to its locker room. He could shoot jump shots with either hand, fake so deftly that he put defenders on their pants and, at 5' 10", outjump players a half-foot taller. It was almost, an opponent would muse years later, "as if you were playing against a kind of enchanted person." Pretty Weasel's younger brother Lamonte got drunk and died in a car accident. Then Pretty Weasel partied his way out of a four-year college scholarship and onto a reservation road crew.

But Jonathan couldn't keep his vow. He felt as if he were locked up in a tiny room inside his body, and it was only when he was playing basketball or drinking that he could break out of it. The first time he was drunk had been in seventh grade at Crow Fair, the weeklong celebration every August when the field on the edge of his town became the tepee capital of the world. Hundreds of tepees were erected, and Indians from far away came to dance and drink and sing with his people deep into the night. Jonathan slipped the bootlegger $4 for a half-pint of whiskey, poured it down—and out poured the talking, laughing Jonathan he had always yearned to be. His mother came and found him at the fair at 3 a.m. Dorothy, a sweet, passive woman dedicated to the Pentecostal Church, began yelling that he would end up just like his father . . . but that was all. In many homes across the reservation . . . that was all.

His sophomore year he moved in with his girlfriend and her parents, to help her bring up their baby daughter. Four months after his girlfriend delivered, she had news for him. She was pregnant again. His whole life seemed hopeless, his daydream of escaping snuffed out. Was it his fault? No matter how hard Jonathan thought about it, he could never be sure. So many things had happened to his people that *were* beyond their control, it had become almost impossible to identify those that were *not*. He watched three brothers go to college and quickly drop out. He watched all three of them take turns with the bottle.

There were no movie theaters or bowling alleys or malls on the reservation. When it became too dark to see the rim on the courts behind the elementary school, Jonathan and his friends would drive up and down the main street of Crow Agency—from JR's Smokehouse to the irrigation supply yard and back again— seeing the same people, the same mange-eaten dogs and rust-eaten cars, until the monotony numbed them. Then someone would say, "Let's go drinking." It was a ritual that had become a display of solidarity and shared values among his tribe, so much so that to say no was to mark oneself as an alien. None of the teenagers had enough money to buy liquor, but all of them had Indian wealth—relatives. Uncles and aunts, cousins and grandparents were as close to most Crows as parents and siblings were to a white child; a boy could walk into five or six houses without knocking, open the refrigerator without asking, eat without cleaning up the crumbs. Jonathan and his friends would each ask a relative or two for a buck, and all of the sharing and family closeness in which the Crows prided themselves would boomerang. Each kid would come up with three or four dollars to pitch into the pot, and off they'd go to the liquor stores that waited for them beyond the reservation borders. It wouldn't take long to see someone they knew who was of drinking age—the boys were related by blood or clan, it seemed, to *everyone*. They whisked their beer or whiskey back onto the reservation, where the statutes against juveniles drinking were less severe, and began gulping it as if they were racing to see who could sledgehammer reality quickest, who could forget his life first.

Jonathan's absences from school mounted. That was how he responded to trouble. He disappeared. His parents wanted him to get an education, but to make the house quiet for two hours each night and insist that he study, to pull him out of his bed when the school bus was rolling up the road—no, they couldn't quite do that. Each of them had dropped out after the ninth grade, but there was more to it than that. Almost every Crow parent had a close relative who had been forcibly taken from his home by white government agents in the early 1900s and sent off to a faraway boarding school, where his hair was shorn, his Indian clothes and name were taken away, and he was beaten for speaking his own language. How many Indians could chase an education without feeling an old pang in their bones?

On intelligence alone, Takes Enemy had made the honor roll in junior high, but now he fell behind in class and was too ashamed to ask the white teachers for help. He lost his eligibility for the first half-dozen games of both his sophomore and junior seasons, regained it after each Christmas and started dropping in 25 or 30 points with a dozen assists a game, leading his teammates flying up and down the floor. His coaches called it Blur Ball. His people called it Indian Ball. And his brothers, three of whom had also been stars at Hardin High, would whip the crowd to wildness, reaching back into imaginary quivers on their backs, loading their make-believe bows and zinging invisible arrows at the other teams; vibrating their hands over their mouths to make the high, shrill *wooo-wooo* battle cry that once froze frontiersmen's hearts; shouting themselves hoarse, making Takes Enemy feel as if he could simply lift up his legs and let his people's ecstasy wash him up and down the hardwood.

He scored 49 points in a state tournament game his senior year and was named the tournament's MVP. The outside walls of his house literally vanished, swathed in posters of congratulation from his fans. "A great major college prospect," said then BYU coach Ladell Andersen.

Do it, teachers urged him. Do it so *they* could once more believe in what they were doing, do it so *all* the Crow children whose eyes were on him could see how it was done. "Just *one*," they kept saying to him. "If just one great basketball player from here could make the break and succeed, it could change *every-thing*. College recruiters would start coming here, other kids would follow your example. You can be the one, Jonathan. You can be the breakthrough."

He was flown to BYU. He stared at the 26,000 white faces strolling across campus. He stood at the top of the basketball arena and looked down, his eyes growing wider and wider, the court growing tinier and farther away. He had never heard of anyone like himself playing in a place like this; he couldn't even fathom it. "He said almost nothing the whole time," recalls Andersen. "I asked him a few questions. He was nodding his head yes when he should have been shaking it no."

The stack of letters from universities grew at his home. Jonathan never replied. His senior year was ending, his sun descending toward the hills. In the long-ago days a Crow hero could go on doing what he did until an arrow or a bullet found him, then let the breeze carry off his soul to the Other Side Camp. But in the 20th century the hero's bullet was high school graduation—and then he had to go on living. "Where are you going to college?" people asked Jonathan everywhere he went. "He'll be home by Thanksgiving," they told each other. "Like crabs in a bucket, that's how we are," says Dell Fritzler, the coach at Plenty Coups High. "Whoever tries to get out, we yank him back down." Even Jonathan's own Indian name—bestowed upon him during his senior season after it had come to the medicine man in a dream—tugged downward at the boy. Iiwaaialetasaash, he was called. Does Not Put Himself Above Others. Go off to college? That would Definitely Put Himself Above Others. No, white people couldn't understand this; Jonathan himself could barely grasp the code: It was O.K. for an Indian to clench his teeth and compete as part of a team, especially an Indian team. But to do it alone, to remove yourself from the dozen people in your living room at midnight and go sit over a chemistry or algebra book—in many families, that tainted you. You were trying to be a white man.

Jonathan's head spun. There were just too many mixed signals, too many invisible arrows from the audience whizzing by. Like most Crows, he'd been brought up not to make autonomous decisions but to take his cues from his immediate family, his extended family, his clan and his tribe. If *they* hadn't decided whether to assimilate into the white man's world or to recoil from it—how could he? And then, his two little children—he couldn't just walk away from them. The small living room he grew up in, with its 65 photographs of family members on the wall—a warm, happy place that the people in those pictures would flow into with no invitation, sit around sipping coffee and exchanging the sly puns and double entendres that his people excelled at, talking until there was nothing left to talk about and then talking some more—he couldn't just leave that behind. "Why?" he remembers wondering. "Why do I have to do it the white man's way to be a success in this world?" Why did all the human wealth he had gathered in his life, all the close friends and relatives, count for nothing when he crossed the reservation borders; why did material wealth seem to be the only gauge? And then his eyes and whys would turn the other way: "Why am I so important to my people? Why do *I* have to carry the hopes of the Crows?" All he had really wanted to do, ever since taking apart a stereo in the 10th grade and staring in wonder at all the pieces inside, was to go to a vocational school and learn electronics. But no, the herd was rolling, the people were waving and shouting him on, his legs were pulling him closer and closer to the ledge. He drank to close his eyes to it. One night at a school dance an administrator found out he was drunk. The next day he was ordered to take a chemical-dependency class.

Where were the people in his tribe who had lived through this? Why weren't they at Takes Enemy's door? Myron Falls Down, a prolific scorer for a Crow independent team in the 1970s, heard the rumors and wondered if he should do something. Six years earlier it had come to Falls Down like thunder through a hangover: that the addiction sucking the life from him and his people went beyond the beer they drank at night after playing ball, beyond the pills some ingested and the weed they puffed, beyond the Aqua Velva and Lysol and fingernail-polish remover some of them swilled; that *basketball*, the way the Crows were using it, had become a drug too. One morning in 1979, at the age of 27, he stood up from the bed where he slept every night with his ball. He went to the two glass-enclosed cases in the living room where his 50 trophies were displayed, and he began throwing them into cardboard boxes. "What are you doing?" cried his mother. She and Myron's nieces raced to unscrew the little figurines from their wooden bases before he could sweep all of them away. He grabbed the five jackets he had won in tournaments, loaded them and his trophies into his car, drove to the dumpster on the edge of Lodge Grass and heaved them all in. He would never take another drink or drug after that day. He would never play, or go to see, another basketball game—not even, 10 years later, the junior high school games of his 13-year-old son. "If there was a connection between education and basketball on this reservation, there would be nothing wrong with basketball," says Falls Down, now a tribal health administrator. "But right now there is none. Basketball is an escape from reality for us. But I never did speak to Jonathan. I felt he or his family would have approached me if they wanted to hear my message."

Pretty Weasel—where was he? The man named Montana's Outstanding Athlete 27 years before Takes Enemy, the one recruited by the University of Utah, Texas A&M and Seattle University, the cousin caught in this same crossfire eight years before Jonathan was born. Relatives and friends had sat at Takes Enemy's dinner table to spill their guts and offer counsel, but the man who with one look or word might have given Jonathan a glimpse at the ledger, at the remorse and relief in the soul of a man who has walked away from his greatness, had signaled nothing. Pretty Weasel stood in the shadows at basketball games, refused invitations to giveaways, belittled his own legend. "Never saw myself play," he said. "Can't picture myself being able to play with those black boys." Years later, at the age of 51 and no longer a drinker, he would wish that he had gotten his degree, explored the borders of his talent. "But I don't give advice," he says. "I guess I feel more like the whites do. That every man can be as good as he wants to. That every man does it on his own."

Graduation day came. Jonathan still hadn't decided. Barely, just barely, he got his diploma. As the teachers watched him carry it across the stage, Anderson, the assistant principal, turned and said, "I hope we're not looking at the first day of the end of his life."

When the dance is over, sweetheart,
I will take you home in my one-eyed Ford.

That sloppy man with the red-rimmed eyes and the puffy face, taller than the others. . . .

That whiskered man with the slurred speech and the thick belly and the slumped shoulders, standing on the riverbank near Two Leggins Bridge . . . that's him. That's Jonathan Takes Enemy.

It's 1989. It's 3 a.m. When the bars close in Hardin, Jonathan and his friends often come here to sing and laugh and drink and dance until the sun comes up. At dawn somebody often hits somebody, and somebody's brother or cousin jumps in to help, and there's a whole pile of them in the dirt. And then they go home to sleep until noon.

But the sky's still dark, they all still feel good. They're singing "49" songs, native chants interspersed with English lyrics, sadhappy tunes to the beat of a drum. Takes Enemy still can't bring himself to dance or sing, but he's thumping out the drumbeat on a car hood. "Way-la-hey-ley, way-la-hey-ley . . . ya-hey-oh-wayla-hey . . ." his companions croon. "When the dance is over, sweetheart, I will take you home in my one-eyed Ford."

The dance is over. It ended four years ago, as soon as it began. Six games into Jonathan's freshman season at Sheridan College, the Wyoming school whose scholarship offer he grabbed at the last minute because it was just an hour's drive from home, he quit. It's all still a blur to him: Hiding from everyone when it was time to leave home. Reporting to college two days late and only because

Anderson found him and took him there. Being stopped in the yard as he left, asked by his teary-eyed mother, "Are you *sure* you want to go, Jonathan? They aren't *forcing* you?" Trying to go from a world where it's disrespectful to look someone in the eye into one where it's disrespectful *not* to. Sitting alone in his dorm room for days, walking alone to the cafeteria, eating alone. Telling none of the white people about his fear and loneliness. Being guided by no one through the bewildering transition from reservation to white world. Knowing before his first game that something was wrong, because he had done something he could never do the night before a high school game—sleep. Knowing that the feeling he had had at Hardin—that he was on a mission, playing for his people— was gone. Returning to the reservation three straight weekends and not coming back in time for Monday practice. Two weekends later, not coming back at all. Walking away from the No. 1–ranked junior college team in the nation . . . but whose nation, *whose?*

"Crawled back under the blanket," said the whites. They've seen Indians do it so often that they have a cliché for it. "Every Indian that leaves has a rubber band attached to his back," says Jonathan's brother James. The Crows have seen their people do it so often that they only shrug. In some strange way, by going away to college and then by quitting, too, Takes Enemy has managed to fulfill *everyone's* expectations.

Somewhere, perhaps upon the hilltop at Custer Battlefield, his daydream still exists. More and more, he bicycles back there, as if in search of it. After all, he is only 24, he tells himself, his life is just beginning—or already half over, according to Crow life-expectancy charts.

His pockets are empty. He bums beer money from his dad, who has stayed clean since entering an alcohol rehabilitation program recently. No one will hire Jonathan. No one will buy him drinks at the bars in Hardin the way they did when he was in high school. Sometimes he walks out of the bars and onto the streets, sees a teacher from the school driving by and slinks into the shadows. He's not a bum, he's *not*. Twice he has been thrown into the reservation jail for drinking, lain on the floor all night in a cell with 30 other drunk men, listened to them moan and retch.

He has gained more than 20 pounds. He still plays ball, lumbering up the floor in Indian tournaments held across the state and the country. After games the team goes drinking—and sometimes, even right before them. He signs up for courses at the reservation's junior college; some he completes, some he doesn't. He has a new girlfriend, Trudi Big Hair, and two more children, Jonathan and Tashina. The four of them sleep in a small room at his parents' house, and no one ever hints that it's time he moved out. Sometimes in the morning the children jump on him in bed and shout, exploding his hangovers. He drifts back to sleep until noon, goes to a class or two, kills a few hours staring at the TV or picking up his welfare check, plays pickup basketball with his friends until dark . . . and then often starts all over again. Each time he drinks, Trudi etches an X on the calendar. Day by day, Jonathan watches his life get crossed out.

Once or twice he has gone to see his old school play. He doesn't go inside. He watches from a half-open door. It's not his court anymore. A new hero has arisen, a boy at Lodge Grass High named Elvis Old Bull. Old Bull took his team to state titles in '88 and '89, was named tournament MVP both years, noticed kids beginning to dress and cut their hair like he does, heard himself called a major college prospect. He has a child, but isn't married; he skips school too much; he drinks too much; his eyes are haunted. Sometimes Jonathan feels as if there is something he could tell the boy—but no, he can't, he *can't*. Old Bull enters a rehabilitation center just after his junior season. The treatment fails. He misses far too many days of school to remain eligible for his final season, but the people need that third straight title too much, and school administrators can't quite bring themselves to sit him down. "You're going to end up just like Jonathan Takes Enemy," people in the tribe keep telling him. He leads his team to the third state title, wins his third tournament MVP trophy, then simply stops going to school. He watches his classmates graduate through eyes swollen from a car wreck from another night's drinking. And the sun arcs across the Montana sky, and the eagle wheels, and the circle remains unbroken.

* * *

Autumn 1990. The sun drops behind the Big Horn Mountains. An orange 1980 Mustang turns onto the highway and bears north across the reservation, toward Billings. There is no caravan behind him. Takes Enemy goes alone.

His face is clean-shaven, his clothes are neat, his cheekbones have bloomed again. He is 25, but he looks like that boy in those high school pictures once more. All summer he has jumped rope, slipping into his backyard to do it at midnight when no one on the reservation could see.

He presses the accelerator. Just a short visit home today; he cannot dally. He needs to get off the reservation by nightfall and back to his apartment in Billings, to Trudi and little Jonathan and Tashina, back to his new life as a student and a basketball player at Rocky Mountain College. Because when the darkness comes and his friends come. . . . "To do this," he says, "I can't be near them. I *miss* them. But I have to be alone." He hasn't had a drink in months. He hears that Old Bull has made a change too, moving to Bozeman with hopes of fulfilling his high school requirements and getting a shot at college ball.

"It's *my* decision to go to college this time," Jonathan says. "I finally realized that I was running out of time. It's not that the reservation is a bad place. There are many good people there. But it's just not a place where you can become what you want to become. It's not a place where you can achieve your dreams."

Last spring he convinced Luke Gerber, the coach at Hardin High, that he was serious. Gerber called Jeff Malby, the coach at Rocky Mountain College, and Malby remembered how the clean water had once flowed across the rocks. He offered Takes Enemy a scholarship to the liberal arts college in Billings with 810 students. So far, it fits Jonathan just right.

He passes the reservation border, glances into his rearview mirror. He knows that some people back there are now calling him an "apple"—red on the outside, white on the inside. He knows what he is leaving behind, what he is losing. Knows it in the morning when he passes his new neighbors in Billings and they barely nod. Knows it when it's midnight and he and Trudi are buried in textbooks, and the apartment is silent. "It's just too quiet here," he'll say. "We're so isolated." And when he lies in bed at night and thinks of his sick mother, he knows it then, too.

His eyes move back to the windshield. Ahead of him, over the rolling hills, across the sage and buffalo grass, he can just make out the soft electric glow of Billings. He's starting to get an idea of what lies this way. He's passing all four of his classes. He's averaging 19.8 points and 4.6 assists for his new team. He's just getting his bearings, but his coaches say that he'll soon establish himself as the best player in Montana and that he's destined to be an NAIA All-America before he's done.

Everything's still so new to him. Paying his own rent each month from the grant money allotted to him by the tribe and the Bureau of Indian Affairs, paying electric bills, buying his own food. Studying until 1 a.m., making sure that Trudi gets off to Eastern Montana College in the morning, that his kids get off to day care and preschool, living in the white man's world, in a hurry, on a schedule.

He wants to go back to the reservation someday and help kids to take the risk, to see both the beauty and the danger of the circle. But he may never live there again. He rolls down his car window. He listens to the air. There is no singing in the land. There is only a quiet, sad-happy song inside a young man's heart.

The Ripples from Little Lake Nellie

The children were playing Marco Polo off the dock where the two ballplayers died. Their mother was sitting with her knees pulled up to her chest beneath a large pink umbrella on the end of the pier. She gazed across the soft green hills that cup Little Lake Nellie, across the cypress and orange trees and the reeds.

"Marco!"

"Polo!"

"Marco!"

"Polo!"

Everything was fine as long as her neighbor kept talking and her rottweiler kept snorting and churning those crazy zigzags in the water. Just fine as long as the sun was high and the children kept playing that silly game, one of them going under for a count of three and bursting up with his eyes closed, crying out "Marco!" and waiting for the others to shout "Polo!" and then flailing toward the voices, groping through the darkness to touch them.

Because then Jetta Heinrich's eyes wouldn't be drawn to the new wood on her dock or to the big brown barn and the rise of

---

This story first appeared in 1993, four months after Cleveland Indian pitchers Tim Crews and Steve Olin died in a boating accident.

land just across the tiny lake where one of the ballplayers' widows lived. And she might not get that sick feeling in her stomach and the echo of the thud again in her ears, the one she heard that night, standing on her back porch in her bathrobe. She wouldn't have to leave like she'd had to nearly every time she'd tried to come out on the dock since then. . . .

"Marco!"

"*Polo!*"

. . . A dock her husband had constructed with a ramp leading up to it instead of steps, so her aunt in a wheelchair and her shuffling grandfather could join them. A dock with a bench at the end so they could sit together and watch the children belly-flop into the water and play silly games. A place to build a family.

Were this story a movie, it would open with a scene 20 years from today. Patti and Grover and Wick and Laurie and Bobby would be sitting around a fire near the cypress trees on the bank of the little lake in Clermont, Florida. They'd all be graying and wrinkled by then. They'd all have angle and distance on what occurred that night at the dock. In the campfire glow you would barely make out Bobby's scar, the one that loops across his forehead like the seams of a baseball. Laurie would be trying to explain what it was like sleeping for months in the same bed with three little bodies. Patti and Wick would be getting hopelessly tangled trying to remember the words to the song they each listened to a zillion times right after it happened, only you wouldn't quite know what *it* was, and you would have to wait two hours and two dozen flashbacks to make sense of it all.

But not even four months have gone by. There is no angle yet, no distance, no movie cliché. There are splinters of wood still flying, people still crying out a name, still groping through the darkness. The ripples haven't even begun to reach the edge of Little Lake Nellie.

So let us just reach into the swirl, choose a moment and begin. A Florida morning, a baseball clubhouse, a week after Tim Crews and Steve Olin died when their heads struck a dock during a family outing on a spring training off-day. Grover—that's what everyone around the clubhouse calls Cleveland Indian manager Mike Hargrove—is gazing out at the surviving members of his bullpen, wondering how in hell he is ever going to bring this team back from its grief. On Eric Plunk's chest is one of Steve Olin's T-shirts. On Ted Power's waist is the belt Oly wore when he broke into the major leagues. In Derek Lilliquist's hand are the two steel balls Oly squeezed to strengthen his wrist. On Kevin Wickander's feet are Oly's shower clogs. Thank God, they didn't know Tim Crews any better—another sweet human being, just like Oly. Thank God, Tim had just joined the team.

And now there's a ghost walking slowly toward Grover. Face white as bone, shoulders stooped, cheeks sunken, eyes dead as stones; a good breeze would blow him away. It's the third man who was in the boat that night, the 35-year-old whom the Indians had hired as a free agent three months earlier to be their No. 2 starter, a Los Angeles Dodger teammate of Crews's the previous two seasons. The one who pleaded, "Keep breathing, Crewser, *c'mon, keep breathing!*"—barely aware that two quarts of his own blood were all over the boat, that his own scalp was ripped back like the top of a tennis-ball can.

"I'd like to talk to the team," Bobby Ojeda said softly.

Sure . . . of course, Bobby, fine, Grover heard himself say . . . but *good Lord.* Grover glanced over the ghost's shoulder again at the team. He felt the lump, the goddam fist, rising in his own throat again. His whole life, a childhood amid the cattle ranches and oilfields of Texas, a manhood amid the cleats and tobacco-stained teeth of professional ball, he had been weaned on a truth, a way of surviving, that was being blown to bits here.

One day. That's what Grover's manager in Class A ball had offered him to get from Gastonia, North Carolina, to Perryton, Texas, and back when his grandfather, Papaw, died. You couldn't do that in one day, so Grover clenched his jaw and kept playing. A few years later his wife's dad died when Grover was a first baseman with the Texas Rangers. "That's not immediate family," said his manager, Billy Martin, when Grover asked for time off to attend the funeral. How many teammates even bothered to call him when he was traded in 1978 after five seasons with the Rangers? Two. *Two.* Baseball had too long a season, was too dependent upon mechanics, for spilling emotions; a high five now and then, an obscenity and a stream of brown goo, that's all a guy was supposed to let out. Even last year, when Grover risked a little kiss with his wife through the screen behind home plate after a spring training game, damned if that fan hadn't caught him and howled, "Get a room!"

If a man was around that long enough, he *became* it, even a good guy like Grover. When his wife's eyes welled up in front of a movie, he made the wisecrack. When his teammate Danny Thompson died of leukemia in the off-season in 1976, Grover drove from Texas to the funeral in Oklahoma because that was the proper thing to do, but the agony, the enormity of what this did to Danny's family, never hit him, and he drove back home feeling as flat and arid inside as the land around him, wondering if something was wrong, if something was missing inside, but . . . crap, that speeding ticket he'd gotten on the way there . . . aw, screw it all. . . .

He wanted what Bert Campaneris got. He wanted, at the end of his career, for an umpire to walk over to him in the dugout the way he had seen Bill Haller do one day to Campy—his teammate, the Ranger shortstop who never whined, never cried, never even smiled—and offer a handshake and say, "You're a real professional." That was Grover's goal in life.

So what was happening to him now? The other day, for instance, when he was bawling like a baby, with his son in his lap. And the day after, head buried in his pillow and crying his eyes out on his bed at his spring training apartment, when his wife walked in, and right after her one of his relievers, Kevin Wickander, and Wick's wife, Kim. The four of them all ending up on the bed, talking and sobbing and wrapping their arms around each other. *That* was professional? Two things were warring inside Grover on the bed that day with the wives and Wick, the last player left on the roster whom he had managed in the minors, now that Oly was gone. "We've . . . we've got to get over this, Wick. . . . We've got to get *busy*. . . . You're my last *pup*."

For a year and a half, since Grover had become the Indians' manager, he and the front office had been telling the world how tight this young team was, how much like family. They had signed a core of 18 players to relatively modest multiyear contracts and planned to keep them together, use their closeness as a weapon against the big-market teams with the cash flow to keep famous free agents shuttling in and out. But lots of team managements yapped about family and waived you in a swing and a miss. Who could possibly trust that?

Now one of the family was in a box, and the other was ashes in an urn in the mountains of Oregon, and Grover had to look inside himself and discover if the sermons he had preached were true. If they were a *family*, how could he be a *professional*? He could only be a father who had lost two children. He sat on a chair in the middle of the locker room the morning after the accident and waved to his players to come sit close around him on the floor, like a kindergarten teacher and his kids. And now the emotions he had always wondered about were coming like a freight train, and the only choice was whether to stand in front of the train or leap out of its way. He stood there and let it happen in front of everyone, kept on talking about what the players meant to him even when the words were hitching and then turning to sobs, and then, one by one, they all did the same. God, it felt like family, the way they all kept drifting in and out of each other's apartments that week, the way Grover and his wife, Sharon, were always there for the players and their wives and the widows, ready to pack or cook or clean or hug or cry with anyone who needed it. It could never be the same after that morning in the clubhouse with Grover. Good or bad for a baseball team, nobody could be sure, but never the same.

Grover backed way off, let the players miss a cutoff man or a signal in those final exhibition games, but now Opening Day was just a week away, time to start sucking it up and setting the jaw . . . and here stood that ghost in front of the team.

It was not so much what Bobby Ojeda told the players that day—how it had happened that night on the boat, how the three of them had never even glimpsed that dock in the darkness, how he wanted them not to pity him or think about him at all. It was the way he said it, the utter deadness in his voice and eyes, the total absence of hope. Not a word of encouragement. Not a word about coming back.

And then he was gone. The players looked at one another. The clubhouse filled, again, with silence. How many million *attaboys* and *let's-pull-it-togethers* would it take to counteract that?

They would charge onto the field for Opening Day in Cleveland, the relievers lifting their thumbs to heaven to signal to Oly and Crewser that everything was going to be O.K., 73,290 people standing and crying and roaring for them and for the two widows clutching empty jerseys at home plate . . . and would get crushed 9–1 by the Yankees. The Indians would lose 43 of their first 81 games, committing 71 errors, pressing to do what they couldn't and not even doing what they could. Injuries chopped down what remained of the staff—six pitchers, at one point, on the disabled list—as little pangs turned into deep pain; who could bring himself to mention a strained tendon or a tender lat in the wake of death? No one pointed a finger in the clubhouse. The team, fused by grief, remained one. But there was no resurrection. No clichés. No movies to be made in last place.

Grover would see a player making an idiot, an absolute idiot, out of himself on the field in May, open his mouth to tell him that . . . but then an image of that player from the day when they gathered around Grover's chair in the clubhouse would come to him, a memory of how much compassion that man had, and instead Grover would hear himself say, "You're *not* what you showed on the field today. I *know* you."

But he couldn't help wondering, as loss piled upon loss, as day after day passed without an offer of a contract extension from the front office that spoke so much about family, if he should've just chewed the guy's head off.

He came home after a loss one day in May and put his arms around Sharon. He had opened a letter before the game from a fan complaining that Grover had betrayed his responsibility to young people by downplaying Tim Crews's blood-alcohol level the night of the accident, and rage had rushed to Grover's face. He had grabbed the phone, tracked down the fan and screamed obscenities at him—how dare this moron judge him from a thousand miles away when there was so much pain, so many lives lying crumpled all around him. Now, for the first time in their lives together, his wife felt his body come unstrung, all his 215 pounds falling against her, and she felt as close to him as she ever had. "I don't know if I did the right or wrong thing about the alcohol," he sobbed. "I don't know anything. . . ."

Were there any standings, any stats, for good human beings? On a tired Sunday evening after a game, when his four-year-old, Shelly, wanted to read a book or his 11-year-old, Andy, wanted to play ball, Grover used to sink into his living room chair with the newspaper or a book and grunt "Yeah . . . later. . . ." until it was their bedtime. Now he got up and did it. Now he swallowed hard and stared in wonder at the note tucked inside his bedroom mirror, written to him in May by his own father, a man who had never before come close to uttering such words to him: "I saw you on television the past few weeks and you seemed to have the weight of the world on your shoulders. You can only do so much with what you have. When you get down and everything keeps falling up tails, remember, He's with you. . . . With love, Pop."

From the corner of her eye the old woman kept looking at the man seated next to her on the cross-country flight out of Los Angeles. Pulled low over his brow was a dark cap with a long bill. Under the cap, pulled tight over the crown of his head, nearly down to his eyebrows, was a blue bandanna. Zippering under and out from it, a terrible scar. On his nose was a pair of John Lennon glasses. She thought he might be a member of one of those gangs.

His finger was tracing a Delta route map, looking for the longest arc, the place farthest away from his home that he could go without a change of planes. He had refused to let doctors give him blood transfusions—he simply didn't believe in them. He might pass out if he tried to change planes. He might get lost. He might end up anywhere.

In his little carry-on bag was a book, a couple of pairs of underpants and socks, a few shirts, a plastic cylinder of sleeping pills and the passport he had sneaked out of his home in Upland, California, without his wife seeing. He had been so calm when he said good-bye to her and his little girl. They had never guessed.

He didn't want to talk. He just wanted to read. He just wanted
to stare out the window and beat himself to death, thinking of six
kids without fathers. But the old woman was so kind, and even
though he often preferred to be alone, he had been the kind of guy
who liked to pull out a chair when a stranger approached for an
autograph or to ask a question and say, "C'mon, sit down."

"What do you do for a living?" the lady said now.

"Well . . . I used to play baseball . . . but then I had an accident."

"Oh." She looked at him again. *Ohhhhhhhh.*

She knew. The whole world knew. She started to tell a story.
He didn't want to hear a story, but she was so kind. When she was
two years old, her mother was eight months pregnant. And then
. . . then her mother was dead. "A kid never loses the pain of that,"
the old woman said. "Never. But do you know what? When you
grow up, it makes you stronger."

For just a second, his eyes flickered.

He got off the plane when it landed on the East Coast. He
went to a bank. He cashed a check. A big check. Absurd. Still
making $1.7 million a year. No credit card. No trace.

He met his brother-in-law. "Are you crazy?" his brother-in-
law said. "They'll never let you in the country. They'll arrest you
at customs. They'll give you a body-cavity search. Do you know
what you look like now in the mirror?"

No. Two weeks straight without looking in a mirror. He
bought the Delta ticket. He stuffed the wad of bills into the carry-
on bag, next to the underwear, the socks, the shirts, the book, the
passport, the plastic cylinder of sleeping pills. It was opening week
in baseball.

You're not serious, Laurie. You can't go down to the dock.
Not already. Not today. Christ, she's Clint Eastwood.

No, somebody said, she's tougher than Clint.

John Wayne, then.

No, tougher than John.

John Eastwood. That's who Laurie Crews is, they were kidding. She's John Eastwood.

The five men glanced at each other. Christ, she was serious. The lake. The dock. Just a few hours ago, they had buried her husband.

The uneasy teasing stopped. They started walking. Fernando Montes, the Indians' conditioning coach, and Perry Brigmond, a buddy of Tim's—the two men who waded in that night and dragged the boat with the ballplayers ashore. Kirk Gibson, a teammate of Tim's for three of his six years on the Dodgers, and Mark Ostreich, a workout pal, and Bobby Ojeda. Bobby took a few steps, and everything spun. Laurie took one of his arms. Kirk took the other. They walked that way to the edge of the water and stared across at the dock.

This was Laurie, pure Laurie. Don't put it off. Step right back up to it. Talk to Tim and Steve. Fix it, *now*. "You're comin' back, Bobby," she started saying that day. "You're *gonna* pitch again, hear me? Don't you worry about me. I got people comin' out of the woodwork supportin' me—worse 'n termites. You worry about you. I'll kick your butt if you don't come back. I *mean* it."

You looked at her body, tan and wiry, at her eyes, deep blue and honest, and you knew she did. People kept asking how she had the stomach to stay there, on the 45-acre ranch overlooking the lake and the dock. She kept asking, How could I not? You could smell Laurie and Tim's dream, just driving up the dirt road to their house. Fresh-painted horse fence. New cedar barn. New cedar house. Baby oaks. Runt magnolias. Lacy grass. Three little children. A dream all planted and spindly and ready to grow.

Every off-season Sunday morning for three years Laurie and Tim had done the same thing. Pulled the classified-ads section out of the newspaper, circled every property that sounded faintly like their dream, eaten a big, greasy country breakfast and spent all day searching. It had to be a place where Laurie could raise horses and Tim could fish bass. Where two grown-up Florida country kids could walk dirt and raise kids. "A safe place," Tim kept saying. Not like Los Angeles, where he had pitched the last six years. Where kids drove Porsches, kids did crack, kids died. It had to be a place to build a family.

They found it one day. They worked on it for more than a year. They moved in in February. A month later Tim was dead. Now Laurie was going to live the dream for them both.

This is what you do with pain. You take it by the scruff of the neck, slap it around and put it to work. More horse fencing to go up. More tomatoes and cucumbers to be picked. More grass and shrubs to be planted. More quarter horses to be bought, sold, fed, hosed, trained. More pets to be taken to the vet. More homework to be done with the kids. More hugs to be given out. It's not healthy to be depressed, she would say, so I won't be depressed. A million people called her each day, but all they ever seemed to get was the answering machine: *Hi, it's Laurie. I'm doin' fine. Busy as ever. . . .*

She would come back to the house at the end of the day, exhausted, her eyes seeing Tim's maroon-and-silver Ramcharger in the driveway and shooting the words to her brain before she could stop them: *He's home!* She would lie in her bed at night, the three kids at crazy angles, lie there smelling their skin and their breath. Tricia, the nine-year-old, refusing to talk about it. Shawn, the five-year-old, saying, "Don't worry, Mommy. Don't cry. He'll never be away. He'll always be in your heart." Travis, the three-year-old, telling people, "My daddy's in church. He'll come out when he's done playing baseball with God."

Sometimes Laurie ached so bad to hold Tim that she would go to the closet and smell his clothes. Other times she went into the shower, let the warm water wash away her resolve, just let it all go, and go, and go. . . .

Midnight. Phone ringing. "Bobby? You're not working out yet, are you? Look, I'm gonna hang up this telephone and get on a plane and come out there and train with you if you don't get goin'. You're gonna hate yourself one day if you don't come back. No more pity parties. I'll kick your butt. I *mean* it."

She couldn't quite put into words why it meant so much to her and Patti Olin, to Tim's parents, to everyone, that Bobby come back. It was almost too big, too *genetic.* Laurie was the daughter of Dutch parents born in Indonesia, both held for years by the Japanese in a prisoner-of-war camp, both hungry, at the end of it all, for America. Laurie's father had taken migrant farm work in

Florida, anything to survive, earned an engineering degree, carved out a good life. That's what everybody had come for, he figured, to a land full of the children and grandchildren of people who left their families and hometowns behind rather than surrender to circumstance, obey fate. A land full of people who kept turning to sports, to see Bo Jackson dragging his artificial hip back to the plate, Jimmy Valvano dragging his cancer-racked spine back to the microphone, to see men and women overcoming injuries, odds and setbacks, athletes reenacting the national allegory, reconfirming it, *taking charge.* So where was Bobby in April when Laurie flew to Los Angeles to see the Dodgers' home opener and to visit him at his house in nearby Upland? Bobby's wife, Ellen, shook her head. No Bobby. No trace. Gone.

Two a.m. Phone ringing. It was Patti. Thank God for Patti. Somebody Laurie could tell that she had dropped from a size 9 to a size 4, that her stomach was burning like a furnace, without feeling as if she were asking for a pity party. Somebody she had never even met before that horrifying afternoon. The only person on earth who understood. "What time is it, Patti?"

"It's late. . . . Sorry. . . . You said if I was going through a bad time to call you no matter what hour."

"That's right. Start talkin'. You gettin' out of that house yet? I tell you, you gotta move down here, and I'll build you a house across the lake, and we'll get you all fixed up. So tell me how you're doin', girl."

"Who do you know here, sir?"

"No one."

"Why are you here?"

"Heard it was a nice place."

"How long will you stay?"

"I don't know."

The customs officer stared again at the photograph in the passport. Stared again at the man in front of him. Barely a resemblance. But this was Sweden. Go ahead.

The man took slow, small steps to the taxi. He checked into the best place he could find in Stockholm, the Grand Hotel. For a day and a night and a day, he put off what he was going to do. He was still so dizzy. He was still so weak. When the sun was setting on the second day, it was time.

He set two packs of cigarettes and two bottles of wine on the table in the alcove of the room. He stared out the window. Water everywhere. Boats. Docks.

All the adversity in his life, all those other brushes with death and pain, they didn't prepare him for this. They were nothing. The time in the early 1970s, when he was just a kid on a minibike, driving off a bridge. The time he and his dad hugged the floor of their fishing boat on a lake south of Fresno, listening to the bullets whine past, inches from their ears, because some lunatic, for the sheer hell of it, felt like squeezing off 10 or 15 rounds at two guys in a boat. The time when he was a teenager and had to heave away a can that had shot up in flames in his hand, because they were out of charcoal lighter for the grill and, well, why not use the gasoline? The time when he was in a Corvette and hit a telephone pole, the time an ambulance plowed clean through the trunk and backseat of a car he was riding in. The time, with the Mets in the thick of the '88 pennant race, when the hedge clippers slipped, turning the middle finger of his pitching hand into a stump dangling from another stump. He remembered coming home at 2 a.m. from road trips in '90 when the Mets had buried him in the bullpen, climbing onto his Harley-Davidson in the suit he had to wear to comply with the team dress code, howling and roaring through the streets of his neighborhood until the sun came up. . . . All Little League stuff. Penny ante. No howling now.

Goddammit, if only . . . If only the Indians still trained in Arizona, like they always had till this spring, and hadn't chosen to move to Homestead, Florida, and if only the hurricane hadn't headed straight for Homestead and demolished the complex, and if only the team hadn't stumbled into Winter Haven—just an hour from Crewser's ranch—to train. If only it hadn't rained that afternoon, and they had gone fishing in daylight, as they'd planned. If only they hadn't already been past the dock when the truck headlights flashed on the shore, the signal that Tim's buddy, Perry, was ready to be picked up, if only they hadn't had to turn around. If only Crewser and Steve had slouched when they sat, as he always did. If only he *hadn't* slouched—goddammit, what right did he have to he alive?

This is what you do with pain. You sit alone in a hotel room in a foreign country, and you start drinking wine and smoking cigarettes and staring out the window, talking out loud to the two dead men you were sitting with thigh-to-thigh, saying the most painful and horrific things you can possibly think of again and again, for six or seven hours, because if you can do that and get out of the chair at the end of it, you've put on another layer. And if you can do that the next day and the next, you can create a person who you're really not, but the person you need to be to go on. And it's worth it, worth everything you lose when you do that, because you don't lose everything. You don't reach for the plastic cylinder of pills you keep looking at, which would make your eyelids finally begin to sag, make all the *if onlys* drift away, and everything else too, forever and ever.

He lurched from the chair at 4 a.m., the room spun, he headed out the door. He walked for miles through the bitter cold and darkness—water everywhere, boats, docks—hanging by the thread, the thinnest, most ordinary thread, the old woman's words on the airplane: One day, because of it, the kids will be stronger. And when he came back, it was sunup, and he fell on the bed, his heart beating so hard and irregular that he thought it was coming right through his chest. Oh my God, he thought. I'm going to die in a hotel room 7,000 miles from home.

On one shelf lies Steve Olin's folded game jersey. Next to it lie his hat, a ball he signed, and his baseball card in a frame. On another shelf lie his baseball pants and several of his T-shirts. On a third shelf lie his fishing-tackle box, his spinners, spent shells from his rifle, his fishing license, his photograph with a deer and his locker nameplate. On a hook hangs his practice jersey.

This is not the Olins' house. It's the Wickanders'.

Someday, when Wick has a little boy and the boy is four or five, Wick's going to start pointing at the shelves and telling him about a wonderful man who drove an hour to a ranch on a lake one day, his only off-day all spring, because he wanted to make sure that the newest member of the bullpen felt welcome. He'll tell the boy about a season that happens now and then, or maybe not even that often. The oldest member of the bullpen, Teddy Power, had already put in 16 years with 10 different teams in pro ball when it happened, and he said he had never seen anything like what they shared that summer. A summer in 1992 when five men who loved the same things—boats and tobacco and motorcycles and trout streams and hunting and silly pranks and four-wheeling in the mud—found a groove that made them the American League's best bullpen, and became best friends as well. A summer when they went on fishing trips together and threw pies in faces and sabotaged TV microphones and branded their names in bullpens with red-hot tarp stakes and shouted *Ch-ching! Ch-ching!* all the way to the mound in the middle of games whenever one of them had broken some screwy bullpen bylaw that would cost him five bucks in kangaroo court. The Pen, they called themselves. We poked our dirty little raccoon noses, Wick would say, into anything we could. Five men: Wickander, Olin, Lilliquist, Plunk, Power. Five boys: Wicky, Oly, Lilli, Plunky, Teddy. In the bubble-gum-chewing contest, Wicky and Oly tied, 71 pieces in each of their mouths.

And then, just like that, the little family was gone. Oly was dead, and Wick, who couldn't get over it, was traded, and Teddy, even though he was 38 and might've known better, kept throwing with pain to make up for it and strained his triceps muscle, and Lilli and Plunky were left to blink at all the names and faces checking in.

"You'll have the most excellent day ever." That was the fortune on the Bazooka bubble-gum wrapper that Oly opened that day last summer. "Here, Wick," Oly said. "This is for you." And Wick believed him. He tucked it in the liner of his cap, won his first big league game that very day, framed the wrapper and put it on his wall.

That's how it was with Oly and Wick, the Pen's two best buddies. Oly wouldn't touch the third base line or flip the warmup ball to the bullpen catcher when he entered a game, so Wick wouldn't either. Oly etched an arrow under his hat brim to direct the ball to the plate, so Wick had to have that too. They had been together since 1989, at the Indians' Triple A farm in Colorado Springs. Oly was a sixteenth-round pick, a devoted husband with skinny shoulders and a submarine delivery and ordinary stuff, who believed in himself deep down. Wick was a second-round pick, a classic bachelor with barroom radar and killer looks and wicked stuff, who, deep down, didn't. Wick leaned on Oly. Literally. They would both go down to one knee and take turns resting an arm on each other's back in the outfield during batting practice, head beside head. Like Siamese twins, Teddy would say. Like listening to two guys talk who'd been next-door neighbors all their lives, said Lilli.

Wick could almost feel *not* feeling that arm on his back, even weeks after Oly was dead. Could almost taste *not* tasting that cheesecake and milk they used to order as they watched a movie after games on the road. Could almost hear *not* hearing that wonderfully whiny little-boy voice Oly used to affect each day when Wick entered the clubhouse. "Wickyyyyyy . . . Coooooome heeeeeere, Wickyyyyy. . . ." Which usually meant that Oly had thought of something wicked for Wick to do, and off they would go into a corner, whispering and giggling, and a few hours later the pitching coach would look down into his new pair of shoes and find the rat that the Pen had caught and cooked in the Angels' bullpen. Wick was happy to face the music. Happy as a puppy to chase the stick for Oly.

Who was there for Wick when he shattered his elbow in a cement runway at Anaheim Stadium in 1990 and then ran up $28,000 worth of bar and restaurant bills in one year, drinking himself all the way to the rehab center in Cleveland? It was Oly. Who was there for Oly in Triple A ball in '89 when Patti was pregnant and he wanted someone to move in with her while he went up to the big leagues? It was Wick. Finally, when Wick listened to Oly's advice, quit skirt-chasing and married his high school sweetheart, Kim, in May '92, Oly was there as Wick's best man. Oly was Wick's conscience, said Grover, who had managed Wick in A ball, Double A, Triple A, the majors.

You don't want to hear too much about Wick's first few days after Oly died. About waiting and calling and waiting for Oly to come home that night from the Crewses' so they could all go out to dinner. About Wick rolling over and over, screaming "No!" on the floor when Oly's name flashed on the TV screen that night, then helping Kim to the bathroom so she could throw up. About packing the things in Oly's locker into a box in an empty clubhouse six hours later, before dawn, and about the three straight nights when his eyes refused to close. "He was my family," Wick sobbed when it was his turn to speak at the funeral.

This is what you do with pain. You set up a locker for your dead best friend, with his nameplate and his glove and his uniform and his team jacket and his shoes and his framed photograph on a stool. Even when the team travels, you tape the nameplate over the locker next to you and set up the shrine, so no one ever forgets. You keep talking about him to the other players because they taught you in rehab never to repress your feelings. You keep walking around the clubhouse, even weeks later, with 5×7 photographs of Steve to send to the hundreds of well-wishers who have written, and offer them to players: "Thought you might like a picture of Oly." You get your brains beat out on the mound.

There was something almost heroic about it; Wick's grief possessed him. Eyes started rolling in the Indian clubhouse. Guys were starting to get the creeps. Guys were trying to forget. Mourning is a private project in America, not a communal one . . . but then, wouldn't everyone in the world, whether he admitted it or not, want a Wick to keep him alive when he was gone?

Grover called Wick into his office. He talked about counseling, about going on the disabled list.

"No," said Wick. "Oly wouldn't want that. He'd want me to pitch."

"But Wick," said Grover, "you can't work this out on the mound."

So what are you going to do about Wick? sportswriters began asking Indian management. Eight and two-thirds innings pitched, 15 hits allowed, 3 home runs. Can't send Oly's best buddy to the minors while he's in mourning, they said. It sure would look cruel.

Late afternoon, on May 7, Wick was waved into Grover's office at Chicago's Comiskey Park. Grover was brief. Barely blinked. There were others in the office. Wick had an hour and a half to catch a flight and join the Cincinnati Reds. He had been traded for a player to be named later. Best thing they could possibly do for him, Grover said.

Wick packed his bag in a stupor, said good-bye to the guys and walked out of the clubhouse. "Wick!" It was someone calling him from behind. Grover's eyes were welling, his arms lifting to hug. "If you ever need anything . . . you know . . . you know you're like a son to me."

The Indians clubhouse was so cramped for space, the delivery man for the local dry cleaner began using Oly's memorial locker to hang pressed shirts and suits for the players to retrieve. By the end of May, Grover had the locker dismantled altogether.

In Cincinnati, Wick started pitching better, feeling happy. Not ripping up records in either department, but he won a game, got some guys out, started smiling. He still wore Oly's shower clogs, sunglasses, wristwatch and T-shirts, but he sent the rest to keep in his off-season home in Phoenix. Someday he would let Oly's kids take from it whatever they wished.

He knew now that no baseball team, no bullpen, would ever again feel like a family, and he realized why Oly had kept urging him to get married and start one of his own. Kim was right beside him on virtually every road trip now. If she hadn't been there when Oly died, he knew he would've started drinking again.

God. He was remembering Oly's thousand-dollar bet at their wedding that Kim would be pregnant by their first anniversary. Easy money, Wick had thought, because they had no intention of having kids for at least a couple of years. When the anniversary came, six weeks ago, Kim and Wick held hands. Oly had lost— she wasn't pregnant—but when they thought about it, they actually grinned. In a few more months they were going to start trying. The baby's name, if it's a boy, will be Olin Wickander.

*   *   *

Yes. That was it. Rip it right across the neck. Now straight down, from crown to chin. Now again, right through that smile. Now the eyes. Good-bye, jackass. Good-bye.

He used to love that charcoal portrait on his office wall. Himself when he was a big league pitcher. Himself when he was happy. He used to look at it and think with satisfaction about how far he had come. The man now making a million-seven a year, overlooked completely in the 1977 draft and signed the next year for $500. The man who used to live in Winter Haven, Florida, with a wife and two babies in a motel room wallpapered with drying diapers because they couldn't afford the Laundromat. The guy who used to grab handfuls of Sucrets from the jar in the Class A clubhouse and throw them in his mouth. Not for a sore throat. For dinner.

He put the frame back. He had made it home, somehow, from Sweden. He stared down at the confetti, then up at the wall. That was good. That was him. Exactly right. The empty frame.

Every day when he was home, it went like this. He would get out of bed, walk down the hall to the reclining chair in his office and sit there. Reading John Grisham novels. Staring out the window. Staring at the empty picture frame. Letting the phone ring. All day in one room, and then back to bed at night, to lie there turning. Another pill. Wake up sweating. Start all over again.

If only he could have it out in one showdown—one night, one week, one month—and then move on. But it didn't work that way. You could tear yourself to shreds in Sweden, tear yourself to shreds in your office at home . . . and it just went on and on and on.

He hadn't called his three children from his first marriage in weeks. He barely touched his 23-month-old daughter by his second wife. He and his wife barely saw each other. They hadn't separated. They just weren't together for a while, while he tried to figure things out.

His family kept begging him to open up, to share his pain. If he told them, if they knew. . . . No. All for him. Only for him. He was sorry about what it was doing to them, but do you want the truth? He felt so numb, so hard, it didn't really matter.

There were two people in the world he could let in. They talked on the phone every couple of days, he and the wives of his dead friends, sometimes for an hour or two. Anything they wanted, he kept telling them. Name it, he would do it. *Money?* No, the Players Association life insurance policy would take care of them well. *A nanny?* He knew a great woman, he would send her there next week. No, they already had help. *Him?* He would fly there in a minute, take the kids anywhere, let them be around a man.

No. They both wanted only one thing of him. The same thing Tim's mom had asked. The hardest thing. They wanted him to pitch again. To come back.

He flew to Cleveland, moved into a rented house and got the plastic surgery done on his head in late May. He still refused all interview requests, read no newspapers for a while. He waited until late in the afternoon, when nearly everyone in outpatient physical rehab at Lutheran Medical Center was gone. He would give it a try for a few days. He stretched the left shoulder that had undergone arthroscopy in April. He walked on the stair machine. His sweat dripped. He looked out the window. He had always read and heard that when you narrowly avoided death, you cherished the things you used to take for granted, you wanted to smell flowers. Why had they lied?

His physical therapist was ready to have a catch with him one day. She wanted to go outside. It was beautiful out there. He shook his head no. Not outside. They took the ball and the gloves and went down to the cellar. Down with the pipes and the bricks and the shadows.

For the first time since March 21, he gripped a baseball and cocked it behind his ear. It felt so trivial.

Looking back on the memory of
The dance we shared 'neath the stars above
For a moment all the world was right
How could I have known that you'd ever say good-bye?

And now I'm glad I didn't know
The way it all would end, the way it all would go

Our lives are better left to chance
I could've missed the pain
But I'd've of had to miss the dance.

Holding you I held everything
For a moment, wasn't I a king?
But if I'd only known how the king would fall
Hey, who's to say, you know I might
Have chanced it all.

Alexa moved. Patti woke. Oh God. Another day. She rose and
went downstairs to the compact disc player. It was all set. Push a
button and that Garth Brooks song, "The Dance," played over and
over. They had never really talked about death, but one day Steve
had turned to her and said, "When I die, play that song at the
funeral." She was still playing it, every morning. A hundred straight
times, it played one day. This is what you do with pain.

Nearly everyone in Cleveland knew her face now. They asked
her for autographs, they wanted to comfort her. She hated the
helplessness, the thought that any moment she could be ambushed
by grief in front of anyone. She hated crying in front of people.
She hated anyone feeling sorry for her. She hated knowing that
they were thinking, There goes poor Patti Olin—nine-month-old
twins, three-year-old daughter, a twenty-six-year-old widow.

The song, in a funny way, gave her power. She pushed the
button. She listened. She cried. She turned it off. *She* decided when
and where and how to grieve. Just a tiny bit, she took charge. "I'm
in intensive therapy," she would tell people who wanted her to see
a psychologist, "all by myself."

Bobby wanted her to see a movie called *Indian Summer*. That
would be therapy, he thought, but he wasn't in Cleveland, and he
told her she couldn't go alone. "Why?" she asked. "Is the movie
too close to home?"

"It *is* home," said Bobby. "Don't you go alone, Patti. You
hear me?"

O.K., O.K. She longed to be as strong as Laurie, and without
even knowing it, maybe she was. Four hours after the accident,

with the police lights still glaring off the lake a few hundred yards outside Laurie's house, Patti ordered Fernando Montes not to change the channel when the body bag came on the screen. She faced 77 reporters in Winter Haven three days after the accident. She kept that note on the refrigerator door that Steve had scribbled to her: WELCOME TO OUR NEW HOUSE! But Laurie was 33. Laurie knew who she was. Laurie had been a schoolteacher, a mother for nine years, and now a ranch owner—hell, a cowgirl! Patti was a . . . a baseball wife.

A *great* baseball wife. She loved being that. She was proud of it. A few days before Steve died, there she was, standing in the rain, watching him give his arm a workout in a minor league game. Pack up another apartment, haul the kids; she never complained. But who was she now? Where did she live?

She packed everything after the accident in Florida and went home, back to her family in Portland, Oregon. But what was *home*? It wasn't just her, was it? A long time ago, when you left home to live in places like Colorado and Florida and Ohio, it was to prove you could make it on your own. Home was all right for a week or two, but after that, sometimes it almost felt like failure.

She put the kids and all their belongings in a plane and flew back to Cleveland. The house was brand-new, empty. She and Steve had bought it in the off-season but never lived there. She went back to the meetings of the Indian wives' organization, as she had before. Back to the wives' Bible-study classes. Back to the wives' section to watch ball games. That was her family, wasn't it? They were rootless, like her. Always looking for a new set of baby-sitters, grocery stores and doctors, like her. Always at the mercy of their husbands' last streak or slump, like her. It almost seemed unfair to lean on the neighbors who had nothing to do with baseball, because you could be gone tomorrow and not be able to pay back the favor. But among teammates and their wives, it was O.K., because it was all understood.

She went on a road trip to Chicago in May with the other wives. The only woman without a husband on the plane, and on the bus, and going back at night to the hotel rooms. She found herself, in the seventh inning of games, looking to the bullpen to see Steve

warming up. Sometimes she had to stand and leave the stadium,
barely able to keep her legs from running—all the same old tired
goblins, all the *whys* and *what ifs* from that day at the lake roaring
in her head. What in hell am I doing? she asked herself. I'm not a
baseball wife. I don't belong here. Why am I pretending?

Laurie and her kids came to spend a week in June at Patti s
house just outside Cleveland. Six little kids running and crawling
everywhere. Two women chasing them. It was brutal. It was great.
It was nuts. Laurie gave Patti pep talks: You're so smart, so tough,
so pretty, all you need is a direction. Get a job, anything for a while,
volunteer, go back to school, get out of the house. Then Laurie
broke down after they went to a ball game together, and she realized she needed Patti even more than she had thought.

They got a baby-sitter and went to Bobby's. He opened the
door. He had said he was coming back, but those eyes. . . . Laurie
walked right up to him, punched him in the arm and kicked him
in the butt. Patti said it in a different way. "If you quit, Bobby,"
she said, "why can't we?"

She could say that to him. After all, she would say, they were
family. One night Patti went to see *Indian Summer*. On the screen,
staring out at a lake, was a woman—just about Patti's age, Patti's
hair color—whose husband had died a year before. A man was
telling the young widow about a lady who used to live on the shore
whose husband had died too and been buried in the middle of the
lake. "Poor woman," the man was saying to the young widow.
"Spending the last fifteen years of her life waiting to die, so she
could go into the lake with her husband. Fifteen years of her life
she wasted. We might as well have just thrown her in the lake the
same day as her husband."

Patti blinked. She felt it coming, in her chest, in her throat,
in her eyes, right there in a theater, in front of everybody. She
glanced to one side. A hand had been waiting there beside her, she
realized, even before the man had finished saying that. Bobby's
hand. Bobby's Kleenex.

There are black and white pipes, bundles of wires, scabbed
paint and glaring fluorescent bulbs all along the tunnel leading to

the home dugout at Cleveland Stadium. On a gray, sweltering afternoon, five hours before a night game on June 25, Bobby Ojeda walked in a Cleveland Indian uniform down the tunnel, into the dugout, out of seclusion. The cameras snapped. The microphones leaned. The tape recorders clicked on. He said it had to be done.

Eyes of the Storm

Here comes this lady into your life. You don't know that she has been up all night peeing, racked with pain in her lower back. You don't know how many people told her she was nuts to get on an airplane and fly to your hometown at a time like this. You don't know that an hour ago, when her water broke, she was crouched in an eight-seat King Air blotting her legs with paper towels. Hell, you're *16*. You don't know that she's spitting Nature in the eye and kicking Time in the teeth.

She's sitting on your sofa as you come through the door from school on a September day in 1990, and she grins and grinds her teeth against the contractions. How could you know that it's already too late—that Pat Summitt's got you, she's got you forever?

Michelle Marciniak takes a seat and looks around her living room. She's a senior at Allentown (Pennsylvania) Central Catholic High, an hour north of Philadelphia, a guard who in six months will become the Naismith and Gatorade player of the year. But that's not enough for Michelle. In her dream she has both the acclaim that goes to the best player in the land *and* the championship that her high school team keeps falling short of. She would

This story first appeared in 1997.

love to put her dream in Pat's hands, but in Pat's hands already rests the *other* player of the year candidate, the *other* All-America who plays Michelle's position.

Michelle knows something weird is going on the minute she walks in the door . . . but what is it? Her mom, Betsy, and her older brother, Steve, are wearing the same nervous, crooked little smile. Michelle's cocker spaniel, Frosty, is yip-yapping laps around the premier coach in the history of women's basketball. Pat's bouncing from the sofa to the bathroom to the telephone and back. Her assistant coach, Mickie DeMoss, is whipping through Tennessee's recruiting scrapbook as if she's sitting on a mound of fire ants: *Here's the arena, here's the library, here's the '89 national championship— O.K., Michelle, any questions?* Michelle's dad, Whitey, is sitting across the room jingling coins manically in his pocket. You try it. It's not easy to jingle coins while you're sitting down.

Suddenly Nature mounts a furious comeback, Time starts kicking Pat in the teeth. "Mickie," she blurts, "we have to go. *Now.*" Suddenly they're babbling to the teenage girl that Pat's baby is coming, and Steve and Michelle are racing to his car to lead the Tennessee coaches to—to the hospital, right?—heck no, to the airport, because Patricia Head Summitt is going to have this baby when and where she wants it. Suddenly Steve and Michelle are swerving around curves, blowing through red lights and stop signs and DO NOT ENTER signs, swiveling their heads to look back at Mickie, who's freaking out at the wheel of the rental car, and Pat, who has her feet on the dashboard and is groaning. They all screech to a halt near the airport's private hangars. Mickie runs up the steps into an airplane. Wrong airplane. She pops back out. "I'll call you!" Pat shouts to Michelle. She strides into the King Air, and off she roars into the sky.

There are a hundred ways to write a story about a hurricane. We could watch it gathering shape and strength from afar and chronicle its course. We could follow at its heels and document its wake, or attempt to speak to all who experienced it and make a mosaic of their impressions. But perhaps the most direct and true way is to see and smell and feel it through one person—one girl who ran both from it and straight at it; one girl sucked into its eye and then set down on its other side; one girl, now a woman, who has had time to sort out what it did to her life.

Those who are playing for Pat Summitt now at Tennessee—members of the 1997–98 team, which finished the regular season 30–0 and is favored to win an astonishing third consecutive national title, the sixth in 12 years—cannot see the hurricane clearly because they're still inside it. They're hugging a tree for dear life, waiting for the wind and water to recede. Someone else, on a dry, sunny day a few years from now, can ask them to describe what it was like to play for this woman whose five national championships are surpassed in NCAA basketball history only by John Wooden's ten; whose .814 winning percentage in 23 seasons ranks fifth among all coaches in the history of men's and women's college basketball; whose number of trips to the Final Four, 14 and counting, will most likely never be matched, seeing how she's only 45. This woman who never raised a placard or a peep for women's rights, who never filed a suit or overturned a statute or gave a flying hoot about *isms* or *movements*, this unconscious revolutionary who's tearing up the terrain of sexual stereotypes and seeding it with young women who have an altered vision of what a female can be.

So we'll leave her for now, we who can't grasp yet what women like her will mean to the rest of us. We'll leave her doubled over in pain on an airplane, clenching every muscle she's got, trying to recall everything her mother told her about birthing babies so she can do the *opposite* until she's back on the ground in Tennessee. And we'll return to the teenage girl by the phone, awaiting Pat's call, trying to fathom what this strange day portends.

It's so hard, when so much air has leaked out of your dream, to inflate it again. For the previous two years, whenever Michelle was frustrated or angry on the court, whenever her high school coach yanked her midway through the third quarter because he didn't believe in stars or 40-point scoring nights, all she had to do was look up in the stands and see her mother forming that little T with her forefingers. It meant Tennessee, but it really meant Pat. It meant NCAA championships and All-America honors and Olympic gold medals, because that's what girls got when they were handpicked by Pat.

Ever since that day in December '87, during her freshman year, when Michelle persuaded her mom to take her on an unofficial visit to Knoxville and she watched this tall, handsome, crisply dressed woman coach a game and a practice, Michelle's aim in life had been to play for Pat. That practice had blown her mind; never had Michelle met a woman—hell, a *human being*—so intense, so authoritative, so certain and yet so caring. Pat walked into a room, and everything about her—her ramrod posture, her confident smile, her piercing blue eyes and her direct manner of speaking— said, "I love what I'm doing and this is what I'm here to talk about, and you'll pay attention while I'm talking or you'll leave the room." Michelle could picture her as president—no, not of the university but of the country! And imagine this: Coach Summitt told her girls to call her *Pat*!

For hours the teenager would thumb through her bible, a scrapbook full of photographs of Tennessee women's basketball and of warm notes from Pat. To heck with rival recruiters who warned her that Pat would snuff out her flamboyance on the court—envy, pure poison envy. She was going to play for the lady, case closed . . . until that afternoon in the spring of 1990, the end of her junior year. It was the day after Michelle's second unofficial visit to Knoxville, and on the way home she stopped in Hampton, Virginia, to play in an AAU tournament. She had decided it was time to announce her decision to the world when . . .

"Did you hear about Tiffany?" It was her AAU coach, Michael Flynn, addressing Michelle just before she took the court.

"No, what about her?" said Michelle.

"She committed to Tennessee."

"That *can't* be true! I was just there yesterday!"

"Well, it is. She committed today."

Michelle felt as if she were choking, as if she might faint. Tiffany Woosley was the girl who would vie with Michelle for every player of the year award during their senior seasons. A Tennessee girl, for crying out loud, who played point guard, the same position as Michelle; no way there would be playing time for two freshman guards! Pat must have betrayed her! Pat must have tipped off Tiffany that Michelle was about to commit, and now Tiffany was the first one, the special one, the local hero with the inside track, and Michelle's dream was up in smoke!

She cried her way up I-95 on the journey home. Bitterly she studied the list of 200 other universities offering her scholarships and searched for a team with no dictator, no system to submit to, somewhere she could play the splashy, spinning, behind-the-back-and-between-the-legs game she loved, light it up for 30 a night and stick it to that cruel lady who . . .

Who now, six months later, has just hopelessly muddled Michelle by nearly dropping a baby in her lap! "If she didn't really want me, why did she go through all *that*, Mom?" Michelle asks as the two sit up past midnight, waiting for Pat to call. Michelle has always believed in omens, in signals from God. "Maybe this means I was *meant* to go with her," she says. "I almost feel like I'm the godmother of this baby."

At 1 a.m. the phone jangles. It's Pat, calling a 16-year-old player a half hour after giving birth to a boy. It's Pat, whose doctor has just told her that it was only because the baby's head was turned sideways in the womb that she didn't deliver him into the hands of an assistant coach at 20,000 feet.

"Congratulations!" cries Michelle. "I can't believe this! Thanks so much for calling me! Good-bye! Congratulations, Pat!"

So Michelle signs with Pat and becomes an All-America guard at Tennessee, correct?

No. When Pat pictures Michelle, she sees so much of herself—the girl who would challenge boys to races and arm-wrestling matches and tackle football. That's why Pat can't bear to disappoint Michelle, why she tells her that she wants her very much, but she can't promise her playing time or stardom. So Michelle agonizes, Michelle flip-flops, Michelle visits Tennessee a third time, hugs Pat, kisses the new baby . . . and signs with Notre Dame. And waits all of two weeks into her freshman season to break NCAA rules by calling Pat to tell her she has made the biggest mistake of her life, and how unfulfilling it is to be the star of a confused and divided 1–5 team, and how she wants to transfer right this very minute.

Pat reports the violation, but Michelle, stubborn as fungus, calls her again, and . . . well, almost everything between this lady and this girl is going to be complicated and racked with labor pains, so let's jump forward a year and a half, leap over Michelle's transfer to Tennessee and the season that, in keeping with NCAA rules, she has to sit out as penance for the switch.

It's the fall of 1993, and Michelle finally is living her dream, and here is how the dream begins: It begins with 4:30 a.m. wake-ups, with relentless wind sprints through the dark on the Tennessee track. It begins with the frightening realization that there is no excuse, none, a fact that team manager Todd Dooley learns the morning he awakens crumpled by stomach cramps and forces himself out of bed to show up at 6:30 and tries to explain to Pat why he's a half hour late, only to hear her shout, "You don't *ever* be late! Next time you just bring that toilet with you!"

It begins with Michelle walking into the Lady Vols' locker room complex and stopping to stare at all the framed photographs on the National Championship Wall and the White House Visits Wall and the Final Four Wall and the All-Americas and Olympians Wall. It begins with Pat reminding her, sometimes even testing her, about who it is up there on the walls, whom it is she *owes* excellence to. It begins with Michelle knowing that Pat kicked the 1989–90 Lady Vols out of their palatial locker room for five weeks and squeezed them into a tiny visitors' dressing room. They hadn't deserved the palace. They hadn't worked hard enough.

It begins with Michelle looking over her shoulder as she dribbles in a scrimmage and wondering what in blazes this woman is doing, three feet behind her, down on one knee and squatting lower and lower as if the view at sneaker level might reveal some hidden flaw, slapping the floor with her palm at her latest find, hanging on Michelle's next decision as if life itself were riding on it, leaning right with her as she cuts and leans in for a layup, and then, *daggone* it, the anguised squinch of Pat's cheeks and punch of her fist if Michelle misses, the disappointment even sharper than Michelle's. And the thing is, that intensity never flags, not for a day or an hour or a minute. Suddenly, in the midst of a seemingly splendid practice, Pat might shout "Hold it! Stop! Everyone stop!" and stride toward Michelle, the way she strode one day toward forward Lisa Harrison.

"Lisa!"

"Yes, Pat?"

"What have you done for your team today?"

"Well, uh . . . I . . . I don't know."

"That's *exactly* my point!"

Whoo boy. Who else demands that her players sit in the first three rows of their classes and forbids them a single unexcused absence? Who else finds out about every visit they make to the mall for a new pair of jeans, every trip to a restaurant or a movie, and always mentions it the next day, so that it seems they can do nothing without her knowing it? Who else, at the end of a three-hour practice, times the suicide sprints on the big scoreboard clock? Who else films every practice and then sits through it all over again, so that if a player is fool enough to question a single one of her criticisms, Pat takes her right to the videotape in her office and stops the dang thing so often to prove she's right that it takes an hour to cover the first 10 minutes? Who carries *five* VCRs on road trips and watches tape of her opponents while she works out on the treadmill while she scribbles POINTS OF EMPHASIS on a notepad while she talks on the phone with an assistant—all after she has read a book to her son, Tyler, and put him to bed?

Imagine living with that. For the longest time even Pat couldn't imagine who could imagine it, until she found R. B. Summitt, whom she married in 1980, her sixth season at Tennessee. A man secure in his own profession as vice president of his family's bank, a man born to the first female pilot in Monroe County, Tennessee, a man unthreatened by a woman with a life all her own. Sure, sometimes he goes off the deep end in the heat of action and yells things at opposing teams that she wouldn't, but Pat can live with that. She knows what it is to enter another realm during a game. For her, it's the one time when Time lets go of her, when it even seems to stop.

Yes, Michelle could almost smell what the pair of Vanderbilt researchers found when they hooked up some visiting coaches to a cardiac monitor one year back in the '80s. Pat's heartbeat and blood pressure, the fastest and highest of all the coaches' during the action on the court, plummeted when a timeout was called, to the lowest of them all. There's no huddle you would rather be in with 20 ticks left in a tie game. First, Pat would tap the 60-plus years of coaching experience with which she surrounds herself, consulting swiftly with her staff: DeMoss, with her uncanny ability to see what all 10 players were doing on the floor; Holly Warlick, who had the game seared into her soul as Pat's point guard in the late '70s; and Al Brown, who could study video and spot the neck twitch that indicated that the opposing team's forward was about to drive left. Then Pat would make her decision, kneel on a stool in front of her players and pull them into her dead-sure eyes. The Lady Vols would drink in this calm assurance and intensity. Ten players would walk back onto the court. Five of them knew that their coach had just given them the way to win.

Michelle is determined to be one of those five, to let Pat jump down her throat and pull out her dream. To nod and chirp "Rebound!"—as every Lady Vol is expected to do when she's corrected—louder than anyone. To look Pat flush in the eye because there's nothing that makes the lady crazier than a player who looks away from The Look, who tries to evade those two blue drill bits digging into her skull. Pat actually dips her knees, lowers herself to catch the girl's yellow-belly eyeballs, locks in on them and lifts them, and if that fails, she barks, "Look me in the eyes!" She wants to see the girl's eyes blaze right back at her, to say, "All right, lady, I'll show you!" To blaze like hers did back when Daddy would inspect the tobacco plants from which she had been pulling suckers for eight hours under a 90-degree sun and find the one damn sucker she had missed—that's what Pat wants to see. In a critical moment, if she doesn't get what she wants, her neck goes blotchy red, and a vein pops out, and you can look at it and see her heart kicking.

Michelle will do anything to appease that heart. She'll go over, under, through any obstacle and come up pumping her fist. Crash, her teammates start calling her, and the Tennessee basketball fans love her. She'll hang out at Pat's office like a faithful puppy, write

Pat birthday and Christmas and Mother's Day cards. She'll stick a note on the windshield of Pat's car a week before practice saying EIGHT MORE DAYS! I CAN'T WAIT! and make Pat grin for an hour—heck, sounds exactly like something Pat would say! She'll do anything for Pat . . . except give up her game.

It drives Pat bonkers. She leaves her office and jogs across campus, wondering, What is it with this girl? You keep telling her to slow down, to make better decisions, to forget the spin move, to throw the simple 10-foot chest pass instead of the blind 40-foot bounce pass, and she keeps nodding her head, but 30 seconds later, there's the dang thing again! Never met a girl so strong-willed in my life.

One day a man named Bill Rodgers, a Knoxville car dealer whose passion and part-time occupation he calls "performance enhancing," looks at the results of the Predictive Index personality test he's administered to Michelle and Pat. "It's amazing," he tells Pat. "It's like looking at a young *you*. Michelle's more concerned with image, with wanting to be loved, but as for almost everything else—ambitious, competitive, outgoing, leadership, stubbornness, willingness to take on all the responsibility under extreme pressure—you could literally be mother and daughter!"

The bond between them keeps deepening. Pat just smiles. If Michelle is just like her—well, then, Pat knows just what to do. She'll ride her harder still, harder than she's ridden anyone before. "*Defense?*" Pat hollers. "You call that defense, Michelle? I thought you wanted to be a leader. How can I take you to war with me? *Don't* try to tell me! I've been coaching longer than you've been *alive!*

"You're gold-digging again, Michelle! Are you going to be the showboat or be *on* the showboat? Well, I'll just sit you, Michelle. Because I know you love to play and *hate* to sit—right, Michelle? That *kills* you, doesn't it, Michelle?"

In front of anyone, this could happen. In front of 10 strangers, Knoxville business leaders and their spouses invited into the Lady Vols' locker room as "guest coaches" on game nights, most of them staring at the floor and praying Pat doesn't suddenly turn on *them*.

She half kills Michelle that first year. Makes her sit for half of every game as a backup shooting guard, sit and watch Tiffany Woosley run the team at point guard. Michelle's determined not to cry in front of Pat, because Pat would never cry; when she did, her daddy only spanked her harder. Michelle digs her top teeth into her bottom lip when Pat tears into her. It's the same thing Pat has done so many times in her life that there's a little indent on the right side of her lower lip. Michelle turns away and grinds her teeth—how could this be happening to the girl who won the Greg Tatum Award in eighth grade as her school's most Christlike child? She holds everything in until she gets home, then cries her eyes out. She drives her red Honda to a stream in the Great Smoky Mountains near Gatlinburg, sits and listens to the water and thinks, What is it with this crazy woman? I'm giving everything I have, but everything's not enough for her. There's something driving her, bigger than what drives anybody in the world. What is it?

It's growing mutually, magnetically, their frustration with and affection for each other. If Michelle could just pigeonhole Pat as the tyrant, it would be so much easier. But Pat's the woman you wish you could cook like and water-ski like and chat up the cashier like and toss off one-liners like. Pat's the life of the party.

How does she do it? How could she turn your name into an obscenity on the court, then walk off it and become your mom? How could a woman be transformed that completely, so that when you sit in her office, she leans toward you to connect with you, the flesh around those piercing eyes wrinkling in concentration, and invariably asks what *you* think the team needs and then, as you're getting ready to leave, asks if *you* think her beige shoes go with her white skirt. Not to con you or charm you, because you would eventually sniff that out. She asks so intently that it seems the two of you are the only ones in the universe, so honestly that you smell the unsure girl beneath the awe-inducing coach.

Then, bang, you and she are done, and her eyes are flashing to her day planner, the one she keeps gorging with duties, 10:25 appointments crowbarred between 10:15s and 10:30s. All etched in perfect calligraphy, this hand-to-hand combat with Time, with neat arrows pointing to peripheral obligations that she can attend to simultaneously, without assigning them a minute of their own, with _key meetings underlined_ and _very important_ appointments blinking exclamation points!!!! Soon Michelle and all her team-mates are carrying day planners, opening them together at Pat's command to fill up a stray half hour here, a vagrant hour there, even to transcribe her annual reminder in late October: _Don't for-get to turn back your clocks one hour!_ Soon it's an epidemic, this guilt over a moment lost.

Where's she from, this woman? What incubated her? Man-hattan or Chicago? A surgeon daddy and a mama lawyer? No, people tell you. She's a _farm girl_. A farm girl from middle Ten-nessee, where the sun is the clock, Nature calls the rhythm, and women know their place. How can that be? "Take me there," Michelle asks Pat one day. "I want to meet your family and see where you grew up." Michelle's changing her major to psychol-ogy. She has to figure this lady out.

"Can't," says Pat. "NCAA won't let me take you. Someday we'll do it, Michelle. When all this is done."

So Michelle must play detective, cobble together scraps. The memories of Pat's former players, an anecdote from a newspaper article, the reply to a brave question she might throw at Pat. Little clues, like that scar on Pat's left knee. Slowly—it takes years—a picture begins to appear. A fuzzy, grainy picture . . .

. . . of a face, a young woman's face, hair sweat-plastered around its edges. A young woman alone at night in a gym. She's running 15 more suicides because she missed a foul shot at the end of her two-hour workout. Pat has flung off her knee brace; it's a crutch, she tells herself, and she's never going to wear it again. Now you can see that scar, blazing red.

A year has passed since she tore her anterior cruciate liga-ment during her senior season at Tennessee-Martin. A year since the orthopedic surgeon examined the knee and told Pat, "Forget it." It's 1974, and many men playing big-time sports are finished after tearing an ACL. A woman? Just forget it.

Fix it, Tall Man told the surgeon. Tall Man is what the hired help called her father, Richard. Fix it right, he said, because Pat's *going* to play for the U.S. in Montreal in 1976, when women will play basketball for the first time in Olympic history. Pat swallowed hard because until Daddy said it, she didn't know she was going to do that. When her best friend, Jane Brown, walked into the hospital room a few minutes later, Pat blurted, "That doctor's crazy as heck if he thinks I'm not going to play ball again!" Then everyone left her room, and she hobbled to the window, drew the curtains and cried herself to sleep.

Now she has to make Tall Man's prediction come true. She has to lose 15 pounds, rehabilitate her knee and work out twice a day to make the Olympics . . . while she's teaching four phys-ed courses at Tennessee, while she's taking four courses to get her master's degree, while she's coaching the women's basketball team. Three-mile run at 6 a.m., weights at 6:30, shower, rush to the gym to teach, dash to the lecture hall to take the exercise-physiology and sports-administration classes, sprint back to the gym to coach a two-and-a-half-hour practice, hop in the car to go scout a local high school player, burn rubber back to the gym for two hours of basketball training and sprints, shower again and hightail it home by midnight to study for the biomechanics midterm.

She's 22. She was hired to be the women's assistant basketball coach, only to learn a few weeks later that the head coach had resigned to pursue her doctorate, so the head job's hers. She has no assistant. She has never coached a game. She's scared, the way she was that day when she was 12 and Tall Man dropped her off in the middle of miles of hay, pointed to the tractor and the hay rake and said, "Do it," then drove away. What's she going to do now, 10 years later? The only thing she knows. She'll be her father. Her players can be her.

At first it's glorified intramurals, a tryout sheet posted on a bulletin board inviting women to play in front of four or five dozen fans on a shadowy floor crisscrossed by badminton, volleyball and basketball lines. Pat digs in. She sweeps floors, tapes ankles, sets out the chairs and towels, washes the uniforms on road trips. She drives the team to road games in a van, her head poked out the window to keep her awake on the drive home at 2 a.m. Behind her, her players glance at each other when the rain stops and the windshield dries and the wipers keep squeaking, squeaking, squeaking. No one musters the courage to utter a word.

She doesn't lose 15 pounds. She loses 27. She sits on the edge of a table, pokes her foot through the handles of a sack full of bricks and lifts till her knee screams, but never when her players are around to see her. She makes the '76 Olympic team—a cocaptain and the oldest player, at 24, on the U.S. roster that shocks the field and comes home with a silver medal. She takes the Lady Vols to the Final Four seven months later, in her third year as coach. She gets her master's degree in physical education. She has learned she can do it: She can overpower Nature and outmuscle Time—at least for a while, just like men do. She has learned, thanks to her father, about human will. How can she settle for filling her players with *want* . . . now that she knows the psychic power of *expect*?

You think she's tough *now*, Michelle? Oh, please, the Lady Vols with crow's feet tell her at the annual alumnae reunions. You should've seen Pat back *then*! How about that time she found out we had that all-night party, and she set up trash cans at each corner of the court and ran us till we puked in them? How about that all-night, eight-and-a-half-hour drive home after we lost in Cleveland, Mississippi—no stops, bladders and bellies be damned? What about the 2 a.m. practice after we drove three hours back from the loss at Vandy, the game Pat's father saw and told her he'd seen a better game the night before between sixth-graders? Yeah, ever notice how quick she was, after the games her father attended, to ask people, "What did my dad say?" What about that time we fell apart in the second half at South Carolina, went straight to the locker room when we got back the next day and had to put on those smelly uniforms that had been locked in the trunk all night, and Pat hollered, "Now you're going to play the half you didn't play last night!"

Pat leads the Lady Vols to the Final Four six more times over the next nine years—and wins none of them, her teams always just a little short on talent. Forget the first Olympic gold medal in U.S. women's basketball history, the one won by Pat's '84 team—heck, a half hour later Pat forgets it. Just imagine what all those fruitless Final Fours do to Tall Man's daughter. If you're Pat's roommate during the early years in Knoxville, before Pat has a husband at age 28 and a child at 38, before there are videos of opponents to watch until she's cross-eyed, you love it when another big game's approaching. Because when you wake up, the white tornado has struck again—the whole apartment's gleaming!

Price tag? Oh, you bet. Don't you think there are times, when the grease stain on the baseboard has her on her knees at 1 a.m., that she wants this thing that's got hold of her to let go? "Times," as Pat's brother Charles puts it, "when you want to knock Daddy's head off." Times when the pain from tension in Pat's left shoulder grows so sharp that she must schedule a deep massage—like, five hours before every game. Times when she's sitting on an airplane next to two women who are solemnly weighing the floral pattern against the plaid for the master-bathroom drapes, and their relationship to Time is so dramatically different from Pat's that she feels as if she's from another planet. Times when people talk about her as if she's a freak, as if she's a man.

As if she's, say, Bobby Knight. That's what they say when she seizes Michelle by the front of her jersey, twists it and snarls at her during the game against Louisiana Tech in the NCAA regionals in Michelle's sophomore year. The photograph runs in newspapers all over the country. "Spinderella and her wicked stepmother," the Knoxville press calls Michelle and Pat. From all over the country friends and relatives send the picture to Michelle and her parents, demanding, *What is this woman doing to Michelle?*

Pat flinches. Why, she wonders, can't people look at the photograph in context, why can't they understand that she's as swift to drop her whole life and rush to her players' sides when they have problems as she is to drop the roof on them when they screw up? That she's Miss Hazel's daughter every inch as much as she is Tall Man's? That she grew up watching and imitating her mother, who was the first to visit the sick or the dying, first to pick, pluck, prepare and deliver a meal of butter beans and fried chicken and mashed potatoes and homemade ice cream to the worried or the grieving?

Pat calls Michelle's mother to try to explain. "She's all yours, Pat," says Betsy, but privately she and her husband are aching for their child and wondering about Pat, too. Doesn't Pat understand that Michelle isn't just like her? Doesn't she know that Michelle's father is tough too, an old college fullback, but that every night he gave his girl a good-night kiss?

Life's funny, though, and something else happens in that 1994 NCAA tournament game after Pat grabs Michelle's jersey: Michelle grabs Pat's heart. She comes in at point guard when the Lady Vols are gagging in the second half, down by 18, and nearly saves them single-handedly before they lose by 3. Furious drives to the basket, long jumpers, brilliant passes, knee-burning steals.

Pat sits there shaking her head, the truth moving from her mind into her gut. Michelle is the only one out there refusing to lose; the only one just like her! Pat can't wait. She tells Michelle right after the game: Tiffany's out. You're in. You're my starting point guard next year. "But remember," Pat says, "the point guard's an extension of me on the court. You've never been through anything like what you're about to go through."

Michelle goes home. She places one large framed picture of Pat twisting her jersey and snarling at her on her bedroom wall, and one small framed picture of the same scene on the dashboard of her car. Now Pat's everywhere Michelle goes, everywhere Michelle hides.

We've got an appointment, so let's break into a trot. Let's dash right past another year and a half; let's bully Time, the way Pat does. Let's fly by the day Pat throws her starting point guard out of practice in her junior year, past the day when Michelle finally crumbles and sobs in front of everyone. Let's jump clean over the last day of that same junior year, when Michelle comes within a whisker of her dream but loses in the NCAA title game to Connecticut—still unsure of herself on the floor in critical moments, still whirling between Pat's way and her way, no longer the All-America guard nor even the all-conference one.

There it goes—did you see it?—the day midway through Michelle's senior season when Pat makes her sit on a chair at midcourt, like a bad schoolgirl, and watch practice, then makes her move the chair to the far end of the floor after she whispers to a teammate.

We've got an appointment to keep, an appointment with an ice storm in Mississippi, coldest night of Michelle's life. It's February 1996. Time's not ticking now for Pat and Michelle. It's hammering. Pat has fixed that problem she had of making it to the Final Four and losing, fixed it mostly by persuading the best recruiter in the country, DeMoss, to leave Auburn in 1985 and be her assistant. Pat has won national titles in '87, '89 and '91, but four years have elapsed since her last one, way too long, and she needs her team leader, Michelle, as much as Michelle needs her.

Michelle's desperate. It's her last shot at the title, her last shot to make all this pain pay off. Her last chance to regain the kind of national acclaim that vanished for her after high school, to become a player whom the two fledgling women's pro leagues will come looking for. But how can she? The Lady Vols are 17–3, but they look nothing like a title team—and guess whose fault that is?

Now Pat's team has gotten skunked a fourth time, by Mississippi, and Michelle has gone 0 for 7 from the field and fouled out, having played as if she could feel Pat's eyes burning through her back. The bus is crawling toward the airport, across the ice, through the darkness; crawling as Michelle listens to Pat, a few seats away, ridicule her; crawling as Pat rises and takes a seat next to Michelle and tells her that unless something drastic happens, she doesn't think the Lady Vols can win a championship with Michelle as their point guard. It's hopeless—no lip-biting can possibly dam it now that the gates are open, now that Pat has already brought Michelle to tears twice that day, at halftime and just after the game, and . . . here it . . . here it comes . . . the third wave of sobs.

Michelle doesn't sleep that night. She's terrified. For the first time she has gone past anger and frustration and the hunger to show Pat she's wrong. The girl with the brightest flame is dead inside. She cannot. Take this. Anymore.

At 6:45 a.m. she calls Pat's home. Only fear and despair could make her speak to Pat Summitt this way: "You don't think we can win it all with me playing like I am," she says, "but I . . . I don't think we can win it all with you coaching like you are. You've got to back off me now, especially in front of other people. You can't do that to me anymore." Her breath catches.

Maybe it's because Pat has won so many championships that she can be more flexible now. Maybe it's impossible not to soften a little, stop choking each minute quite so hard, when there's a five-year-old boy in bed breathing the night in and out while you listen and then wrapping you in a hug when morning comes. Maybe Pat has no real choice this late in the season. She and Michelle speak for a while, and then there's silence. Well? "Doesn't mean I won't criticize you anymore, do you understand?" Pat says. "But I'll try it."

With that, everything changes. "As if we were two people in a room with boxing gloves," Michelle will say a few years later, "who finally both come out with our hands up." Pat gives Michelle more rope. Michelle quits trying to tie a triple knot when a single will do just fine. Tennessee reels off 15 straight wins, beating UConn in overtime in the NCAA semifinals behind Michelle's 21 points and then blowing out Georgia to win the crown.

Pat goes up into the stands and gets the first hug and kiss from her father that she can remember. Michelle is chosen the Final Four MVP. Her flying leap into Pat's arms nearly knocks Pat off her feet.

If this were a TV movie, it would end there. You would never get a chance to watch Michelle go home with Pat and finally understand the force, or to gaze down the road and peek around the bend to where the story really ends. But it's not a TV movie. It's summer, four months after the title, and the two women are in Pat's car busting 90 through middle Tennessee, heading to Henrietta. It's O.K. with the NCAA because Michelle has just graduated, and it's O.K. with the state police because Pat Summitt can go as fast as she wants in Tennessee, and it's O.K. between Pat and Michelle, who cried together at the senior banquet a few months before.

From this new place, from this last ledge before Michelle leaps into the pros and adulthood, then maybe marriage and children, she looks over at Pat. The championship glow is still emanating from both of them, but it's no longer blinding. It's good light in which to look at Pat and assess. . . .

Does Michelle want to be like Pat? Does she want to make herself go cold and hard inside when she needs to, or is the cost too steep? Can she have children and sweep them along with her, the way Pat does with Tyler, showering him with love and attention on airplanes and bus rides, taking him and his nanny on road trips whenever he can go . . . then steeling herself and walking out the door alone when he can't? Can Michelle dress like the First Lady, give goosebump-raising speeches, spearhead $7 million United Way fund drives, be competent in *everything*—can she be, does she *want* to be, the woman who's trying to do it all and pulling it off, as Pat is?

They climb out of the car, and Michelle stares across the hayfields and the tobacco barns and the silence. She gazes at the old homestead where Pat grew up, no girls her age within five miles. She sees the hayloft behind the house, blown off its 10-foot cinder-block legs by a tornado. It's where Pat climbed a ladder nearly every evening when chores were done and played two-on-two basketball under a low tin roof and two floodlights, on a tongue-and-groove pine floor surrounded by bales of hay, with three older brothers, two of whom would go on to play college sports on scholarship.

Michelle sees Pat's mother limp toward her on ankles worn to the bone by all the years of stocking shelves on a cement floor in the family grocery store, all the years of tucking her foot beneath the old 10-gallon milk cans, hoisting them off the ground and into the coolers with a thrust of her leg. All the years of milking cows before sunrise, picking butter beans all day in summer, laying down linoleum floors on the houses her husband was building to sell, never resting from the moment she woke till the moment she dropped into bed.

Michelle sees the three farms that Pat's father ran along with the feed store and the grocery store and the hardware store and the tobacco warehouse and the beauty salon, all while he was a school-board member and the county water commissioner. She sees the field where he once disked an entire night, through dawn, and then hitched up the mules and began a day of planting corn . . . until his head jerked up from sleep and he saw that his rows were running together. She sees the white-haired man coming home from his tractor, on which he still spends 10 hours a day after two knee replacements, prostate surgery, two ministrokes and quintuple-bypass surgery. She sees all the command and authority leak out of her coach as Tall Man draws near. . . . *Deference . . . Pat?* In a funny way, it's what Michelle needs to see: Pat's vulnerable. Pat's a regular person. Michelle does what Pat can't do. She walks up to Pat's dad and throws a hug around him.

She sees the schools where Pat never missed a day, not one, from grades one through twelve, because illnesses were like birthdays—her father didn't believe in them. She sees the high school to whose district Tall Man moved the family just so Pat could play basketball, because he never separated what a girl ought to be able to do from what a boy ought to. Michelle sits at the table where the family still gathers often because only Pat, of the five Head children, has moved on. She sees how bare-boned and basic the family's life is, and how silly a spin move can seem.

She gazes across the dirt and asphalt roads where Pat used to take the family car, killing the dashboard lights so her kid sister, Linda, couldn't see the needle nosing 95, and it begins to dawn on Michelle that the wind that has been at her own back for the last three years is really the wind that has been at Pat's back all of her life. And that maybe you don't have as much choice as you like to think—after you've lived that long and that close to a force that strong—about the kind of woman you would like to be. Maybe the wind just sends you flying.

But the significant moment in Pat's story isn't back there, in the past, or even in all those traumatic and giddy moments that she and her point guard shared. The story doesn't end with Michelle—it goes through her, and on to people that Pat will never know, because Michelle is now the carrier of a spore.

A year after she leaves Tennessee and a few months before she joins the Philadelphia Rage of the American Basketball League, Michelle meets a 15-year-old girl named Amanda Spengler, who plays basketball at a high school a few miles from Allentown, where Michelle grew up. Michelle takes Amanda under her wing—plays ball with her, lifts weights with her, talks about life with her and tells her all about Pat.

"She makes you feel there's nothing to be afraid of in life," Michelle tells Amanda. "If you want something, you go after it as hard as you can, and you make no excuses."

She tells Amanda how much she misses that lady now, how much she misses that sense of mission all around her—the urgency of 12 young women trying to be the best they can, every day, every moment. Sometimes in practice with her Philadelphia team, Michelle pretends Pat has just walked in to watch her, and she practices harder and harder. She tells Amanda how she dreams of being a coach someday, maybe even Pat's assistant.

"Let's run," she says to Amanda one day, but she doesn't run alongside the girl. She just takes off, barely conscious that she has already joined the legions of Pat's former players all over America who are spreading the urgency, breathing into thousands of teen-age girls a new relationship with Time. She's barely aware that she's part of a capillary action, like the one that men have had with boys for generations, whose power is too vast to measure. She just takes off, determined to run seven-minute miles for 45 minutes, and Amanda gasps, running farther and harder than she ever dreamed she could, just trying to keep Michelle in sight.

A few weeks later Amanda goes to a high school track with a watch. We're talking about one girl now, remember, but we're *not*. We're talking about a wave. It's midday in the dead of summer. Amanda starts running and realizes after three laps that she has almost nothing left, and there's only one way to come close to Michelle's seven-minute mile. Her face turns scarlet, her body boils, her stomach turns; Nature screams at her to stop. Instead, she sprints. She sprints the entire last lap.

The watch says 7:05 as she crosses the line. Amanda can't believe she ran that fast, and she laughs as she reels and vomits near the flagpole. She laughs.

The Fiesta in the Town of Ghosts

Darkness. Punches from the darkness to my belly. I want to throw up. I want to cry. I want to turn and leave.

"Don't you worry. This fight ain't over, no, it's not. He got somethin' up his sleeve. Ali, he a magician. He—"

A pickax of a right hand cuts him off. My eyelids shut. I feel it land and rip through me.

"A ruse. He playing another game. That Ali . . . oooooh!" A Larry Holmes left strikes Muhammad Ali's head. Me, I can only feel it in the belly. Kneeling in the darkness in an aisle at Madison Square Garden. The only light shafting from a projector to a screen. Next to me, the black man is finally silent.

Ali's jaw sags. Holmes looks at him and, almost sorrowfully, throws his right again. Why? *Why?*

No other sport, no other form of art or entertainment—no, only boxing keeps rubbing our faces in this spectacle. Jim Jeffries, returning to be ravaged by Jack Johnson. Louis, pulverized by Marciano. Frazier, fungoed by Foreman. Masters, again and once more and again, coming back to be humbled.

This story first appeared in 1987.

What makes them do it? What makes me watch it? Duran, Leonard, Arguello, Foreman, Ali, Holmes, each of them walking away and then running back, risking brain damage in their decline. Money did it, people said. Pride. Ego. *Go down!* I almost scream to Ali on the screen. My eyes drop, glance sideways, briefly meet the black man's. Both of us look back to the floor. On the screen, they are stopping the fight. Swiftly I turn and walk into the night.

"What does *tinku* mean?" I asked.

"*Tinku* means fight," the drunk waiter told me.

"Where is the *tinku*?" I asked.

"No, do not go to the *tinku*," the bespectacled engineer told me. I was sitting at a sidewalk café in Cochabamba, Bolivia, leaning forward, eyes wide. An Indian man in an oddly curved cowhide helmet—a replica of the metal ones that Spanish soldiers wore when they conquered South America—had just walked past, and all at once four street urchins were throwing mock punches and a word I'd never heard was moving from table to table.

"What kind of fight is the *tinku*?" I asked.

The waiter, grinning, placed my beer on the table. "Once a year the Indians come down from the hills into a village, put on those helmets and beat the hell out of each other."

"Where? When?"

"Listen to me, my friend," the engineer said. "Let this thought leave your head. People die on the roads that go there. Mountain roads, dirt ones, thin as an old woman's wrist. The trucks have many years, and the tires. . . ." He rubbed the bald crescent on his head.

"Many other fiestas you must go to in Bolivia," the drunk waiter said. "Go to the one in Copacabana, where the people climb the hill carrying rocks and then kneel at the top and pray to Mary and get drunk."

"Or the one in Quillacollo," said the engineer, "where people pour liquor over themselves and then roll on the ground in flour."

"The *tinku*," I said. "Where do I find these trucks that go to the *tinku*? Is it soon?"

The waiter laughed. The engineer removed his glasses, laid them on the table and slowly rubbed his face.

"*Americano,*" he said, "listen well to me. There is no electricity there, no food or water safe to drink. No doctors when you get sick. And for three or four days after you arrive, no way to leave. Think. All this to see Indians make each other bloody?"

I started in darkness on a morning in late July, tossing my gear up to a cluster of dark figures in the back of a truck and then scrambling aboard to squeeze among them. Soon the old engine began to rumble, and we left the town behind. There was no room to sit, so I stood, shivering beneath a coat and blanket, and clutched a rope running down the middle of the truck's bed in order not to fall. I peered through the gloom but could not see who was making this journey with me.

Night lifted. In the Andean valleys that stretched on and on around us, the mist lay like a lake of white gauze. Now and then a solitary form, a peasant huddled in shawls and a peaked woolen cap, waded across the smoky lake. Its vastness mocked him, but he didn't seem to know.

At last it grew light enough to see my Indian companions: wool-capped babies, eyes closed, suckling their mothers; children contorted in positions not human, trying to sleep; teenagers shoving wads of coca leaves into their cheeks, sucking the juices to deaden the bite of winter; men with caps tugged low, cheekbones high, eyes narrowed, staring far ahead; women with the impassive faces Andean women wear—dark, stoic full moons rimmed by black bowler hats and two long braids running down their backs. The women sat upon sacks of grain and onions they would sell to the Indians coming down from their isolation in the hills to beat each other up.

The land lost its smoothness and began to convulse. Here and there we passed small adobe huts with bulls' horns protruding from the tops of thatched roofs to chase the evil spirits. Near the road, families stared blankly at us. The truck stopped, and an Indian hawked long spikes of sugarcane for the passengers to crack open and gnaw. No, this could not be. Now more sacks of food were being pitched over the truck's wooden siding, more round Indian women wrapped in five tiers of skirts were climbing in. The truck began to roll again. No room remained on the truckbed for both of my feet; I lifted one and felt the other begin to ache. *"¡Cuidado!"*—"Care!"—someone shouted too late. I ducked, but the thorn-covered tree branch had already strafed me, clawing welts on my neck.

An hour passed. The chill and mist of dawn were gone, chased off by an angry sun. We corkscrewed up a thin dirt mountain road, peeling sweaters and shirts, eating dust. With his hands, a man near the edge signaled how many inches separated the truck's wheels from a half-mile fall. I drew in my breath. You made your decision, I told myself. Whatever happens, happens.

Instead of looking down, I gazed straight up at the ribbon of road above. Staring down at us over the edge, outlined by an impossibly blue sky, was a pair of figures, motionless. I stared back at them, disturbed. *"¿Hombres?"* I asked, not wanting to point.

"No, espantajo."

"Oh, scarecrows."

"No. scare*crow*. One man, one scarecrow."

I looked up again at the two figures. Everyone fell silent. It was something more in the attitude of their bodies than in their stillness: Which was stuffed with blood and muscle, which with straw? The truck crept along the road, the roar of its motor the only sound. Which of us three, I wondered, would be the first to break the trance?

Stomach coiled, mouth dry, hands twitching. Five minutes until the first Leonard-Duran fight. Closed-circuit projector busted, doors locked, 5,000 black men clenched outside, and me. West Philadelphia. Unlit ghetto. Rumors flying.

"Gonna fix it any minute, gonna open up the doors. . . ."

"Honky rip-off. Ain't never gonna see no fight here. . . ."

Fists pounding the glass. Stomach coiled, mouth dry. *Go home.* Three minutes left. *But the fight. . . .*

Shouts all around me. A surge toward the door, an elbow in my back, a knee in my thigh, an obscenity in my ear. *Go home.* Two minutes. *But the fight. . . .*

A bottle flies and shatters. *Leave now!* The thick glass in the door shudders from the pounding. *Get away!* Shoved forward, knocked backward. *But the fight.* . . .

One minute. A siren. A riot, this is going to be a riot. *What are you doing here? Go! But the fight.* . . .

Cannon shots across the Andes. The truck's exhaust system began to backfire, echoing off the mountainside. A baby began to wail. The sun's eye followed us, unblinking. More turns, turn-and-stop-and-back-up-and-turn-again-tight turns. The truck swayed and groaned, jolting over ruts, sending loose rocks over the precipice. Engine backfiring, stalling, restarting, truck pitching, baby wailing, tires spinning for grip at the edge. *My God.*

"I knew well a man who died on a truck here," said a young man. He smiled. There came a moan, then another moan. Children vomited, falling over each other to make it to the side, failing, one boy throwing up on another's head. My eyes darted. If only I could move. The truck lurched. I crashed against an Indian woman, bouncing her from sleep.

I wondered if I could figure out a way to eject if this truck began to tumble. Carefully I started to step over bodies, through tangles of arms and legs and sacks. My knee sank into someone's back. A pair of eyes glared up at me. My weight came down upon a hand. The man attached to it never blinked. Three more steps, two more apologies. I made it to the side. A loose plank. I wedged my sneaker into it and hoisted myself up near the top of the siding. I looked over the edge, straight down and down and down into a dry river gully.

Every bounce went through me; it hurt my legs and wrists to stay braced to jump. That's O.K., I thought. The others in the truck sat knitting, sleeping. I alone was prepared for a failure in the driver's judgment or the truck's brake pads or. . . .

A screech, a shot of pain, a body flush of terror. I looked down, panting, clutching. A chicken, dying from the heat and closeness, had lurched up in a death spasm and pecked a hole in my leg and nearly sent me over. The Indians looked at me and laughed, and then fell back to sleep.

* * *

To the Spanish ear, the village was called Toro Toro. But in ancient Quechua—a modern version of which is the language most of the Indians in Bolivia speak—it was *thuru thuru*, meaning "mud, mud," and during the rainy season no vehicle ever reaches the village at all. We arrived in Toro Toro beneath a sky turning dark, local boys running escort the last mile, flapping their arms and legs ecstatically at our breakthrough from the outside, from beyond.

Stiffly I climbed down. "How far did we travel?" I asked the driver.

"More or less a hundred thirty kilometers."

Twelve hours, a scarlet sunburn, a coat of dust, a pounding headache, a mountain range and river crossed, with water lapping at the door handles. Eighty miles.

"When is the *tinku*?" I asked. "I don't want to miss it."

"Do not worry," a man said. "It will find you."

The mayor offered me a barren room in the crumbling town hall. No running water inside, no bathroom, no furniture. I smiled my thanks for the blankets and cot, dropped off my bag and walked the streets. Donkeys and goats bent their heads, grazing on weeds that grew between the cobblestones.

Now it was black. Little tongues of candle flame tottered down the streets, tottering shadows closely following. Nearly everyone was drunk. A wooden cup was thrust in front of me. "*Tome*," said a voice. I stared into a cup filled with *chicha*, a home brew made from fermented corn the color of a puddle half made by rain and half by a drunk with an aching bladder. I drank.

"Are you from Toro Toro," I asked my host, "or have you come for the *tinku*?"

He was a thick, well-fed man who grunted as he bent to fill his wooden *chicha* dipper. "I was born here," he said, "but now I return only for these three days. My belt, you will see how I use it. I whip it in circles to keep the people from coming too close to the fighters."

"I do not understand the *tinku*," I said. "Who fights whom?"

"Two peoples," he said. "The Laimes from the south against the Pampas from the north. They are all campesinos from the hills."

"But why do they fight?"

"Years ago they fought over boundaries or llamas or women," he said. "*Tome.*"

I swallowed with him. From somewhere far or close came a melody—relentless, simple, plodding. A few repeated notes a man alone on a moonless tundra might blow through the hollow thigh-bone of an ancestor.

"There is a rumor that the priest will ask the campesinos not to fight this year," he said. "That he will tell them God does not want them to use violence."

"What will the campesinos do?"

"I do not know. Most of them are Catholics . . . but they also believe any blood spilled here is an offering to the earth goddess, Pachamama. No one has died for a few years in the *tinku*, but if someone does, they believe it will be a good year for the crops. Some in the past have even worn brass on their knuckles when they fight. But rocks are worse. It is only very bad when the women become involved, and the people reach for rocks."

We watched shadows stagger past us, and buttoned against the cold. From some unseen source came the melody, insistent, relentless, working its way inside me and digging out a hollow. What kind of instrument would make that music? I wondered. What kind of man?

My host liked to talk. "There are no doctors here," he said. "Usually the Indians that fight treat their wounds with donkey dung. If blood is running from their faces, they try to lick it. They believe it will increase their courage."

He smiled with contempt at the *chicha* yet in my cup. I drank it and he dipped back into the dirt-streaked bucket. "A town of ghosts," I said, nodding at the passing shadows.

"That is so even in sunlight now," he said. "Except during the fiesta, thirty, forty families is all that remain here."

"What happened?"

"Many people lived here when I was a boy, perhaps six thousand. A big market, haciendas. Then one night the Indians came down from the hills. They had been promised an equal distribution of the land, but they were tired of waiting. We escaped and hid by the river. Others. . . ." He made a noise from the inside of his throat, ran his finger across the outside. "Almost everyone else left after that."

"Do the people here have any communication at all with the outside world?" I asked.

"*Tome*," he said. "Yes, there is a telegraph wire."

"Uh-oh. I hope that wasn't the wire our truck snapped today on the road."

He shrugged. "Well . . . they say it is not working."

We stopped talking and listened to the music. "But why do they fight?" I asked again.

"Like I said. Many years ago—"

"But I mean now. Is it still over llamas and women?"

"No, not now."

"So, why?"

He shrugged, leaving only the trudging melody to reply.

Seventeen, suburban, scared and frail, drinking my first hard liquor with the brothers at Baltimore Arena between rounds of Ali-Frazier I. No other sport did this. Only boxing kept drawing me into different worlds. . . .

All night I lay awake, partly because of the bacteria from the *chicha* at work in my belly, more from that music at work along my spine. It drifted to me from one end of the village, then the other; I would sit up rigid when it plodded past my door. Over and over, the same stark five-note cosmic statement: Isolated is a man, isolated is a man. . . .

There was light now, and I had to find the music's source. I walked swiftly up and down the streets, turned corners and finally came upon it: the campesinos who had come from the hills to fight. Drunken, red-eyed, they staggered about in small circles, knees bent, shoulders hunched, blowing through clusters of wooden tubes that resembled miniature organ pipes turned upside down. Behind them, women, equally drunk, flailed the air with flags of white rag, their leader snapping a sorry whip. I stood on the fringe and stared. Feathers and nails, trinkets and braids of cloth stuck out of the bands of their white peaked hats. On their backs, the women toted firewood and babies in colorful blankets. The men wore bright sashes and three or four layers of brightly colored pants, each pair hemmed progressively higher to show off the owner's wealth.

At the head of their ranks, a small statue of the village saint, Santiago, was carried high, a blue-eyed general brandishing a sword atop a horse whose hooves crushed the devil. They trudged toward me, looked right through me. One paused and urinated on my sneakers. I jumped back.

"What are they doing?"

"Praying to God," said a man.

I followed them for hours as they plodded, bent and hunched, in a trance induced by the *chicha* and the repetition of the tune.

"When does the *tinku* start?" I asked a street vendor. She rolled her shoulders. I continued my pursuit.

The Indians reached the church on the plaza, staggered in, kneeled and blessed themselves. I heard a terrific bang and rushed outside. One of the Indians was hurling sticks of dynamite into the sky.

I heard a sound like a horned owl desperate for a partner. I rounded a corner and saw a knot of people a block away. My legs began to run. A strong young man stood in their midst wearing a bright green vest and the curved cowhide helmet I had seen once before. He hooted again and kicked at the dirt.

Two women pushed him back and scolded. His chest heaved; he cast an insult at the man opposite him and made the eerie hooting sound once more. Abruptly he shoved the women aside, took three swift steps and threw an overhand right. A man crumpled, and the crowd gathered around him. Blood seeped from his nose. I pushed my way among them and looked down. The man on the ground had no left arm.

I looked up. Most of the crowd had already dispersed, the warrior in green was gone. Is that all? I wondered. A young stud coldcocks a cripple and it's over? Head down, I walked back to my room. I had come to see men fight.

No sleep. All night the two ends of the cot trying to snap shut, folding me up like a crepe. All night the sound of urine hissing against adobe walls, of dynamite shaking the sky, of whispers, grunts and that tune. Once I scrambled to my door and swung it open. A man hitched up his pants and ran, a woman scampered into the shadow of a doorway. Soon it would be dawn and they would be kneeling on the cold stone floor of the church.

Stiffly I walked outside and threw cold water on my face. The bread in my bag had hardened, the cheese was turning pungent. My stomach howled for food, and the smell of it cooking on the streets drew me to it. A toothless woman shoved a plate of something mushy, wet with grease, before me. I considered it for a moment, then turned away.

Around me, regathering chaos. Who were these people who obliterated the lines between dynamite and reverence, dance and insult, sex and fistfight, night and day? I leaned against a deserted building and felt alone.

Without purpose, I wandered. I found myself standing at an intersection, staring dully at an Indian woman beating sugared egg whites and finger-painting them on rings of bread. I whipped my head around—*tinku!*

It began of itself, a milling and strutting of Laimes on one side and Pampas on the other, balled fists, outthrust jaws, jiggling legs, heaving chests, spat insults, hoots from the throat. The crowd—the corner men, the matchmakers and referee—all suddenly materialized. The matchmakers pushed men forward, comparing sizes and ages for fairness; the corner men whispered encouragement; the referee, my drinking partner, whipped his belt to shoo back the mob. The fighters, eyes glazed from *chicha*, mouthed Quechua curses and stared one another down. Two young men fixed the Spanish-replica helmets on their heads, the onlookers shouted, and the fighters lunged for each other. No feeling out. No sweet science. The Pampa threw a roundhouse right that missed, a second one that landed; the Laime toppled. The crowd whooped, the Indian next to me grinned ear to ear and pounded me on the back.

The town's only cop sauntered by, borrowed a man's cap and waved it over the unconscious loser. "*¡Sin patas!*"—"Without kicking"—he warned, then sauntered on. Finally the knockout victim rose, embraced the winner and smeared blood from his nose on the victor's shoulder. I smiled and beat my hands together.

A man who lived in the city shook his head. "I guess you cannot blame them," he said. "They live so isolated all year, they need this." I nodded without thinking about what he'd said.

Now the fights came off like firecrackers: a quick matching, a few jeers, a flailing of fists, a loser dropping, then hugging and humor. Few understood the kinetic advantage of a short, crisp, well-timed punch; the blows gusted in long, wild, angry loops. The fighting space moved with the fighters, the bloodied faces multiplied. Boys of 11 and 12 were hustled into the ring, men of 49 and 50. We in the crowd leaned on one another, cheering, grimacing, laughing.

Some helped up their foes and we applauded. Some kicked them and we screamed. One young man pulled a packet of white powder from his pocket, sniffed a little, wobbled into the ring and was flattened in two punches. Then a fat Indian woman waddled in to break up a fight. She caught a left on her ear and went spinning.

The church bells rang. Eleven a.m. Sunday, time for Mass. No one left the *tinku*. For the first time in a day and a half, no plodding music, no walking dead. Up on my tiptoes, I bobbed and weaved for the best view, knowing I would never see anything like this again.

From the corner of my eye, I saw a man throw a punch, miss the head he was aiming for and catch mine, a glancing blow to the temple. Everyone laughed, a few rubbed my head. I feigned wooziness and laughed, too.

Just then, the man who had accidentally punched me took a right hook to the mouth and crashed. Almost lightheartedly he sprang back to his feet and posed for me, grinning blood. Then he wrapped his leathery hand around mine and shook it.

Now heads were turning, I heard murmurs. The crowd went quiet. I craned my neck. The young stud in the green vest, the one who had coldcocked the armless man the day before and demolished three two-armed opponents of his own size and age today, was adjusting his helmet and shoving up his sleeves. I looked to the Laimes' side. A well-built man in his 40's, starting to go soft and gray, stepped forward and took four practice jabs. Something about his eyes—he never blinked.

A man behind me tapped my shoulder, pointed to him and nodded. I understood. This was their Louis, their Ali, their Frazier—past his prime, coming back to take on the young buck. Is he crazy? I wondered; that young guy is a killer. He's going to get his head kicked in, and nobody's even going to pay him. Why does a man who doesn't have to fight—have *to fight*? The crowd edged closer. And why do other people let him?

The fighters circled. The man with the belt forgot all about waving it and stared. The old champ took two cautious steps forward and let go a crisp combination, enough to make the young buck backpedal and think. The people pursed their lips and nodded—yes, yes.

On they went this way, unlike the other fighters, considering every thrust. And then a right like a rockslide came down on the old champ's cheek; he buckled to the dirt and it was over.

The people grew silent. The young man strutted. The old one's face we still couldn't see. He stood at last, blood running from his mouth. Our Louis, our Frazier, our Ali. . . . I let someone's head block my view.

When I looked again, he was peering at the blood he had wiped with the back of his hand, hopping on one foot, then the other, grinning. Everyone was cheering and laughing and beating him on the back; I heard myself laugh, too. No, people don't fight for pride or money or ego. People fight, and people watch them fight, to feel. And if being human is to be born, grow strong, level off, then decline, fighting is a thing too much like being human to expect a man to stop and walk away before his ride is over.

There were a few more fistfights, and then there was a quiet intersection, an Indian woman beating sugared egg whites and finger-painting them on rings of bread.

In the morning our truck rolled out of the village. I stared through the slats, watching the Indians trudge over the ridge of hill, the other side of which I couldn't see.

Out of the Shadows

Who's to say? Maybe it's enough for you. After all, they're playing the game on a shiny hardwood surface, and it moves with such beauty and ferocity across that surface . . . maybe that's sufficient. Perhaps you can stick your hand on a radiator and know all you need to know about heat. But if only you could hear, in the silence between sneaker squeak and ball bounce, the other drama being played out. If only you could see what brought each of these 10 people to this shiny wood, what makes them race and leap and dive across it, then you would know the true heat and beauty of the game.

There's no time for that, of course. But what if you understood, say, just one of the 10? Then you would have at least some notion of this other place where the game unfolds, this furnace room that heats it. Say, for instance, the most obvious player out there, the littlest and quickest one, the relentless feet and the ponytail— did I fail to mention that this is women's basketball? No, too late, you missed her. She's already over there in the corner, the one in the Stanford uniform playing jaw-to-jaw defense, pressing even

This story first appeared in 1997.

when her team isn't pressing, the one thieving and threading through everyone else, dribbling behind her back, between her legs, deceiving left, dishing right, running the whole damn show—no, you must look quicker. Over there, streaking up the sideline now, everyone's All-America in high school, one of the leading characters in a best-selling book, the daughter of one of America's most distinguished writers, the sister of the damned, the niece of the doomed—missed her again, huh? Right baseline now, the 5'6" point guard who helped steer Stanford to the Final Four the last two years only to be shipwrecked each time in the semifinals, and who's hell-bent to not let it happen again this year, this month, her final shot. Too late, too late again—she's just too quick, and there are just too many pieces to her; the eyes cannot fix Jamila Wideman with one look.

Even when you *think* you've caught her, you haven't, because how can you see black when you're looking at white, or see a murder in a man-to-man press, and how can you hear the point guard's brother saying, "I feel helpless for the destruction I have caused, and hate myself for it," or her other brother saying, "In a single overwhelming instant I realized what I was—the sole black male Wideman of my generation not behind bars or beneath the ground," or her father saying, "Fear marched along beside guilt. . . . Fear that I was contaminated and would carry the poison wherever I ran," or her mother saying, "I'm not going to check either box! The baby's not black! The baby's not white! I don't care who you send in here to convince me!" And how could you possibly, as Jamila flies past midcourt on a two-on-one break, flip to page 2 of one of her dad's novels and read words that could have been ripped right from her throat: *See, cause I wanted to scream. I wanted to cut loose and tell somebody how scared I was. . . . Needed to scream worser than I ever needed to pee—or needed anything I can think of. But I knew if I'da screamed I'd be gone. If I screamed I'd be like them other poor suckers screaming and flying away. That scream would take me with it.*

Stop. Stop right there. Calm is what's called for here. A little distance. The writer who's going to have any chance of understanding the furnace can't jam his head inside it.

But it's easy for the writer to lose his bearings when he's an outsider stepping inside the door of a family of writers such as the Widemans and trying to write what is too close, too suffocating for them to write. There's John Edgar Wideman, the black father and two-time PEN/Faulkner Award–winning author, upstairs in his writing room in Amherst, Massachusetts, working on his 14th book. There's Judy Wideman, the white mother who at 52 earned her law degree and ranked second in her class, down the hall from John, writing briefs in her battle against the death penalty. There's their son Danny, at 28 the editor of a published anthology of black authors' works, bent over his notepad at his new home in Durham, North Carolina, writing his own books of nonfiction and fiction. There's Danny's brother, Jake, 27, writing haiku and short stories as he serves a life sentence in Florence, Arizona. And there's their sister, Jamila, 21, in her apartment near Stanford, writing in stream-of-consciousness flurries in her journal. But perhaps the smoke is still too dense where the Widemans are, the blank page too flammable for this story to come from their hands.

An entirely different story could be written from inside the guts of the couple whose son was murdered by Jamila's brother. Who can imagine what it was like for them to send a child to summer camp 11 years ago and then get a phone call saying he was dead? But this is not a story about the death, nor a back-and-forth story about the families, nor any attempt to put the Widemans' grief up against the grief of the parents who got that call. It's a story about a young woman trying to lead her team to a national title, one who knows now that so much of who she is, as a person and a player, is connected to her family history and to a tragedy. So here the writer goes, stepping gingerly, sensing how much there is to be learned about a game, but beyond that about a person, and a family, and a country, all engaged in a similar struggle, the struggle that everything rides on, to see if all their pieces, their many pieces, can be held together . . . or if they must blow apart.

Start simply this time. Start one summer evening, 1986, with a 10-year-old at a summer camp in the woods of Maine, the only girl among 350 boys. Jamila, the one exception, because her mom's father, Mort Goldman, owns and runs Camp Takajo, and because she can run circles around half the boys, and because she can bunk in the nearby cottage her grandfather built so her family of five could live at the camp each summer. It's not just any evening. Tonight's the musical variety show, and Jamila's got the curtain-closer. Her 17-year-old brother, Danny, one of the camp counselors, will accompany her on piano. Her uncle John Henry will be playing trumpet. Too bad her 16-year-old brother, Jake, won't be there—he's off on the camping trip out West that the older campers traditionally take—but she knows her parents will be. Everything she and her two brothers have ever done, Judy and John have been right there, hooting and hollering for all they're worth. . . . So where are they now? Jamila wonders, her eyes sweeping the audience seat by seat.

She's going to sing "If You Don't Believe," a song she loves by Deniece Williams. Jamila, you see, has this dilemma, the same one her brothers have. Her dad is black, and for a week each year, they visit their relatives in one of America's bleakest ghettos, the Homewood section of Pittsburgh. But Jamila's skin is white, or perhaps a pale olive—you might guess she's Italian—and she has lived her 10 years in a middle-class white section of Laramie, Wyoming, the ranching and college town where her father teaches literature and creative writing. How can she straddle Laramie and Homewood? Already she's beginning to form a way of talking, slipping in a *y'all* here and there, droppin' a consonant at the tail of a verb, nothing extreme, just a gentle, middle-ground diction that flies just fine in either world. Already she has sucked in the sociopolitical discussions whizzing around her dinner table, drawn a deep breath, climbed onto the cafeteria stage of her elementary school at lunchtime, grabbed the microphone and talked half of the school into walking out to demand a holiday on Martin Luther King Jr.'s birthday. Done it so adroitly, in fact, that her principal immediately called an assembly so the issue could be discussed before the entire school. Already she has stood up, when her fourth-grade teacher tried to downplay the horror of U.S. slavery by emphasizing how many other civilizations have engaged in the practice, and declared, "My family were slaves once!" Standing this evening in front of a campful of affluent Jews and singing this black woman's soul song is one more hook-and-eye attempt to stitch the pieces together.

Nervous? Sure she is. But not *too* nervous. Jamila is accustomed to the head-turning, the stares, the buzz each time she races onto the basketball court for the layup drill before a game against another all-male camp—*That little squirt, that GIRL, she's on their team? She's going to START?* She can live with that. She has been watching her dad play every weekend in pickup games against college players half his age. She's been mimicking his moves, practicing one-on-one, no-holds-barred, against her two older brothers. She's been provoking the whole crowd at Laramie High to roar with each of the little squirt's 15-foot shots at halftime of her brothers' high school games, and to boo Danny and Jake's team when it comes out of the locker room and displaces her on the court.

She's a precocious child with deep, dark, sensitive pools for eyes, calm and wise way past her years. At five Jamila could already do what the great point guards do, what most adults go to their graves without mastering: make the imaginative leap from her own consciousness to someone else's. One day the Widemans were wedged in an endless line of cars on a bridge, exhausted after a long day of travel, and the children were listening to their father fume about all the people blocking the way. "John, John, why don't you hush up?" came a squeaky voice from the backseat. "Don't you know you're just traffic to all those other people?"

"Even as a baby," her father says, "Jamila was looking into another dimension." Perhaps because she already had. She had come into the world nine weeks too soon, born in a bloody mess that nearly took both her and her mother's lives, arriving with a malfunctioning heart valve and necrotizing enterocolitis and then swiftly contracting salmonella poisoning. A doctor at Colorado General Hospital in Denver had studied the X rays of the 2-pound, 14-ounce creature and announced that even there, in that cutting-edge neonatal ward to which an ambulance had rushed Judy Wideman from an hour and a half away, there was no good reason to hope. But somehow, inside the incubator's glass walls, those arms, thinner than John's pinkie, and that little head, so tiny that Judy's mother knitted a cap for Jamila by sizing a small orange, and that wrinkled torso hung on. It astonished John, and then it didn't astonish him, when he saw his preschooler wave and call out cheery hellos as they drove past the cemetery in Laramie each day—"Hiya, Vass!"—conducting little conversations by name with the people beneath the stones.

In infancy she began to enter yet another realm that few children do. Every year during her family's visit to Pittsburgh, their Volvo station wagon would pull off a city street into a vast, barren stretch of cracked concrete. Jamila would get out of the car and stare up at the 40-foot walls, the barbed wire, the armed guards atop the ramparts, and then walk through the thick steel doors, the metal detector and the sentries' piercing stares to visit Uncle Robby, John's brother, sentenced to life in Western State Penitentiary for being an accessory to a murder in a 1975 robbery. She took it all in—the deadening chill of the prison, the guard barking "That's enough!" if her relatives hugged Uncle Robby a few seconds beyond the limit, or touched him at any time after that hug, or circled their chairs around him to talk. She felt his warmth each time Uncle Robby flopped on the visiting-room floor and played with her. "An instant simpatico between the two," John recalls. "Jamila would go right to him and ask him the questions the adults couldn't, like 'Why are you here? How long will you be in the cage? Are you happy?' She was the one who transcended the circumstances and saw her uncle as a person and made the guards and the bars disappear."

Already, at 10, she's taking in her parents' anger over the warehousing of so many black males in U.S. prisons with little or no attempt at rehabilitation, the anguish over injustice and prejudice and the concept of the "good seed" and the "bad seed" brothers that led her father to write his 1984 account of his and Robby's lives, *Brothers and Keepers*. Already Jamila has observed that Mom's the one who always goes to the motel reception desk to get a room when the family travels, and Dad's the one stopped by cops for no discernible reason except DWB, driving while black. Already, in fourth grade, she accompanies Mom to law school. Some remarkable harvest will come forth from this daughter—that's clear to her parents. But where, where are they this evening for her big camp number, and why do Danny's eyes keep cutting and running each time she asks? She goes onstage anyway. "She sang so beautifully that night," remembers Danny.

If you don't belieeeve all the tears in my eyes
I cried for ya!
If you don't belieeeve all the nights with you gone
I sighed for ya!
And if you don't belieeeve while you're away
That my life gets emptier with each breath that I take . . .

She bows before the audience's standing ovation, returns to
the family's cottage and finds her parents. She'll never, ever sing
like that again.

Jake? The brother who flopped on the floor with her to play
with R2-D2 and C-3P0, her *Star Wars* action figures? The boy who
divvied up teams with her and played out the NCAA tournament
brackets, one-on-one, in the driveway? *What* happened to Jake?
He's missing, vanished, and his camping roommate, Eric Kane, is
dead from a . . . *what?* A knife buried in his chest? Where could
Jake be? Could the bad man have killed Eric and kidnapped Jake?
Will they find Jake dead somewhere too?

Right here, right now, we could launch a novel. We could
make an entire chapter from each of the pieces of this puzzle and
try to comprehend why the second son of Judy Wideman, the passionate and tenacious woman who has drywalled the old Fish and
Game building in Laramie to expand an alternative school, pro-
cured the school's loans and leases, driven the kids on field trips,
helped teach the reading class and served as president of the
school's board . . . why the second son of John Edgar Wideman,
the All-Ivy basketball star at Penn from 1961 to '63, the Phi Beta
Kappa who would become only the second black in a half-century
to win a Rhodes scholarship, the subject of an article in *Look*
magazine entitled "The Astonishing John Wideman" before he
graduated, the future winner of a MacArthur Foundation "genius
grant" . . . why the brother of Danny Wideman, named Person of
the Year by the *Plainsman Times* of Laramie in his senior year
of high school . . . and why the brother of Jamila Wideman, the
snatched-from-death's-jaws wunderkind . . . why Jake Wideman,
a soft-spoken, seemingly gentle boy with good grades, unafflicted

by drug or alcohol problems and already starting on the varsity basketball team as a high school sophomore, would wake up in a Flagstaff, Arizona, motel room and kill a sleeping companion with whom he hadn't even quarreled. . . . We could write that novel and still be left clutching, on its final page, a puff of smoke. We could shift point of view, attempt the imaginative leap into any of the Widemans' blood and tissue during the months that follow the murder, go from Jamlia jolting awake night after night, racked by nightmares and insomnia for nearly three years, to her father walking alone through the Maine woods, dropping to his knees, digging his fingers into the soil, sinking his face into the earth and praying to the universe, "Take me, take me, take me in Jake's place," and still never even sketch the horror and the heartbreak. But this isn't a novel. This is just journalism, and every sentence only raises five more questions that need five more pages to answer, pages that simply don't exist.

So let us remain here, just near enough to the fire and the anvil, just long enough to glimpse what manner of young woman is being forged. Because the hammer blows are ceaseless. The news that her brother will be tried as an adult rather than a juvenile: Would that happen, Jamila's family wonders, were Jake not a black man's son? The realization that her parents now must fight tooth-and-nail to keep Jake from being executed. The news that Jake has also confessed to a murder that occurred a year earlier in Laramie (for which charges will eventually be dropped after he recants and exculpatory evidence comes to light). The reports that Jake has twice attempted suicide in jail. The news that a $70 million civil suit against the Widemans, which could bankrupt the family, is being filed by the victim's family. The news that articles are appearing in newspapers and magazines all over the country poking through the ashes of the Widemans' family life, pointing to the rage expressed by John in *Brothers and Keepers*, searching for the answer, the explanation, the certainty that will permit everyone else to sleep restfully at night, assured that this murder or something like it couldn't happen to one of their children. Every one of these hammer blows finds Jamila, even as the adults think, *pray* that she's too young to feel them all. Guilt, shame, fear, anger:

They're all in her journal. She'll realize that years later, when she looks back at her words. They're all in her 10-year-old heart.

So it's recess time, sixth grade, and the new girl in school, the little spindly one, is walking into the schoolyard. Jamila and her family have just moved to Amherst, Massachusetts; they had been planning to do that even before their world exploded, so her father could begin teaching at the University of Massachusetts. She is two weeks late for school because of the family chaos, and this morning the whole story is breaking in the *Boston Globe*, and she's walking on eggshells, the new girl, the one whose past has just vanished behind her in Laramie, disappeared so abruptly that she never even had a chance to say good-bye to most of her friends— the family gone in a cloud of rumors and gossip. She's the silent stranger, wondering who among her new schoolmates has seen the newspaper, who knows her secret, who's going to nudge whom and say, "Don't go near Jamila. You know what runs in her family," like the two kids she overheard just before she left Laramie. At recess the boys go one way, toward the basketball court. The girls go another way, off to talk. Jamila pauses. The precocious little girl, the one who would step onstage to sing or lead a protest—where is she now? Gone, gone. Jamila stands there, looking around . . . then freezes her insides and heads for the basketball court. The boys sneer, roll their eyes, giggle. Jamila doesn't budge. Then the game begins and she's moving, whipping passes, flicking in jump shots, and for 20 minutes, a half hour, everything, everything goes away.

The boys take the new girl in; she's a novelty, she's one of them. What about the girls, though, staring at her as if she's a traitor? Jamila has a secret, and people with secrets can't afford to have enemies. That's it: Since she's basketball buddies with the boys, she'll play matchmaker for the girls. She'll be everyone's confidante, everyone's listener and problem-solver; it's so much easier to walk the mile in their shoes than in her own. "I got good," she says, "at being evasive. It's so hard when so much of who you are is tied to something you can't express." Banter, that helps too. She'll keep it quick whenever she can, quick and easy and light. She'll blend in without explaining herself. She'll hide right in plain sight.

God, how she'll need to. The day a classmate walks up and blurts out, "Isn't your brother a murderer?" and the day her teacher wheels a TV in front of the class and shows a movie about a teenage boy who commits murder and is condemned to death, she's certain everyone is staring right through her. Where can she turn? Suddenly she's an only child in a new house strangled by silence—Danny off at Brown, Jake in prison—a home where anguish seems to feed on the family's very flesh and blood. Her mother contracts a life-threatening illness; Jamila's grandfather Mort (who as owner of Camp Takajo is also a target of the $70 million civil suit, which will eventually be settled out of court) learns that he is suffering from heart disease, which will soon kill him; and her father is racked by pain from stenosis, a condition that causes muscle deterioration in his left arm and the left side of his chest and forces him to suffer each time he tries, like Jamila, to find refuge on a basketball court, to make everything, everything go away. "Imploding," says Danny. "It seemed as if my whole family was imploding."

A teacher notices Jamila playing basketball and recommends that she do something audacious: try out for the Amherst Regional High girls' team as a seventh-grader. No seventh-grader in the school's history has started on the varsity in a team sport. Jamila walks onto the court that first day of tryouts, braces glinting, bones showing, 4' 6" and 80 pounds, her mom the only parent in the gym, watching like a hawk from a corner seat. "All you could see," recalls the coach, Ron Moyer, "was this wisp of a thing, a ponytail and a basketball, and then once in a while you'd see a body. She was a water bug. Nobody could take the ball from her. The two senior captains came up to me after the first practice and said, 'Coach, you're going to keep her, aren't you?' I said, 'Who?' They said, 'You know, the little one.' I said, 'Well, I'm intrigued.' I got so intrigued, I was hypnotized for the next day and a half. The major concern wasn't whether she was good enough to start on the varsity, it was whether she'd be maimed for life if anyone fell on her. I told her mother what I thought: She's too quick to get hurt.

"When I think back on Jamila, I just smile. Always ready to go. Always the first one on the court and the last one off. It was clear that here was a kid who had learned from her parents the price you have to pay for excellence. I could get her to do everything and anything except put the ball in the ball rack at the end of practice. The boys' team could be walking on the floor to practice, my dinner could be ready at home, but I couldn't get her to leave the court."

Here's the safe harbor for the little girl while the storm howls overhead. Here's where she can have intimacy and feeling without ever articulating intimacy or feeling, where she can let everyone know who she is through sweat and gesture, through a bounce pass under a defender's arm to a teammate streaking backdoor. Senior year, playoffs, dead ball, game already sewn up: That's the only highlight footage we're going to run here. Nothing from the game in her sophomore year in which she single-handedly halts Monument Mountain High's 81-game winning streak by dervish-dribbling through her opponents' famous full-court press. Nothing from the game against Springfield Central High two years later in which she lickety-splits her team to a 15-point first-half lead and her coach makes a mercy substitution, sitting Jamila down, only to notice the opposing assistant coach crab-crawling in front of the official scorer's table toward the Amherst bench and whispering, *"Pssst!* Coach Moyer! Leave her in! Our kids want to see her play. Our kids want to say they played against her." No, none of that. Just the dead ball during the playoff game her senior year in one of those big airport-hangar arenas. Twenty-two-point Amherst lead, 6:29 left in a game in which Jamila has notched 25 points, 11 rebounds and 7 steals, in which three girls have tried and failed to cover her, and she has held the enemy star to six points . . . when an errant pass whizzes out of bounds, rolls 30 yards, then vanishes down a long tunnel. Good, a breather, some aerobics for the ref, a ball boy, a fan, right? But there goes Jamila like a cannon shot, leaping over a barricade, disappearing down the tunnel and reemerging on the fly with the ball a second later. "Pure adrenaline," she tells the media afterward. "I wanted the ball back. I wanted to finish the game." Insane, a teammate calls her intensity, her perpetual motion.

Then, as always, she sags in the locker room, the fastest one becoming the slowest, staring off into emptiness, nothing bad left inside her, because there's nothing left inside at all. Jamila, who can't discuss her internal narrative with a therapist or with her brother Danny or with her parents, who wraps herself in a thick coat, mittens and hat on winter weekends and takes jump shots and double-pump scoop shots in the driveway. Jamila, who will go six years as a high school varsity starter without missing a practice or a game. The one Wideman who isn't getting sick, who isn't imploding.

Thank God, Jamila thinks, for Jenny Pariseau, her backcourt mate, her best friend, so effervescent, so good at saying something smooth, something outrageous, veering the conversation somewhere else when it's skidding toward Jamila's family. She feels so light with Jenny at her side, silly enough to lose some of her wariness. On a team bus ride the two of them swarm all over the new assistant coach like Gypsies on the Paris Metro, pilfer the wallet from her pocketbook, memorize all the numbers and facts on her identification cards and then astound her by playing Siamese swamis—go on, ask us anything, we know all about you. Your middle name? Where you were born, your mother's name, your Social Security number? The swamis know all, no problem.

Cute. Coach is laughing, kids are laughing, Jamila's laughing, her guard dropping a little lower. It's at times like this that the innocent question might come out of nowhere: *So, what about you, Jamila. Do you have any brothers or sisters?*

Uh . . . yeah . . . I have a brother at Brown, playing ball there.
That's it?

Well . . . there's another brother, living out in Arizona. . . .
What's he do?

Nothing much, just hanging out. . . .

Is that dishonest? What if the person asking her already knows and is thinking, *Liar, liar, liar?* What if someone ambushes her, spills the truth in the cafeteria, at a table full of classmates? What if she doesn't mention Jake, and that person drops by her house and notices him in a family photograph? *Talk* about him? She can't even bear to *think* of Jake, alone in that place, surrounded by. . . . But who can really know her if she keeps this piece of herself hidden? Should she wait and see if a new relationship is going somewhere before she tells—but then, if it does go somewhere, doesn't it only grow harder and harder to tell? Where does she take this kind of pain and confusion when she's the star, cozy in a fine house, the child of the privileged? What does she say when one of her best friends demands, "What is it, Jamila? Why don't you ever talk about your feelings? Why do you keep everything inside?"

And oh, by the way, do people need to know that Jamila's half black, too? Why does she have to indulge in the foolishness of declaring that, of making herself vulnerable to everyone's narrow notions of race—*oh, so THAT'S why your uncle and brother are in prison and your cousin Omar has been shot dead*—when she's Jamila, an individual, none of the above? But knowing that if she fails to make the declaration, the steel trap is set, ready to spring, just waiting for the moment when another new acquaintance does a double take at the tall, handsome black man waiting outside the locker room and whispers, "Jamila, who is *that*?" Knowing, if she fails to make the declaration, she must squirm through a book or a dinner-table discussion at home about some character who toadies up and tries to pass for white. But how can she explain to other kids what it's like to whiplash from a week at one grandma's house, surrounded by boarded storefronts and cracked sidewalks and fire-gutted buildings, a house crowded with aunts and uncles and nephews and nieces and teenage cousins with babies, loud with laughter and music and games of whist and sometimes with gunshots and sirens in the night . . . to another grandma's house a five-hour drive away, a million-dollar, six-bedroom home surrounded by trees and grass and next to a stream—and make them understand how warm, how loved she feels in both homes?

Why is it her task, why now, in adolescence, when all a kid craves is to be like everyone else? If she just keeps playing the role of hoops star, team captain, Rock of Gibraltar, academic whiz, the ever-calm one everyone else depends on, the one who always selects the right words or gestures to bring out the best in her teammates, the wise and nonjudgmental Jamila who's wonderful at discussing *their* issues, *team* issues, the girl whom every faction at Amherst High—the skateboarders, jocks, druggies, geeks—trusts with its problems and feelings . . . doesn't that grant her a free pass when mirror time comes?

Nigger. When a peer casually tosses off that word, or pockets a whole race inside a stereotype, or bangs the drum for the death penalty—is it her duty to stand up and protest, to attract all the attention that makes her skin crawl, to clear her cobwebbed throat and sing what she feels: *Excuse me, that's my kind you're talking about, my dad, my brother, the kid sealed away for life without getting the psychological help he needs, and if you're going to divvy up the world that way, us-and-them it, then you have to count me, everybody's All-America, everybody's confidante, on the other team.* But if she does that, if she refers to her brother's needs, will she be seen as being unfeeling to the dead boy and the plight of his family, for whom she also aches?

This is the zigzag that occurs in Jamila's mind with virtually every social encounter, the ricochet through levels and layers that occurs behind those calm, dark eyes and long, curly eyelashes, beneath each spoken word. One day, after putting it off for years, after leaving *Brothers and Keepers* on her bookshelf to gather dust, she finally picks it up to read. Some pages bring tears to her eyes, some pages make her wince, as she reads of the terrible price her father has paid for running away from his history. Of all his huffing and hiding in the halls of academia and on the plains of Wyoming in order to cope, and how it's all undone when his brother, Robby, can no longer even squint and see the American dream that John seems to have by the tail, undone completely when Robby shows up on John's Laramie doorstep as a fugitive in 1976, just a few months after Jamila's birth, only to be arrested a day later and imprisoned for life. She reads of John—who in 1963 told *Look* magazine, "So far the things I've wanted to do haven't been held back from me because of my being a Negro. So the problem is not my own problem, not something I feel I have to cope with or resolve"—looking back two decades later and confessing in print what lay just beneath those words: "Fear marched along beside guilt. Fear of acknowledging in myself any traces of the poverty, ignorance and danger I'd find surrounding me when I returned to Pittsburgh. Fear that I was contaminated and would carry the poison wherever I ran. Fear that the evil would be discovered in me and I'd be shunned like a leper." Hadn't she seen the toxin suddenly spill when she watched Dad play pickup ball? Hadn't she seen or heard about him calling wind fouls—demanding the ball back if the breeze blew his shot astray—screaming at opponents, picking up an overaggressive 6' 10" player and slamming him onto the court?

It's beginning to happen now, in Jamila's last two years of high school: She's growing more aware—damn her Wideman wits— that each one of those zigzags pulls her one step farther away from purity, from just *being*, and drives her right back to the one place where she can feel that purity: the straight lines, the shiny wood. Jamila's growing more aware—damn her family's penchant for swallowing shards and regurgitating words—of the cost of fleeing your past, your genes, your shadows, your Robbys and your Jakes. And then she opens a book by a man named Ralph Ellison.

> It goes a long way back, some 20 years. All my life I had been looking for something and everywhere I turned someone tried to tell me what it was. I accepted their answers too, though they were often in contradiction and even self-contradictory. I was naive. I was looking for myself and asking everyone except myself questions which I, and only I, could answer. It took me a long time and much painful boomeranging of my expectations to achieve a realization everyone else appears to have been born with: That I am nobody but myself. But first I had to discover that I am an invisible man!

Hit the floor! Incoming salvo! From that opening paragraph of Chapter 1 of *Invisible Man*, the novel she's assigned to read in 11th grade, about a black man who realizes that no one sees him as an individual, she feels the ground shaking, the walls crumbling, the sudden rendezvous with self. The realization that because of society's fears, and her own fears, not only is Jake the Invisible Man, but she is too! "Invisible," she says, "because such a big part of my life was unspeakable and unknown. Basketball was the only part of me most people knew. I couldn't articulate a thing until I read that book. It became a bible for me. It made me begin to confront questions: Do I fit into an easy box, or be who I am, or become so many things, take on so many roles, that I become nothing, like the Invisible Man? Where were the other people like me? And then I realized . . . there isn't anybody." She leans over a keyboard to write her five-page report on *Invisible Man*. Six hours and 30 pages later, she's done. Oh, yes, an odd literary compadre, the Invisible Man, for a girl in sports headlines every week, a girl with 150 college scholarship offers.

Hit the floor! Now the Los Angeles riots of 1992 are raging on her TV screen, and her father is out there with pen and pad— it's another jolt telling her that she's connected to those people running wild in the streets 3,000 miles away, that she mustn't succumb to the temptation to be what she looks like, a white kid in the suburbs that the rage and riots never reach.

She writes a poem entitled "Black" and submits it for publication in her school newspaper, never telling her parents. Part of it reads:

I walk the tightrope between the fires
Does anyone know where I fall through?
Their forked daggers of rage reflect my eye
Their physical destruction passes me by
Why does the fire call me?

O.K. Let the ones she has never explained any of this to, which means virtually everyone, read that and scratch their heads. It's a start, at least. But it's not enough. To each game she plays, she carries her fanny pack, bringing to battle all the pieces of her life that she's trying to hold together: the medallion with the outline of Africa, the miniature African mask, the necklace Jake sent her from prison with the carved-peach-pit charm showing a mother monkey carrying a baby monkey on her back, the basketball card of Kenny Anderson (a lefty point guard, just like her), the picture of Michael Jordan and the little book containing the autographs of Nelson Mandela, Desmond Tutu and Spike Lee. But she never shows her teammates these pieces inside the fanny pack. So it's not enough.

A criminal-rights and civil-rights lawyer—that's what she vows to become when basketball's done. She'll appeal Jake's case one day, she daydreams, like any little sister might. She'll delicately but relentlessly carve apart the system that locks away a 16-year-old—who, yes, has done something terrible—and throws away the key without offering him the smallest chance to reform. But she knows she'll never really get the chance to represent him. So this too is not enough.

She holds little conversations with Jake in her head before she falls asleep. She thinks, on her 16th birthday, *This is where the trail ended for him.* Over and over it occurs to her that everything she does from this point on—the run for the state championship, the prom, the graduation, the parties, the first day of college—he will never experience. She sits in the quiet before a big game and reflects on this, rededicates herself to seizing the moment for them both, but this too is not enough. Why doesn't she write letters to him? Why does she hold back when she has the chance to walk alone with Jake through the prison yard during her yearly visit? How do you reach for the stars while you're reaching back to someone who is chained to a stake? How does a girl do it, a family do it, a country?

Funny how basketball is always the answer when there are no answers, the thread running through everything: the game Jamila's family plays at either grandma's house, the game she and Dad and Danny and Jake played on the court in Phoenix the day before Jake turned himself in to the police. The game Jamila and her father could play on the driveway without a hitch in conversation. The sport that gave the Widemans an entrée back into the community, a way to begin emerging from their nightmare—for Judy to godmother a dozen girls, wash their practice uniforms, compile their team yearbook, videotape their games, cook their ritual chicken-and-pasta dinners; for John to feel as if he were passing something on instead of giving it up, to stand tall in a packed gymnasium and whoop for all he was worth, even when Judy ordered him to move out of earshot of her camcorder.

The whole town of Amherst, a community of college professors and old hippies, gets swept up in the gust: the quest of Jamila and her pal Jenny to make 10 other girls want success as badly as they do, to carry the Lady Hurricanes across the threshold they have stumbled on for five straight seasons and win the state title their senior year. The crowds grow so thick that people must be turned away; little girls and boys form lines for Jamila's autograph; and a new girls' youth league is spawned by the surge of interest in the game. A local writer, Madeleine Blais, smells a story, smells a book. Something about sisterhood, about a group of girls shaking off the shackles of sexism and societal conditioning and their own inner fears to hurl themselves at a goal. Dangerous, dangerous. . . . Jamila refuses to open up her heart or her journals, as her teammates do, but still ends up on the cover of the book and of the Sunday *New York Times Magazine*. In the state-championship game she leads her team on an astonishing 37–0 run and finishes with 27 points, 13 steals, 11 rebounds and 8 assists as Amherst annihilates the defending champions by 38 points.

And when it's over, Jamila goes back to her home court, waits until all her teammates leave, then lies down after midnight on the shiny wood and sobs.

Then Jamila was gone. Three thousand miles gone, to a university that offered her one of America's finest educations, finest women's basketball programs, finest climates and, yes, 3,000 miles between her and her past.

Here is what happened to Jamila at Stanford: She chose a double major of political science (to prepare herself for law school) and African-American studies and wrote a research paper on the inhuman conditions at a California prison. She found herself surrounded by people of all races and mixtures of color and listened to them talk of their experiences. She made it known to her coaches and to the sports publicists at the school that her family history wasn't to be discussed with the media. She found herself saving the small mementos, ticket stubs even to mediocre movies and concerts, as if someday her past might vanish if she didn't hang on to hard proof.

She was named captain and starting point guard as a freshman, for which there was no precedent at Stanford. Her scoring dropped from her high school years, but that was fine. It was as if her teammates couldn't wait to get the ball in her hands, knowing she would know the perfect moment to get it back to them.

In her final regular-season game that first year she made a spin move, but her ankle didn't. The injury—a severe sprain and deep bone bruise—cost her a chance to make the U.S. Olympic Festival West team, relegated her to the bench for much of her sophomore year and made Michael Dillingham, the San Francisco 49ers' physician, fear she might have to give up basketball. And it taught Jamila, in the most painful way, just how many pieces those ligaments had been holding together.

"It was as if my voice had been taken away," she says. "Basketball was my voice, and I couldn't speak. I felt so empty, so devastated, any catastrophic word you can come up with. But I couldn't let out my fears." Finally, in February of her sophomore year, she broke down, cried and told teammate Kate Paye her feelings, her past and the story of Jake.

Here is what Jamila learned: that it was terrible to sit on the bench and not even be able to recognize her game when she did play—but she survived. And that Kate didn't recoil when Jamila told her the truth. And that many others had lived through nightmares, but their telling of those nightmares didn't diminish what people thought of them. And this, too: that basketball, though it had saved Jamila from the fire, also had denied her some of the light, consumed so many hours that she'd had no time to get involved with issues of race and justice that cried out to her on campus. Basketball cocooned her in a little capsule with 11 other women, cocooned her sometimes even from herself.

Jamila learned one more thing she might never have suspected: that while so many people around her had no idea what they wanted to do with their lives, she was sure. She had a passion, a commitment to civil rights, a depth of feeling about them that she couldn't have had without her family history. Her pain, once she began to face it, also became her gift.

"I'm finally comfortable expressing myself about it," she says. "I still haven't articulated a lot to a lot of people, but I don't have the fear I once did. I kept waiting for something to change things, waiting to wake up one day and have things fit. I thought going to California would make things easier. But I learned it doesn't work that way. The way I related to people at Stanford was the same, my guarded approach to friendships was the same, my inclination to keep things on a surface level. I finally realized that until you understand why you do things, you have no control over what you do. And realized that there won't ever be a solution to the dilemma. That it's not the problem itself that defines you. It's how you deal with the challenge that the problem presents every day; that's what defines you. Who I am is somebody on the tightrope.

"Solutions are overrated. Easy answers, that's where we go wrong. What happened to Jake, there is no answer to that, but I do know that I'm a lot more similar to him than I am different, and to get closer to the truth, you have to be able to see them *both* as your brother: the victim and Jake. I know my brother has to take responsibility for what he did, and there has to be punishment. But you have to ask yourself, What if he was *your* brother, *your* father? What if you'd grown up with him and knew he was someone besides what he did? Of course I wish all this had never happened, for my brother's and the victim's sake, but for me, I don't know. . . . Who would I be without it? So much of my strength has come from having to face this, so much of who I am. I have an obligation now to deal with these issues. I have a commitment."

Here is what others say of Jamila. "From the very first day, she took possession of this team," says Stanford teammate Vanessa Nygaard. "She pulls us all together and connects us. [Coach] Tara [VanDerveer] always asks us who we'd want in a foxhole with us, defending our lives in a war. It's Jamila. We all say that. She could be having the worst game of her life, and you'd never know it. She has an intimate relationship with everyone on the team. She's close to them—but they're not close to her. She has this . . . this presence about her. Team meetings are *her* meetings."

"A rare person," says associate head coach Amy Tucker. "Extremely rare. The most articulate twenty-one-year-old I've ever met. But very private. She wants to be pictured as a very strong person with no chinks in her armor."

"She'll make a frightening attorney," says Danny Wideman. "So passionate and articulate and with the skill of detachment, the ability to completely inhabit something outside herself, to observe and intuit it without judging, and make it completely her own."

Here is what must be done this month: "The national championship," says Jamila. "We've been to the Final Four twice; I can't be satisfied without winning it all. I feel more pressure on myself to make it happen this time than I did with the state title my senior year at Amherst. I know what I've set my heart on. I know what I've set myself up for. To play in one of the women's pro leagues— that'll be great if it works out, but it won't be like this. This is our chance."

And then? One day, she'll have another little trip to make. If it goes as it has before, she'll wake up in a Phoenix hotel room two hours before dawn and throw on her clothes, with barely enough time to glance at the teddy bear she still carries on almost every road trip, all that's left of that innocent little girl bounding onto the stage to sing "If You Don't Believe." She'll climb into a rental car with her family, who will have flown out to meet her, and fall silent as her father drives the Widemans into the desert. Drives them past the cacti, blind and silent in the dark, through land as flat and dry and lonely as they all feel inside. An hour and a half later, just before dawn, it will rise from the wasteland: the electrified fencing, the razor wire, the concrete bunkers, the watchtowers with the machine-gun-wielding guards in bulletproof vests. The door will open, the Widemans will go inside. Through Jake's walls. Through Jamila's.

They'll hug him as long as the rules allow, then sit at one of the 12 orange-and-green tables and talk of basketball and triumph, but then the conversation will go farther and deeper and bend around. And Jamila will walk with Jake in the yard, which she couldn't make herself do until the last few years, and speak to him alone. And her eyes will well up when it's time to hug him good-bye—a moment somehow more dreadful and less dreadful than it used to be, now that she's not so swift to avert her eyes and run.

Then it will be back into the car, back across the moonscape, and silence again in the family of writers: the keen awareness of voicelessness and voice, and of how those who have a voice must keep turning and leaning toward those who don't, for without them they have nothing of lasting value to tell the world.

A country is so large and made up of so many pieces, it's hard to see what must be done sometimes. If only you could whittle it down, say, to that family crossing the desert in that rental car, then maybe the path would become clearer. But maybe that's still too complicated, and it would be better to whittle it even further, to just one young woman, climbing out of the backseat, pulling on her sneakers, running with a basketball across a shiny wooden surface. . . .

An Exclusive Club

*Never join someone who eclipses you. Align yourself with one
who increases your luster. The man who puts you in the shade
because he is either more virtuous or vicious gains the greater
recognition. He plays the main role, and you are relegated
to support him.*
            —Baltasar Graci, 17th-century Jesuit philosopher

Suppose you had spent the best years of your life gasping for
oxygen. Suppose you had awakened each Sunday morning
knowing you must run 23 miles to feel clean, then lie on a table
and hope someone could rub away the pain. Suppose you had spent
nights brooding over 10ths of seconds, a decade of life under the
tyranny of a clock, and finally you had what you ached for. "You're
the king of the world," as one who did this said. "The fastest miler
in the world." And then, a few years later—or perhaps only a few
months or weeks—it was gone. Someone else was faster. Someone
else was king.

This story first appeared in 1994.

Suppose that one day long after this fever had passed, one day when your hair was gray and your face was a fine web of wrinkles, you opened the mail and found an invitation. Someone wanted you to get on an airplane, fly 15 hours, or 28, in order to stand in the shade of the ones who had surpassed your sacrifice, eclipsed your glory. No appearance fee. Would you do it? What for?

"To be the world-record holder in the mile," said Herb Elliott, the 56-year-old Australian who was just that from 1958 until '62, "a man must have the arrogance it takes to believe he can run faster than anyone ever has at that distance . . . and the humility it takes to actually do it."

What becomes of all that arrogance and humility? One by one, on the 40th anniversary of the most famous mile ever run, the record holders arrived at the Grosvenor House Hotel in London on May 4. Shaking hands, smiling shyly, they stepped into each other's shade.

FILBERT BAYI: I don't have much money. But I have this: I'm among the great milers in the world. That makes me rich.

DEREK IBBOTSON: If it had been any other event, I don't think I'd be remembered now. I'd be lost.

JOHN LANDY: I was a loner, a shy young man. It opened me up to live a life I never thought I'd live.

STEVE CRAM: It becomes luggage permanently attached to your name. It matters not what else you do. You'll be introduced everywhere as world-record holder in the mile. Even after you're hurt or on the downside of your career, you'll believe you can do anything. It can create great frustration.

PETER SNELL: The anchor I have is that regardless of how good you think you are, I at least have achieved something that was world-class and that can never be taken away from me.

SEBASTIAN COE: I'll say it—why not? We are members of one of the most exclusive clubs in the world.

Dawn. Damp. Cool. Windy. Herb Elliott was sitting on his bed, eyes shut, mind quiet, body still. He was meditating. Jim Ryun, the world-record holder from 1966 to '75, was rousing his four children. Noureddine Morceli, the current king, was dropping to his knees, facing Mecca, murmuring his prayers. Bayi, who reigned briefly in 1975, was cooing to his fourth-born, one-year-old Cuthbert. John Walker, who dethroned Bayi and ruled until 1979, was sleeping like a stone.

The bus awaited them outside the Grosvenor House Hotel. Soon it would take them to the Iffley Road track in Oxford, where 40 years ago—on a day not unlike this one—England's Roger Bannister astonished the world by running the first sub-four-minute mile. Four minutes was a barrier that had withstood decades of human yearning and anguish, a figure that seemed so perfectly round—four laps, four quarter-miles, four-point-oh-oh minutes—that it seemed God himself had established it as man's limit, posted it as one quiet, subtle proof of Order against the howl of two world wars. The spectacle was seen by Americans watching their first televisions, by young lovers and old ones entering theaters around the world. At the time it seemed as improbable as . . . well, as 14 of the world's 16 living mile-record holders coming from Algeria, Australia, England, France, New Zealand, Sweden, Tanzania and the U.S. to celebrate it four decades later.

George Dole, a Massachusetts minister in the Swedenborgian Church who was invited to join this pilgrimage—he was one of the six runners who ran in Bannister's epic mile—climbed onto the bus before any of the record holders, full of the knowledge that perhaps no other sport had ever gathered so much of its greatness in one time and place. "Imagine," Dole said, his voice husky with reverence. "Imagine how many gallons of sweat these men represent."

Two would fail to show. Gunder Hägg, the Swede who three times set the mile record (4:06.2, 4:04.6, 4:01.4) during World War II, had not come because he was 75 years old and too wearied by life for the journey. Steve Ovett, the Brit who set mile records in 1980 and '81 and now lodges guests in a renovated mansion in Annan, Scotland, had not come either, officially because he was on holiday but mostly, several who knew him said, because he is Steve Ovett. "Pathetic," growled one of the record holders. "He cheated us all," seethed another.

Slowly the bus began to fill: Michel Jazy, the 57-year-old Frenchman who held the record from mid-1965 to mid-'66, now retired from promotional work with Perrier and Adidas but still the boulevardier in his snazzy mustard-yellow sport coat. Arne Andersson, the 76-year-old retired Swedish schoolteacher who broke the record three times during World War II, in a red, yellow and blue Reebok pullover. Bayi, the 40-year-old Tanzanian, in the blue-and-gold native robe that his wife had crafted, clutching his one-year-old. Ryun, the 47-year-old Kansan, in a preppy plaid sweater vest, his children and wife in tow. Walker, the 42-year-old New Zealander, in sneakers, jeans and a sweatshirt. Morceli, the 24-year-old Algerian, in a mod green-and-purple hooded jumpsuit. Cram, Elliott, Ibbotson, Landy, Snell. . . . Slowly, too slowly, they boarded, now a half hour past their scheduled departure time. "My God," remarked Elliott, "for world-record holders in the mile, they sure are bloody late."

BANNISTER: Each runner worries the others. The anxiety of being pressed and jostled increases; soon it will become too much for someone, and he will make an effort to break away from the field. It is this controlled tension about to break down that gives miling its great excitement. It seems to present a perfect test of judgment, speed and stamina.

LANDY: Almost every part of the mile is tactically important—you can never let down, never stop thinking, and you can be beaten at almost any point. I suppose you could say it is like life.

COE: Blink and you miss a sprint. The 10,000 meters is lap after lap of waiting. Theatrically, the mile is just the right length—beginning, middle, end, a story unfolding.

WALKER: The 800-meter record, the records in the 1,000, the 1,500, the 5,000, the relays—no one remembers them. The mile, they remember. Only the mile.

Finally the bus headed down Park Lane, into the suburbs and then the deep green-and-gold country meadows between London and Oxford, the rain clouds unable to shadow the radiance within the bus's windows or without. "Jesus!" Tony Ward, the British Athletic Federation official who had organized this gathering, yelped every now and then. "What a collection!" He just couldn't help it.

Mutual respect rolled up and down the aisle like marbles, ricocheted over seat backs, pinged off wives, as the bus chugged down the motorway. But even among these men there was a hierarchy of awe. Elliott, having never lost a mile or a 1,500-meter race, having demolished the world record by the largest margin ever, 2.7 seconds, and having chucked it all at 22, had earned a special rung—what more, they all wondered, might he have achieved? "A being," Jazy called him, "from another world." Ryun, having chewed 2.3 seconds off the world record on a cinder track as a skinny 19-year-old—this still made them all shake their heads. Had his training, which included clusters of 20 60-second quarter-miles with almost no time for recovery, not been so "suicidal," several milers agreed, Ryun might well have gone down as the most prodigious miler of all. Snell's blowtorch finishing kick was still held in awe, as was Walker's longevity (129 sub-four-minute miles over nearly 20 years) in an event that left Bannister bathed in sweat on the night before each race and Elliott "incredibly, uncomfortably, powerfully, sickeningly nervous" even as he warmed up. Then, too, there was Morceli's 3:44.39 ravaging of the record last year at age 23, entering a realm, without a rival to push him, that even these men found almost incomprehensible.

Walker, whose career straddled track's amateur and professional eras, had to know more about Morceli. "A V-8 engine on a VW frame," he marveled. "He'll destroy so many hearts, they'll all wish they weren't born in his era. What a tough bastard." Bleary-eyed from the long flight from Auckland, Walker leaned over a seat back in the rear of the bus, trying to learn what had incubated the Algerian. Walker harbored a theory that great milers were born not on tracks but on cross-country trails, amassing heart by slogging through mud, bounding over tree roots—and yes, Morceli confirmed, that was where he, too, had begun. "What do you think of the 2,000?" Morceli wished to know, since Walker once owned that record. "I am thinking of going for that record next." The 2,000 was the son of a bitch of all races, Walker confided, the most grueling on the body.

Sir Roger Bannister, the neurologist who lives part-time in Oxford, would soon be collected and seated in the front of the bus,

John Landy behind him—just as they would sit forever in track history. It was not difficult, even across the expanse of 40 years, even amid the damp fragrance of the English countryside, to catch the scent of an old anguish, baked slowly to resignation. Landy, the Australian, pounding out 15- and 20-mile workouts in pursuit of the record while Bannister, the ultimate amateur, whisked off his white medical student's smock, dashed from St. Mary's Hospital in London to the tube to squeeze in 30-minute sessions at lunch. Landy, the front-runner with the lovely economy of stride of an "Inca courier," as a writer of the time described it, hurling himself again and again at Hägg's record of 4:01.4 and at the magical number that lay just beyond it, unfurling six races of 4:03 or less between December 1952 and March '54 and once groaning, "It's a brick wall. I shall not attempt it again." Landy bursting through the wall with a world-record 3:58 mile on June 21, 1954 . . . 46 days *after* Bannister had smashed the four-minute barrier with his May surprise, a preemptive strike on history a full month before the summer track season was rolling. Landy finally racing Bannister to settle the question two months later in the Mile of the Century at the British Empire & Commonwealth Games in Vancouver, leading Bannister as they swept into the final bend only to see the tall, stoop-shouldered Englishman unbottle yet one more of those delirious finishes that left him all but collapsed.

"I keep rerunning that Vancouver race," said the 64-year-old Landy, "on the theory that if I rerun it a thousand times, the results will at least once be reversed . . . but it hasn't happened yet. I've asked myself many times if I should've laid back that day, not set the pace, but I knew that would make for a slow mile and be unsatisfactory to everyone, and I didn't like the feeling of running behind someone. The trouble is, you make yourself a tangible target when you front-run, and you give yourself no tangible target. We were all the kind of men who set targets and chased them down."

Having run a faster mile than any previous human, Landy mused as the bus rolled on, had helped to transform him from a bashful loner into a man unafraid to try almost anything in life. He taught science. He helped run a cattle and sheep ranch. He

worked on conservation of national parks. He became manager of
the agricultural research department of the biggest chemical company in Australia, chairman of the Wool Research Corporation,
technical director of Melbourne's bid for the 1996 Olympics. He
wrote two books on natural history, one a best-seller, and now acts
as a consultant to Australia's dairy industry and serves on com-
mittees for a hospital charity and the prestigious Melbourne Cricket
Club. "The hardest thing to know, once you've taken something
to the limits, as we did, is when to give something up, when to stop
pushing further," Landy said. "I've tried to put a three-year limit
on each of my projects. I've had a rich life."

On his lap was a sheaf of crisp photocopies, reproductions of
pictures of all the world-record holders blazing around tracks in
their primes. Landy straightened the stack a half-dozen times,
glanced at the men around him speaking French, Swahili, Swedish and English and wondered if he dared to . . . and how it would
be received if he. . . .

"Michel . . . could you be so kind as to autograph these?"
Landy asked. "It's not for me, of course. It's to auction them off
for charity, for medical research. . . . Good on ya. . . . All for charity
. . . wonderful . . . perfect."

ELLIOTT: Why did I run? I ran at first to remorselessly beat
everyone I possibly could.

RYUN: I ran to get a letter jacket, a girlfriend. I ran because I
was cut from the basketball and baseball teams. I ran to be accepted, to be part of a group.

JAZY: I ran so I would not have to fight the war in Algeria.

SNELL: I ran for recognition.

COE: I ran because I was meant to run.

LANDY: I loved to run because, in running, one's effort could
be pinned down and quantified precisely.

IBBOTSON: I ran to prove to my father that I was better than
my brother.

ELLIOTT: I ran later to prove that my spirit was the master of
my body.

MORCELI: I run to be known as the greatest runner, the greatest of all time. I could not eat or sleep for a week after I lost in the [1992] Olympics. I have to win or die.

The bus pulled up to the Iffley Road track, where a battery of cameras four-dozen strong awaited the milers. Bannister's eyes rose to the white flag with the red cross, hoisted up the pole atop St. John the Evangelist Church just for this occasion—the same flag he studied 40 years ago to decide if the wind was telling him *no*. The starting pistol that commenced that race was laid in his hand, and the woman who fed him lunch that afternoon now stood at his side: Oh, do the Brits know how to do history. This was a celebration of the mile, not of himself, Bannister kept reminding everyone, but so much of the mile's magical dust was kicked up by Sir Roger's spikes on that long-ago day that it is no longer possible to sift one from the other.

The cinder track was gone, replaced in 1976 by a synthetic surface. Bannister, limping slightly from the car accident 19 years ago that damaged an ankle and ended his weekend jogging, walked with Morceli across the last 40 feet before the finish line, and the Algerian, perhaps emboldened by the rare air he was drawing in, confided to reporters that he planned to make attempts at records this year in the 800, 1,000, 1,500 and 5,000 meters as well as the mile and two miles. "You have to attempt this when you are young enough," he said softly, "and not let the chance go by."

It was Morceli, always with the shy grin, the bowed head—always showing a deference that few any longer expect from the young—whose presence most gratified his elders. But as sweet as Morceli was, Sir Roger couldn't help himself. His crusading cry as a runner had been that the athlete was just a sliver of the whole man, and the first chance he had, as he and Morceli had posed side by side for photographs the day before, the doctor asked the professional runner, "Do you have any plans for after you retire? What will you do when you are thirty-five?"

"I don't know," said Morceli, all smiles and shrugs. "I have no plans."

"Will you be involved in some kind of coaching?"

"Probably, yes," said Morceli, grateful for the help. "Some kind of coaching."

In the press box above the Iffley Road track, someone asked Cram—the 32-year-old who lowered the record to 3:46.32 in 1985 and recently launched his comeback from a chronic calf injury— what he and the other record holders shared. Cram thought before he spoke, for this forum was no place for pikers. At the previous day's press conference, playing toss-and-catch with the question of how much faster a human being might run a mile, the neurologist Bannister discussed the "genetic variants" that athletes from China and India would bring to the chase, the physiologist Snell discoursed on the body's "ability to transfer oxygen across lung membrane," the Puma Australia managing director Elliott noted that the "interface between the mind and the spirit and the body" was a facet of human potential so little tapped that astonishing improvements might yet be made, and the *International Herald Tribune* writer Ian Thomsen concluded that there was more intelligence in that one group than in all of the football locker rooms in America.

"Lineage," Cram finally said. "The men here today are part of a unique lineage." A lineage cleaner, perhaps, than any other devised by mankind, neater certainly than that of kings, who were continually muddying things by fathering imbeciles or bedding with the barren, or that of heavyweights, who in the twilights of their careers were prone to pass their crowns to bums. There were no split decisions to be argued or myopic judging to be rued. Switzerland's finest watches kept score, and no man could claim the throne until he had surpassed the performance of his predecessor *on his predecessor's best day.*

Next stop for the pilgrims was Vincents Club, the fabled enclave where Oxford athletes have drunk and debated for more than a hundred years, where former Australian prime minister Robert Hawke set the world record for downing a yard of ale, in 16 seconds, where Sir Roger himself was president during his college days and where some of the nicks in the photograph-covered walls are attributed to the celebration of his record mile. Bannister, his eloquence ever ready to combust, delivered a speech. A room jammed with old and new Oxford sportsmen toasted him with champagne and applause, and the Tanzanian army captain, Bayi, juggling his one-year-old and his glass, watched with wonder and a little sadness. "Other countries honor their history so much more than mine does," he said. "In Tanzania I am no one. Maybe one day people will understand. That will be maybe when I die."

In a private dining room awaiting the milers at the nearby Randolph Hotel, the commemorative menus lying upon the tables caught John Walker's eye. Plucking one, the New Zealand rancher began moving quietly from table to table, asking each of the record holders to grace the menu with his signature. Even with his three-inch pinch of midsection, Walker still radiated the air of a rugby player over a pint of black and tan. Of all the milers he still seemed the readiest to go out on the sidewalk and outrun anyone who dared to try him. If Walker was saying, "Sorry, Roger, but can I bother you for an autograph? . . . Sorry, Herb, but . . . ," then who, in this most exclusive of clubs, could feign to be above it?

And so the free-for-all began in earnest, the greats bustling from table to table to collect each other's scribble before the potatoes and vegetables were ladled, Sir Roger begging to bother Morceli, Morceli begging to bother Elliott, and on and on and on.

"John," said Bayi, blinking at Walker, "we've never done this before."

"This is a once-in-a-lifetime event, Filbert," said John.

"Yes," said Filbert. "Once in a lifetime." And he peered down at his pageful of scrawl, racking his brain to figure out whom he had missed.

Lunch concluded, the milers splintered for an hour. Walker, Cram, Landy and Andersson took a guided tour of a few Oxford colleges; the Ryun family went to explore the old haunts of the famous Christian writer C. S. Lewis; and Elliott wandered through the bookstores in search of *Siddhartha*, the Hermann Hesse novel of a man's spiritual journey. At 56, Elliott was circling back, ready to complete the quest he had begun as a runner.

When Elliott was 18, sitting in the stands during the 1956 Melbourne Olympics, his hunger to run had been ignited by the spectacle that unfolded in the 10,000 meters. Vladimir Kuts, a

Soviet runner who had tossed incendiary bombs at German tanks during the defense of Stalingrad, kept surging away from England's Gordon Pirie, then slowing enough to engage Pirie's monstrous fighting instincts, then surging away again. "It was like watching a cat play with a half-dead mouse," recalled Elliott. "Kuts utterly steamrollered Pirie. It appealed to the basic, animal part of me, the part that wanted to grind people to dust. That's what I ran for at first. But then I realized the battle wasn't against others. It was against myself. It was in defeating my own weaknesses, in demonstrating that my spirit could master my body. It's why billions of people watch people run in circles or kick a bag of leather, isn't it? It's for those moments when we realize we're not just watching bodies, when human spirit is revealed."

Kindled by Kuts, Elliott drove to Portsea, Australia, to engage the counsel of a white-haired fanatic named Percy Cerutty, who ranted of Gandhi, Christ and Tennyson, who raised drudgery to philosophy and turned a footrace into a test not of strategy or athletic skill but of human character. He had Elliott racing up and down an 80-foot sand dune, hoisting barbells made from rusting railroad track, reading H. G. Wells's 1,200-page *Outline of History* in his camp bunkhouse at night. "He challenged my totality," said Elliott. "I came to realize that spirit, as much as or more than physical conditioning, had to be stored up before a race. I would avoid running on tracks because tracks were spiritually depleting. I never studied my opponents—they were an irrelevancy to me. Poetry, music, forests, ocean, solitude—they were what developed enormous spiritual strength. How do the modern professional runners today find that spirituality and simplicity, when most everything they do would seem to deplete it? I'd like to talk to Morceli about that this week.

"Once I had satisfied myself in that question—that my spirit *could* dominate my body—there was no great reason to continue. People still ask me if I made a mistake in quitting so young, but they have it all wrong. To keep having to do more, to keep being dissatisfied, what kind of man would that be? He might be called a brute."

He retired, graduated from Cambridge, grew apart from Cerutty—what role could such a Svengali play in the life of a man trying to raise six children, to climb the ladder in marketing with the Shell chemical company and then in the management of Puma in Australia? "Service to your job, your family, that's all part of human experience," Elliott said, "but my life was a spiritual desert until a couple of years ago." This time it was a Catholic priest who reawakened him, with tales of life in an ashram in India, and Elliott quickly sensed that his old quest had been abandoned in its infancy, that the ultimate aim of spirituality is not so much to dominate the body as to learn to let it go. So he traveled to an ashram in India last year. Now every morning at 5:30, he awakens and reads passages from the Upanishads or the Bhagavadgita, ancient Hindu treatises on the struggle for purity and wisdom, and he meditates and tries to let all the motion and memos and meetings melt away.

Just two miles from Cerutty's old oceanside camp, Elliott bought a house on the beach, and each time he walks or jogs past the cemetery where the old prophet lies at rest, he stops and acknowledges what the old man did for his life. "We've grown back together," Elliott said. "I suspect I know what I'll do with my retirement. It won't be a rest. It'll be an adventure. The object would be to totally remove yourself from body and mind, from ego. To think I could ever do that would require total arrogance, but to do it would take total humility. Yes, kind of like. . . ."

BANNISTER: I have always said that man will run the mile in 3:30—given the human body constituted as it is, with perfect training and perfect facilities, the world remaining relatively peaceful and without too many wars, famines and disasters.

SNELL: I think I've seen the fastest miler ever. I think Morceli is the guy.

MORCELI: I think I can take another two or three seconds off of it.

COE: If you start thinking there's a limit, there is one. It's almost self-defeating. It's going to keep tumbling down.

CRAM: It won't come from training harder. It won't come from science or new techniques or new surfaces. We've exhausted those possibilities. But every ten or twenty years, the freak human being will come along. That's what will keep lowering the record.

ELLIOTT: I think I'm the only dreamer. Human beings have a huge reservoir of strength we've never tapped—we've only just begun to play around its edges. I think there's a quantum leap there to be made. We still overprotect ourselves. It would be very unintelligent to run yourself to death . . . but I'm sure we can go a lot closer to it.

"I feel silly," said Morceli. "I feel crazy." The autograph frenzy at the Randolph Hotel had achieved several things. Now all of the record holders knew one another. Now all of them had felt silly and crazy in front of each other. There was not so much to protect. They had all stepped into each other's shade.

The chatter grew louder, the quips began to fly. "Poor Morceli!" yipped Ibbotson. "He's got withdrawal symptoms—he hasn't run in two hours!"

"I'm taken aback," said Snell. "Whenever I saw Herb Elliott before, all I ever thought of was raw aggression, this ruthless killer instinct. He's so jovial now. He's actually quite *gregarious!*"

In Snell's hands, as the bus ferried the milers back to London, was a book with yellow pages and a cover about to disintegrate. It was a 17th-birthday gift from his parents, the first athletic book he ever received: Roger Bannister's autobiography, *The Four Minute Mile*. Now its opening page was covered with signatures.

The musty pages smelled of memories, of an old and quiet desperation for success, of a shy, likable, big-eared, toothy-grinned boy crushed by his father's disappointment in him. The book had been given to him in the midst of two straight years in which he had failed in boarding school, smashing the teenager's chances of entering New Zealand's rigid university system, destroying his father's plan that Peter, just like Peter's dad and older brother, would become an engineer. Running became Peter's salvation. He took the 800-meter gold medal as a long shot at the Rome Olympics in 1960, eclipsed Elliott's mile record on a grass track in New Zealand in '62 and won both the 1,500- and 800-meter gold medals at the Tokyo Games in '64.

Snell had planned to run just one more year after that, to use running as a vehicle to see the world. But as psychological fuel, travel ranked nowhere near in octane to his old petrol, the need for self-esteem. At age 26 he lost nine consecutive races in less than two months and quit, but there was one reward. He found his calling that summer, becoming fascinated by the gadgets and line of inquiry of San Diego State exercise physiologists whom he permitted to run tests on him. It took years, but he slowly screwed up the courage to junk his job in promotions for a cigarette company, sell his house, leave New Zealand and stake every cent he owned on three years of study at the University of California, Davis ("I could fail quietly there," he explained), and then four more, thanks to prize money he won in Superstars competitions in the 1970s, at Washington State. His father—who suffered a stroke during Peter's last year in high school, became mute and died in '62—would never live to see his son's academic redemption. Today Snell, 55, is an assistant professor doing research in exercise physiology at the University of Texas Southwestern Medical Center in Dallas.

"There was such pressure on an athlete then to be a complete man," Snell said. "'When are you going to do something of substance?'—I got a lot of that. Now everything's changed. It's quite respectable to be just a runner. But yes, the world record did liberate me in a way. My thrust is enjoying my work now, not publishing papers or collecting more diplomas, as many of my peers do. If I hadn't proven in running that I was the best in the world, I'd be chasing that forever in academics."

A few feet away, tiny Cuthbert Bayi was emitting ear-curdling shrieks, and Walker was peering again at the odd autograph he had received from Ryun. Above his name Ryun had written "Go with God" and beneath it "John" and the numbers "3:3–8." Other runners had written their world-record-mile times beneath their names, but Ryun's figure was too fast for any 20th-century mile; could it be, Walker wondered, Ryun's best time in the 1,500? No, it was a passage from the Gospel according to John in which Jesus declares, "Except a man be born again, he cannot see the kingdom of God."

Several seats away sat Ryun, his old haunted look gone. He was locked in conversation with Cram, taking up the Englishman's offer to host Ryun's family at his home in a week or two, agreeing how fortunate Cram was to have had countrymen Coe and Ovett drawing everyone's eyes during his years of ripening and how unlucky Ryun was to have assumed the yoke of America's hopes as a teen. Ryun is a little thicker now and wears hearing aids in both ears to correct a 50 percent hearing loss he suffered as a child, but the light in his eyes makes him more handsome than ever. His job, which takes him to schools for the hearing-impaired across the U.S. as a representative of a hearing-aid firm named Resound, allows him to appear in road races all over the country and also to tell the tale of his religious conversion before Christian groups.

Having twice set world records by age 20, Ryun had seen his life swirl ever downward after he lost the 1,500 to Kip Keino in the high-altitude 1968 Olympics in Mexico City. He quit in the middle of several races, was savaged by the U.S. press, stopped running altogether and finally regathered himself for atonement at the '72 Munich Games. His times, as he prepared, remained erratic, the yoke yet too heavy, the joy still not there.

"I'll never forget that day after he ran a 4:19 mile and finished last in Los Angeles in the spring of '72," said his wife, Anne. "He walked out of the stadium, slammed his spikes against a tree and started screaming. I'd never seen such rage in Jim."

Brought up by a strict father in a fundamentalist Christian church, forbidden to attend dances or movies, Ryun had grown into a young man so bound by duty to meet others' expectations that each sigh of disappointment from the world after each race in which he failed to rebreak the world record had crushed him. "And then," he said, "in May of 1972, I accepted Jesus Christ as my savior, and for the first time in my life I had the feeling that God loved me because of *me*, not because of my accomplishments. I felt elated. At the Olympic trials I felt so light that I threw up my arms ten yards before the finish and had to throw them up again! Then I went to Toronto, and on a track that was like asphalt, with the closest runner eighteen seconds behind me, I ran a 3:52 mile—the third-fastest mile ever. A new dimension inside of me was being tapped. For the first time I was relaxed. Everything was right. And then, in the prelim in Munich, I was tripped, and the official [on the appeals committee] who could've reinstated me for the final refused to, and that was it. I had to retire from amateur running then to work and raise my family."

Ryun needed years to overcome his bitterness, to forgive the official. He knew that he had done so only when the man's image flashed up on the big screen as Ryun sat in the stands during the 1984 Olympics and he felt . . . nothing. "I was released," he said.

"Now he runs to spread the word of Christ," said Anne. "He has found a peace that he never felt when he was breaking world records."

ELLIOTT: When I wanted to quit in training, I used to visualize a competitor on my shoulder. And I'd think, I'd rather die than let this person beat me.

IBBOTSON: I used to picture a tall shandy. That's beer and lemonade, in case you don't know.

SNELL: I used to picture handicapped people, people with crutches and wheelchairs, and ask myself, What right do you have to complain about this pain?

JAZY: I would picture Gordon Pirie after Vladimir Kuts had destroyed him in the 10,000 meters of the 1956 Olympics and tell myself to keep going so that would never happen to me.

BAYI: I'd keep saying to myself, Break the wall. . . . There is no wall. . . . The wall is in your mind.

WALKER: A little ways before the turnoff to the road I lived on, there was a sign that said 1500 METERS. It was a three-lane highway, and each time I drove it, I'd pull into the middle lane with about 800 meters left and start passing everyone. Then with 400 to go, I'd pull to the outside lane and beat the crap out of my car. That's the image I kept using. Me pulling out in that car and then flying past everyone.

"Milers!"

"Just a minute! Got to sign all these for Derek," chirped Cram, scribbling madly.

"And vice versa!" panted Ibbotson, signing a batch for Cram. "Where's Snell? Oh, if I could only get Stevie to sign . . . I mean Peter."

"Milers, *please!*"

"Filbert, sign these."

"Herb, could you. . . ."

"That's it. Good on ya, mate."

"All for charity!"

"*Milers!*" wailed the organizer of the affair, Tony Ward. In just over an hour, 730 people in formal attire would begin entering the Great Room at the Grosvenor House for the gala dinner, and Ward needed to brief the record holders on the evening's schedule of events. But now the autograph-seeking had become a raging fever. Now all the milers had stacks of the commemorative dinner programs to exchange and sign.

Ibbotson had spent the previous evening with a straight-edge and 12 pieces of paper, etching 14 rectangles on each page, with each record holder's name and time inside a rectangle to be autographed. "One complete set for each of my children, my grandchildren, my mother-in-law, father-in-law. . . ."

Ward threw up his arms. "My God," he said, "they're like schoolchildren!"

Coe, finally freed from his duties as a second-year member of the British Parliament, had joined the group—nobody had his signature yet! With the look of a startled deer, he sagged into a chair as his brothers in the club fell upon him, and then he caught the infection too. Sydney Wooderson of England, the world's oldest living mile-record holder (4:06.4 in 1937), three months shy of 80, walked ever so slowly into the room, bringing the milers' ranks to 14. "I just can't believe how old I am," Wooderson said, shaking his head. "I just can't believe it." Elliott and Ryun went off to a quiet corner to discuss God.

Finally, after the clan had posed for the official photograph and laid plans for regathering later in the night to cross-sign personal copies of the photo as well, they plunged into the cocktail-sipping crowd. John Walker sighed. "Just watch what's going to happen," he said. "Seven hundred and thirty sons of bitches trying to get our autographs."

Yes, it was that, but mostly it was 730 people laughing, cheering, *glowing.* The big screen showed old footage of the milers breaking and rebreaking the record, one after the other, somehow building in the Great Room a cumulative power, a feeling that there was nothing not possible for humanity as long as it kept producing individuals like the 14 being honored. "Everywhere I looked all night," said Coe, "all I saw were people wearing broad grins. It was like a huge family coming together. It was the greatest sports gathering I have ever been to."

Everyone hushed when it was Bannister's turn to speak. "Old men, they say, forget," said Sir Roger. "It's true we forget the pain and the fatigue and lashing yourself to try harder next time and next, illness and injury, real and perhaps sometimes imagined, the castigations of the press and coaches—all these fade away, because memory is kind. We remember the good times, the sun on our backs, running through the beauty of the countryside, running thousands and thousands of miles. We remember laughter and friends. For us, no matter what life may bring, whatever subsequent shadows there may be, no one can strip us of these memories."

In chronological order of their achievements, each to a standing ovation, the record holders walked to the stage and shook the hands of those who had preceded them, who had pushed them to discover something wondrous in themselves. Fourteen men who had split off from the road, gone off on solitary missions, now part of a team.

"Total kinship," said Elliott. "That's what I felt up there."

"The greatest night of my life," said Morceli.

"These men could show today's athletes where sports fit into a round life," said Cram.

"The bond among us," summed up Coe, "is that which Lady Macbeth describes as a sickness: ambition, the pursuit of excellence. But you had this feeling that these were men very much at peace with themselves. That each of us realized that what we had done was neither greater nor lesser than what had come before us or after us, that we were all part of a human progression."

They rose together for one last ovation beneath the lights, in the brilliance of the shade.

Crime and Punishment

I

Here is a man. Barely a man; he just ran out of adolescence. He stands alone, 2,000 miles from home, beside a swimming pool, in a stucco-walled apartment complex, in a city built on an American desert.

Seton Hall chancellor Thomas R. Peterson buckled under to intense pressure from media and alumni yesterday when he denied admission to star basketball recruit and admitted sex felon Richie Parker.

NEW YORK POST
Jan. 24, 1995

It's too hot to run. But he must run. He strips to his trunks. He steps into the pool. His body leans forward.

The University of Utah ceased its recruiting of former Manhattan Center basketball star Richie Parker in light of a barrage

---

This story first appeared in 1996.

234

of media criticism and pressure from the university president regarding Parker's sexual abuse conviction.

NEW YORK NEWSDAY
May 6, 1995

His hands ball up. His elbow draws back, pushing against the water. Slowly his foot begins to rise from the floor of the pool.

George Washington University officials informed high school basketball star Richie Parker yesterday they "regrettably" would stop recruiting him and blamed "unbalanced publicity" for a wave of criticism that hit the school for pursuing the youth, who had pleaded guilty to a sexual assault.

THE WASHINGTON POST
June 30, 1995

His foot gradually descends to the bottom of the pool. His other foot begins to push off. His shoulders tighten. The water pushes back.

Richie Parker will never wear a UTEP basketball uniform. UTEP has bowed out of its recruitment of the controversial basketball player, athletic director John Thompson announced Friday.

EL PASO HERALD-POST
Feb. 24, 1996

His knee slowly lifts again. His arms silently pump. He's trying to run laps through water.

USC on Wednesday terminated its recruitment of former New York City All-American point guard Richie Parker, a convicted sex offender. The decision came after . . . two days of sometimes heated exchanges among athletic department personnel.

ORANGE COUNTY REGISTER
March 28, 1996

He climbs out finally and pants for air, in the desert that once was the bottom of an ocean.

II

Here is a periodic table. It's the one you would see near the blackboard in any high school chemistry class, a listing of the 109 elements according to atomic number. Why is it being inflicted on you here? *Patience.* Remember, this is a story about higher education.

Near the lower left-hand corner of the chart is an element named cesium. Among its own—the metals surrounding it in the chart, such as sodium and potassium—cesium is a quiet, unassuming element. But because it has just one electron on its outer shell, one electron aching to leap to any atom that is lacking a full outer shell of electrons, cesium is a bomb in a suitcase when it leaves its neighborhood. On contact with oxygen, cesium will cause an explosion. Introduce it to chlorine, fluorine, iodine or bromine—and look out! Almost everywhere it goes, trying to rid itself of the baggage of that one electron, another eruption occurs, and only those who understand what cannot be seen can make any sense of it at all.

III

Here is an assistant principal. She works at Manhattan Center, the East Harlem high school Richie Parker once attended. Teenagers deposit their leather jackets in Ellen Scheinbach's closet in the morning for safekeeping, come to her at lunchtime for oatmeal cookies and advice. The phone's constantly ringing, teachers are always poking in their heads. "A lunatic asylum!" she calls her office, ambling about with her spectacles dangling from a neck chain. But now there's silence, and it's Richie's mother, Rosita, shuffling on her bad knees, clutching her envelope of articles clipped from the *New York Post* and the *Daily News*, extending them toward the assistant principal and asking her to explain.

Ellen Scheinbach is an authority figure, one of the few Rosita knows. Surely she can explain how *all this* could result from the one day in this building, in January 1994, when Rosita's 6' 5" son, a junior then—a well-liked boy known for his silence, his gentle nature and his skill on a basketball court—was walking through these halls, having gone to the nurse's office with a sprained ankle and having found the nurse not there, was returning to class when he paused . . . and turned. And headed toward the bottom of a stairwell in the back of the school, where he and a schoolmate, Leslie Francis, soon compelled a 16-year-old freshman girl to perform oral sex on them. And how 15 minutes later, the girl came running up the stairwell, sobbing, and soon thereafter Richie and the other boy were being led away in handcuffs. And how from that moment on, virtually everywhere Richie would turn to rid himself of the baggage of those 15 minutes, another explosion would occur. How careers would be smashed, men fired, dreams destroyed. How some relationships would splinter and others almost spontaneously be fused. How secrets would burst from hidden places, and rage and fear would tremble in the air behind her lean, quiet son. The assistant principal can explain all this to Rosita, can't she?

Ellen throws up her arms. The incongruity of it all still confounds her. Richie Parker? Richie didn't drink. Richie didn't curse. Richie didn't get into arguments or fights; he had never even gotten detention. She knew lots of kids who would play peekaboo with a toddler in the bleachers for a few minutes, but Richie was the only one she knew who would do it for an hour. The only time she had ever seen him exert his will—to *force* any issue—was on a basketball court, and even there he did it so softly, so smoothly, that she would be startled to learn at the end of a game that he had scored 35 points. He would be rated one of America's top 50 high school seniors in 1995, a notch or two below Georgia Tech signee Stephon Marbury in New York's schoolboy hierarchy.

Two investigations—one conducted by a George Washington University lawyer and another by the lawyer of the stairwell victim, not to mention the searchlight sweep of Richie's life by the media—failed to turn up a single thread that would indicate that

those 15 minutes in the stairwell were part of a larger pattern.
Richie himself had insisted on his innocence at first, but he eventually pleaded guilty when the charges were lowered from first-
degree sodomy to first-degree sexual abuse in January 1995. His
sentence was five years of probation. So now Rosita's standing on
the other side of Ellen's desk, holding a half-dozen full-back-page
pictures of her son under screaming SEX FELON headlines, asking
her what the world has come to that one rotten act by a 17-year-
old could take on such monstrous proportions and why Seton Hall
has just reneged on its promise of a scholarship for Richie as long
as he didn't get a prison sentence . . . and it's only the beginning,
because now the great American morality play is ready to hit the
road, with actors and actresses all across the land raring to perform their roles, eager to savage or salvage the teenager from 110th
Street in Manhattan—often knowing nothing more of him than his
name. Ellen keeps shaking her head and blinking. Sports, having
somehow become the medium through which Americans derive
their strongest sense of community, has become the stage where
all the great moral issues have to be played out, often rough and
ugly, right alongside the games.

Ellen had tried to protect Richie from that. She had tried to
smuggle him out when the media surrounded her school. She sat
beside him at games when he could no longer play, to shield him
from the media's popping cameras and questions. She went to
Seton Hall and told administrators that she would trust Richie with
her daughter, if she had one. But it was hopeless. In the same way
that cesium needs to rid itself of that one dangling electron on its
outer shell, Richie needed to take his sin to a university, to one of
America's last "pure" places, and have it absolved so he could find
his way to the promised land, the NBA. In the same way that fluorine longs for that extra electron to complete itself, the universities and their coaches were drawn to the basketball player who
could enhance their profile, increase their alumni contributions and
TV revenues. And the mutual attraction would keep causing ex-
plosions, hurling Richie and yet another university far apart, and
Rosita would keep returning to Ellen, her eyes filling with tears.
Hasn't her son, she would ask, done everything demanded of him?

Yes, Rosita, yes, he fulfilled the requirements of the criminal justice system and of the out-of-court settlement of the victim's civil lawsuit. He had met monthly with his probation officer, met regularly with a counselor, made both a private and a public apology to the victim, an acknowledgment that regardless of the details of the incident, he had done something profoundly wrong in that stairwell. He had promised to speak out against sexual abuse and to make financial restitution to the victim with a percentage of any money he might generate one day in the NBA. He had earned A's and B's at Manhattan Outreach Center, the school he was sent to in the wake of the court ruling, met NCAA qualifications on his fourth try with an SAT score of 830 and, when all the major universities began shutting the door on him, enrolled at Mesa (Arizona) Community College, which refused to let him play ball but allowed him to be a student. And, yes, both the victim and her lawyer had requested that the country's media and universities let him move on. "He's rare among people who've committed a sexual offense," says Michael Feldman of Jacoby & Meyers, the victim's attorney. "He admitted that he did something wrong and committed to help the victim. How does it assist women to refuse him an opportunity now?"

"We believe Richie is truly sorry," the girl's father had told the *Daily News*. "We're religious people who believe in redemption. We don't believe in third chances. We do believe in second chances."

So how can Ellen explain to the 49-year-old woman with the envelope full of news clippings that the second chance, the fresh start, the comeback, the stuff of magazine covers and made-for-television movies, the mother's milk that immigrant America was nursed on and cannot—to its everlasting credit and eternal confusion—seem to wean itself from, has been denied to her son?

"What can I do?" Ellen cries. "I can't get the reporter from the *New York Post* fired. I can't speak to women's groups who are saying he shouldn't have the right to go to college and play basketball. What *is* a women's group, anyway? I know plenty of women, but what's a women's group? I can't call [Georgetown coach] John Thompson and tell him to give Richie a chance—you think he's going to listen to some little old Jewish lady? So I'm just left with this horrible frustration. It's like trying to comfort the survivor of a plane wreck when Rosita comes here. There's nothing I can do.

"He was seventeen when this happened. For fifteen minutes of rotten judgment, he's been crucified! These women's groups are talking about O. J. Simpson and Mike Tyson, and they're using Richie's name. When teachers here heard what he was accused of, they said, 'Are you kidding?' This is a kid who always tried to fade into the background, who wouldn't push back if you pushed him. Even when he wanted something, he'd just stand there and wait till you *asked* what he wanted. Look, I don't know what happened in that stairwell, but if he did it, he must've had a brain lesion. This kid is not a threat.

"If he were white, would this story have been written this way? But no, he fit the perfect stereotype. He has no money, and he's a black male teenager, so they could have a field day. What do people want—for him to fail, so he's out on a street corner? Are they saying you can never redeem yourself? If he wanted to be a doctor instead of a basketball player, would they say, 'You can't take biochemistry class'? Basketball is his talent, and while he's on probation he's entitled to play that the same way he'd be entitled to be a musician or an artist. Everyone thinks the NCAA is so macho. I've never seen so many wimpy men in my life."

Once, just once in the two and a half years of watching everything around Richie go to pieces, has Ellen feared that he might go to pieces too. She had never seen him cry, never heard him blame anyone else, never sensed a chip on his shoulder. But when it was clear that the Board of Education was about to suspend him from Manhattan Center in the middle of his senior season and that the media swirl was sucking down his teammates too, he came to her office with his mother and read his letter of resignation from the team. When he finished, he finally broke down and clutched his mother. "If not for you," he sobbed to her, "I don't think I could make it."

In the end, Ellen decides, perhaps there isn't much she can do to help Rosita, but there's something Rosita has done to help her. "I've learned a lot from her," says Ellen. "I've learned that no matter how frustrated and upset you get, you just keep turning to your kid and saying, 'I love you, and no matter what happens, there's one place for you that's safe.' When my son has a problem now I just try to hug him and say, 'Whatever decision you make I'll stand by you.' Because *it works.* I've seen it work. It saved Richie Parker."

IV

Here is a copy editor on the sports desk of a major city newspaper. She's smart, and she's funny, and if an office push-up contest or footrace suddenly breaks out, hopefully after deadline, she's the one you want to put your money on. Of course, because she's a woman, the sensitive stories go to Jill Agostino for editing. Anguish? That's a Jill piece. Morality issue? Absolutely Agostino. Not that it's ever actually stated in a sports department that men are bereft in those areas. It's just sort of understood.

So she gets the Richie Parker stories to polish for *Newsday.* And as she's scanning the words on her computer screen in early 1995, she begins to feel something tightening inside her. It's the old uneasiness, the one she dreads, the one she has no time for here, now, as the clock hands dig toward deadline; the one she might try to run into the ground tomorrow when she's doing her five miles, or scrub away in the quiet of her Long Island apartment, or stow away and convert to fuel someday, something to help flog herself through an extra hour of work when she has to prove her worth to some sexist idiot who dismisses her as a token woman in a man's world, a newspaper sports desk. But not now. Not here. No way.

She begins to sense it here and there between the lines—the implication that Parker is being treated unfairly—and her uneasiness starts to turn to quiet anger. She doesn't sleep much that night, doesn't feel like eating the next day. Another Parker story comes her way a few evenings later, then there's an afternoon drive to work listening to radio talk-show callers chew the issue to death, some of them actually sticking up for the kid, and her quiet anger curdles into a rage that no one knows, no one sees.

The writers like Jill. She's not one of those editors who must tinker with a story to justify their existence. One *Newsday* reporter writes an article that comes right out and says Parker is a good kid who made a mistake and deserves a second chance, and he calls Jill as she's editing it, cheerfully asking her how she likes his piece. There's silence on the phone. And then it erupts from her, something she has never even been able to tell her family.

"I've been raped," says Jill. "I don't agree with you."

"Oh, I didn't . . . Jill, I'm sorry," he says.

She feels like a jerk for making the reporter feel like a jerk, but it's too late now, the anger's out on the table, and it's not finished. *Mistake?* How can anyone call it that? Leaving your headlights on or forgetting your keys, *that's* a mistake—not humiliating a woman the way Jill had been nearly nine years earlier, at age twenty-two, by a man on a boat on Queechy Lake in upstate New York. She goes into her boss's office, seething at a society where a man like Mike Tyson can walk out of jail a few years after raping a woman and be greeted by a thunderous roar and a paycheck worth millions of dollars, and TV commentators can blather on about all that *Tyson* has been through, as if the perpetrator was the victim and the real victim was yesterday's oatmeal. "I want to write a column," she tells her boss. "People need to know what it's like for the victim. I was raped."

His jaw drops. Well . . . uh . . . sure, Jill, but. . . .

She barely sleeps that night. Her husband, Michael, says that if she's sure she wants to do this, he's behind her. She's sure. She sits on the couch the next day with a red pen, a blue pen and a notepad. The red ink is for *her* pain—the italicized sections interspersed in the column that recount that night on the lake where she swam as a little girl: *"I wanted to throw up every time I smelled the mixture of Grand Marnier and tobacco smoke on his breath as he held me down. . . ."* The blue ink is for Richie Parker: "How often do you think Parker will think about this incident once he's on a college basketball court? For the victim, not a day will go by without that memory. . . . Parker's punishment should last until his victim is able to walk alone up the street, or through a parking lot, or down a dimly lit hallway and feel safe. Until the nightmares cease. Until a day goes by and she doesn't think about the horrible things these boys made her do. But it won't."

What are you doing? a voice inside her asks when she has finished writing. To her, this is not an act of courage, as some would take it. To her, this is Jill Agostino publicly admitting her most private pain just on the chance that it will make some men begin to comprehend how it feels to be violated, how it eats into a woman's life forever, how it can make her hold her breath when a stranger steps into an empty elevator with her, make her want to run when a man rolls down his car window and asks her for directions, make her stare into a mirror some days and hate her body because somehow it betrayed her.

She can't surrender to the urge to crumple up the notepad paper, because if she does, the man in the boat wins again, and she can't let him keep winning. He has won too many times, at night when she sits up rigid in bed from nightmares she can never quite recollect—only raw terror and the faint echo of all the world's laughter. He won every time she bought another size 8 blouse for a size 4 body, every time she froze when a colleague she didn't know well threw an arm around her shoulder, every time she couldn't sleep and had to caffeinate and will herself through the next day so that no one, except perhaps her husband, would ever dream that she was anything but the sharp, competitive woman that the world always sees.

Now comes the next agony. She can't let her family find out in a newspaper story. She must call her mother and father and brother and sister and tell them about the rape and why she buried it. She must listen to her mother cry and feel guilty for not protecting her daughter from something she couldn't possibly have protected her from. A few days later the story appears. Seven hundred and fifty thousand readers learn Jill's secret, and countless thousands more—including old boyfriends, old coworkers, old roommates—come across it in the newspapers across the country that run the story. Some of her colleagues are moved to tears by her column. Some confess to her their own buried stories of rape.

The eddies never seem to end. Radio talk shows call her to be a guest and ask her about her rape, and she has to keep reliving

the worst moment of her life. The victim's lawyer calls to compliment her on her story and asks if she would testify in his client's
civil lawsuit against Parker. When that's settled out of court, he
asks if she'd consider doing that in another lawsuit in which the
jury needs to feel the long ripple of a rape, and she says yes, because how can she refuse to help someone who has endured what
she has or allow so many people to keep insinuating that it's the
violated woman who is to blame? *Sports Illustrated* calls a year
later and asks to interview her, and she has to worry how that will
affect the way her colleagues at her new workplace, the *New York
Times*, will look at her, worry that *this* is who she is now to people,
this is *all* she is. Each new episode will mean another week of barely
eating, barely sleeping, a few more nightmares and 10 or 15 extra
miles of running, but she can't back down. She has never met Richie
Parker and no doubt never will, but Jill Agostino is paying for his
crime, oh, yes, she's paying.

V

Here is an assistant coach from the University of Utah. Once Donny
Daniels, too, was a black teenager from a crowded city who lived
to play basketball. And so even though he is a 40-year-old father
of three, including two daughters, on this spring day in 1995, he
is walking into his past when he walks into the Parkers' apartment.
He finds Richie just as quiet and respectful as all his sources vowed.
He sits in the living room with the 108 basketball trophies that
take Rosita hours to dust. He looks into the kitchen where she cooks
pots and pans full of baked chicken, ziti, collard greens, banana
pudding and sweet-potato pies on Sundays and has half the
neighborhood into her house, just like it used to be when she was
growing up in North Carolina. He gazes around the home where
Rosita and Richie's ever-so-quiet father, Richard, and Richie's two
older sisters, Monica and Tanya, who have both attended college,
eat and tease each other and laugh.
    Donny talks to Rosita, who for years telephoned after Richie
to make sure he had gone where he said he was going, who tried

to seal her son from all the bad choices blowing around outside the window. No, Donny can't see her running a half-dozen times to the emergency room with high blood pressure at each twist her son's story takes; can't see her bent in half with chest pains six months after Richie's arrest, paramedics rushing through that front door and clamping an oxygen mask over her mouth, driving an IV needle into her arm, pushing a nitroglycerine pill under her tongue, trying to stave off the heart attack or stroke that's on the verge of occurring as her son watches, even more scared than he was on that long night when he lay awake smelling urine in a New York City jail. He can't see her lying in the hospital, realizing that if she doesn't stop letting the newspaper stories affect her so deeply, they're going to kill her. But listening to the mother and the son, he can feel it.

And it's all that feeling that Donny lets out when the *New York Post* reporter gets a tip and calls him a few days later to ask, "How can Utah consider rewarding a sex felon with a scholarship?" All that feeling from a man who senses that his and his university's integrity is being assaulted. Of course, he has never walked into the *victim's* house and felt what a heart might feel there. "There are two victims here," he tells the reporter. "He doesn't evaporate into the atmosphere. He's not a piece of dirt. He has feelings and emotions. . . . They both made a mistake; they shouldn't have been there. But everyone's worried about the girl. What about him? . . . You don't see her name or picture, but Richie Parker is plastered all over. . . . She probably will get a doctorate and marry a successful guy and live in the Hamptons. . . . Will he ever be able to forget it? . . . Who's hurt more for life?"

Imagine the explosion this quote causes back in Salt Lake City, the ripping apart of molecules. Imagine how rapidly the college president and athletic director must run from that quote, how swiftly Richie's chance to attend Utah vaporizes, how many columns are written citing Richie as the prime example of America's coddling of athletes and Neanderthal treatment of women. Imagine how tightly doors shut to discuss what must be done with Donny.

He is luckier than others will be. He is placed on probation for a year and ordered to attend sensitivity training sessions with

a director from the Women's Resource Center on campus. Donny
Daniels gets a second chance.

A year later, when a writer from *SI* calls, Donny says he was
wrong for saying what he did but wishes to say nothing more, and
his boss, Coach Rick Majerus, the most affable of men, seals his
lips as well. Better to fence off the area and let the pieces lie where
they fall, to be covered by the sediment of time.

VI

Here is a university president. Here is the picture of Teddy
Roosevelt on his office wall. Which is which? Who's who? Mus-
tache. Spectacles. Hair combed back. Eyes atwinkle. Robust body.
Bent for bold action. Oh, so *that*'s how you tell the two of them
apart: Stephen Trachtenberg's the better politician.

He's the man who transformed the University of Hartford and
George Washington, the one who gives big-idea speeches and writes
ethics essays for books, magazines and newspapers. He knows
something about everything. Even chemistry.

Yes, he's going to do it. He's going to give this Parker kid another chance, and he's going to satisfy the alumni and faculty
and the women's groups and the media and the talk-show callers, and even the victim. He's going to introduce cesium to fluorine, and—*eureka!*—nothing's going to go *ka-boom!*

And why not? He's a master at problem-solving, a genius at
persuasion. "He has a tremendous capacity to anticipate a whole
variety of outcomes and the implications of those outcomes," says
George Washington vice president Bob Chernak, "and then calculate how to move an issue toward the most favorable one. He's
always three steps ahead of you. He's thinking of ideas in his sleep."

Stephen inherited a university with a profound identity cri-
sis, not to mention a 1–27 basketball team, in 1988. In the wake
of his brainstorms, applications have nearly doubled, contributions
have soared, average SAT scores have rocketed and the hoops team
has become an NCAA tournament fixture. A new challenge? Bully!
A fray? Fine! He would wade right into it and convince people he

was right, the way he did during the student sit-ins at Boston University back in the 1960s as a bearded associate dean, persuading protesters not to risk a violent confrontation with police. He has built up a tall pile of chips at George Washington, and he's willing to ante up for Richie Parker.

Sure, he's eager to help his basketball team, but it's also something else. Sure, he's the son of one hell of a Brooklyn life insurance salesman, but he's also the son of a social activist, a mother who sent him to summer camps with black kids and wanted him to become a doctor who would treat the poor, not to mention the grandson of a Ukrainian Jew who fled to America for a second chance. His record of helping kids out of deep holes is long. At Hartford he gave a scholarship to a young man with an eighth-grade education who had been convicted on drug-dealing and burglary charges. That man, John Richters—who played no sport—went on to graduate summa cum laude and get a Ph.D. in psychology and now works as a program chief at the National Institutes of Health in the study of chronically antisocial children.

A young deer—that's the image that forms in the university president's head when Richie enters his office in May 1995. Barely audible, Richie expresses contrition and an earnest desire to attend George Washington, and he's so hopeful that he buys a school hat and T-shirt. All the questions march through Stephen's head as Richie walks out of his office. Is it a college's job to mete out more punishment than the legal system does? Perhaps not, but isn't it a university president's job to make sure that a parent doesn't send an 18-year-old daughter to live in a dorm room next door to a sex offender? What if it were *his* daughter? If a sex felon shouldn't get a basketball scholarship, what about an academic scholarship? What about a thief, a mugger, an embezzler? A custodian or a waiter can return to his normal life after the legal system passes judgment, but a gifted basketball player cannot? Pro sports are fine for felons to play, but not college athletics? What kind of message does it send out when a sex offender gets a scholarship? When you remove the emotion from the question . . . but maybe you *shouldn't* remove the emotion from the question. All this confusion, does it signal a society lost in the wilderness . . . or one finally mature enough to look at questions it has always shut its eyes to? His mind gnaws at the bone, at every last bit of gristle. Beneath it all, he can sense what's going on, the vague feeling people are beginning to have that their love of sports—the sense of escape and belonging that they provide—is doubling back on them like some hidden undertow, pulling them all out to sea. It's not the ripest time for redemption.

But he takes a deep breath and begins constructing a master plan. He sends a university lawyer, a woman, to New York City to compile a massive dossier on Richie. If she finds any smudge, besides the stairwell incident, George Washington can retreat—but he keeps checking with her, and she doesn't. Shrewder still, he decides that *he* won't decide Richie's fate; he'll leave that to a blue-ribbon committee, one that he structures as if he were a supplicant at a Hindu shrine, bowing to a dozen different gods, to every possible political correctness: seven blacks and eight whites, seven females and eight males, including a professor of law, an assistant chief of police, a minister, a campus chaplain, an academic coordinator, a faculty clinical psychologist, a director of multicultural student services, a superintendent of schools, two judges, two trustees and three students. "A Noah's Ark committee," he calls it. If the menagerie chooses to accept Richie, Stephen will have him redshirted for a year, ease him into campus life, save him from the jackals waiting at enemy arenas. And then, as the frosting on the cake, even before the committee makes its recommendation on Richie, he offers the victim, a valedictorian of her junior high class, a scholarship when she graduates from high school. A university lawyer warns him that one won't look pretty in a tabloid headline, but Stephen is determined. Win-win for everyone, right?

Do you recall Chernobyl? It all begins to rain down on Stephen Trachtenberg: the *New York Post* reporter, radioactive telephone calls, faxes and letters, scalding editorials, icy questions from the board of trustees, student petitions and condemnation from the faculty senate. Stephen, the father of George Washington University, is being called immoral, a fool, a calculating liar. Even his wife, Francine, in his corner all the way, warns him that he has underestimated what he's up against, that, politically speaking, he has made the wrong call. He's losing sleep. It's usurping his entire day and all of his night. The story moves to the *Washington Post*'s front page—*that's* trouble. If only he could buy enough time for his plan to incubate, for the score of Richie's last SAT test to arrive and the Noah's Ark committee to see the results of the nearly complete investigation, but no, Stephen looks to one flank, then the other and sees a remarkable alliance closing in on him. The feminists *and* conservatives, "the forces of the left and the forces of the right," he says, "coming together like the jaws of a vise." Eight years of working 12-hour days to build George Washington's image is being frittered away, and image is money. And he can't even try to persuade the public that he's right—the NCAA gag rule preventing school officials from discussing a recruit has stripped him of his greatest gift. Could he even lose his job over this, if the jaws keep closing? Could he?

One by one, those in his inner circle who admire the risk he has taken, or have simply indulged it, urge him to halt, even as his investigator's reports on Richie keep coming in, convincing him more than ever that it's right to go on. Finally it's just Stephen out there, hanging on to Richie by his fingernails as everything around them shakes. At last, he has to let go. Stephen looks at himself in the mirror. It's not Teddy he sees. It's not the man who could persuade almost anyone of anything. "I gave Richie Parker a moment of hope," he says, the light going out of his eyes, "and then I took it away."

VII

Here is the victim. No, here the victim is not. She has never emerged from the shadows of that stairwell. She will not emerge now. Of her you shall only know this: For months after the incident she endured nightmares and telephoned threats from people who blamed her. She is an excellent student, but her grades dipped, and the taunts from schoolmates forced her to transfer from one high school, then another. She undergoes therapy. As she gets ready for her senior year, her family will not even reveal the borough where her current school is located.

She hopes to become a doctor. Her father is a social worker
who deals with abused children, her mother a hospital nurse. Six
years ago they and their daughter left Ghana and came to America,
looking for another chance.

VIII

Here is a number. Such a nice, plump number. Say it: *500*. Let
them scoff at Dave Possinger, let them cringe at his intensity, let
them ask him, like wise guys, to total up the traffic lights in the
towns where he has coached, but this would be proof he could
clutch all the way to the coffin: *500*. One more win is all he needs
to reach that number. One more.

And no, this won't be 500 by dint of sheer endurance, a box
turtle's milestone. Eighteen years is all it took Dave, an astonishing average of 28 victories a year. He is the best coach you never
heard of, a 52-year-old man marooned in the bush country of NAIA
and junior-college basketball by bad luck and an old whiff of scandal. But it's summer, and the 1995–96 season is just a few months
away, and on opening night his Sullivan County (New York) Community College team will no doubt pulverize Dutchess C.C. as it
does every year, and he will join the invisible club: *500*.

He has envisioned the moment all summer, even as the man
he has just chosen as his assistant coach, Charles Harris, has begun
to grow intrigued by the never-ending newspaper accounts of a
kid in New York City named Richie Parker. Richie is the last thing
on Dave's mind. Dave has just coached his team to the national
junior college Division III championship and is loaded to repeat in
1995–96, and he has no reason to think that Richie will end up
with him in bush country, at a low-level community college. Start
making contacts and see what's out there, especially for the year
after this, is all he has asked of Harris, a likable 40-year-old black
man who Dave is sure will make a superb recruiter.

Everywhere Dave goes that summer, even on his vacation in
the Philippines, he imagines the magical night that is coming: The
limousine his girlfriend is renting to take him to the game. The

official hoisting of the national-championship banner, his second in four years at the junior college in Loch Sheldrake, New York. Former players converging to congratulate him, a capacity crowd rising to recognize him. The plaque, the ringing speeches, the commemorative T-shirts, the late-night dinner for 100 in the Italian restaurant. "It dominated my thoughts every day," Dave recalls. "Even in places in the Philippines where there was no running water, no electricity, I'd see kids playing basketball and I'd think about five hundred. It would stand for all the years, all the kids, all the hard work." It would stand for his nine seasons at a New York NAIA school named St. Thomas Aquinas, where his 295–49 record helped make the program the country's winningest of the 1980s, on *any* level—yes, Dean Smith at North Carolina was second to Dave Possinger. It would stand for his four-year run of 133–5 at Sullivan County and ease the pain from the '89 scandal that forced him out after a single year at Western Carolina, his one shot as an NCAA Division I coach, even though it was his assistant, not him, who was cited for minor recruiting violations. Perhaps 500 wouldn't mean quite so much if he had a wife and children, but no, it's just him and his basset hound Free Throw, and 500 stands for his life.

A few hours' drive south, at a showcase game for unrecruited players, his soon-to-be-named assistant Harris is watching the one obvious jewel on the floor, Richie Parker. It's crazy, thinks Harris, who remembers inmates from the local prison taking classes at Sullivan County C.C. when he was enrolled there in the 1970s. "Everyone has something in their closet they're not proud of," Harris says, "and everyone deserves a second chance." A long shot, but what a coup if he could offer the kid the second chance that the four-year colleges wouldn't.

Harris gets clearance, he says later, from Sullivan County's athletic director, Mike McGuire, to have Richie apply to the school— not as a scholarship student but as any normal student would. Searching for a way to contact Richie, Harris calls the *New York Post* reporter. It's like the mouse asking the cat for directions to the cheese.

McGuire says now that if he heard the name Richie Parker, it didn't register. And that he definitely never gave Harris permis-

sion—even though Harris had been unofficially approved to go on
contract in two months and had already invested countless hours
and a few hundred dollars from his own pocket on phone calls and
recruiting trips—to present himself to a *New York Post* reporter
as a Sullivan County assistant coach and declare that Sullivan
County was "committed to working" with Richie Parker.

You know what happens next. You know about the reporter's
call to the president, asking if he knows that Sullivan County is
recruiting a sex felon. You know about the next day's headlines,
the ducking for cover. Richie, of course, will never play at Sullivan
County. Harris's fate will hang in the balance for a few months
while the school wrings its hands. In October, after he has spent
weeks monitoring the players in study hall and working at practices without pay, hoping for the best, Harris is told he won't be
hired.

Harris, with head-coaching dreams of his own, is crushed.
Dave, who feels responsible for Harris, is devastated. There have
been other slights from his superiors at Sullivan County, he feels,
but to do this to a well-meaning man trying to give a kid a second chance—how can he go on working there and live with himself? But then, how can he walk out on his team two weeks
before the season opener and deprive himself of the Holy Grail:
500?

Simple, Dave's friends tell him. Win the opener, then quit.
What a scene it would be, the man of the hour strolling to the
microphone, saying, "Ladies and gentlemen, thank you. *I quit!*"
But Dave's conscience won't let him do it. "If I start something,"
he tells his friends, "I have to finish it."

Five days before the opener, he quits. He can't sleep. A few
days later he smirks and tells a reporter. "Your job is to tell me
why I shouldn't jump off a building." His team goes on to win the
national championship again, without him.

His record hangs there, rolling around the rim—499 wins and
116 losses—but athletic directors look right past him, searching for
a younger man. Eight months later he still hasn't even received an
interview. He takes a job as a regional director for National Scout-

ing Report, a service designed to help high school kids get—what else?—college scholarships. "But there's still a claw in the back of my throat," he says, "a claw telling me, 'You are a basketball coach.'"

A week after he quits, Dave goes to his dresser drawer. He opens it and stares at what he purchased in the Philippines a few months earlier, and he makes a decision. Damn the math, they can't take it from him. It's there now, glittering in 18-karat gold from a chain around his neck: *500*.

IX

Here is the girlfriend of the boy who has pleaded guilty to sexual abuse. She's tall and lean, a beautiful girl who's so composed that everyone always assumes she's older than she really is, until that day when people are running to her in the hall, telling her to come quickly, something terrible has happened, and Richie's in the principal's office talking so helter-skelter that none of it makes sense, and the police are on their way, and she's nearly in hysterics.

He's the schoolmate Jaywana Bradley fell in love with in 10th grade, the one who taught her to play basketball so well that by her senior year she will be named by the *Daily News* as one of the best schoolgirl players in Manhattan. Who knew, perhaps they would go off together to trumpets, the king and queen of Manhattan hoops moving on, hand in hand, to set up court on a college campus . . . until this.

But what, exactly, *is* this? Jaywana keeps finding herself in bed, crying, wondering. People keep asking her, "You gonna leave Richie?" Some call her a fool if she sticks with him, and a few boys walk right up to her and say, "Why you goin' out with a rapist?"

She can't quite answer that. Maybe it's because her mother and father believe in Richie, her dad accompanying the Parkers to court hearings. Maybe it's just sitting there in the Parker apartment all those evenings, playing spades with the family and watching TV, feeling that relentless presence of Rosita—like a rock, a magnetic rock. Listening to Rosita talk about the past,

telling how her father died when she was one, how her mother
died of diabetic complications when she was thirteen, how her
twin sister stepped in front of a car and was killed when they were
five, leaving Rosita clutching the sleeve of the coat with which
she had tried to yank back her twin. Maybe Jaywana, just like
Richie, simply keeps absorbing Rosita's relentless message: "Make
your life what it's meant to be, and don't let anyone or anything
stop you."

Maybe it's two young people pulling closer and closer together
the more that forces try to drive them apart. Maybe she's a sucker
for that playful, silly Richie, the side he only shows close family
and friends. And maybe it comes from holding him, wiping away
his tears the way she does when George Washington closes the door
on him and she ends up getting the big-time basketball scholarship to Massachusetts that was supposed to be his.

He goes off to Mesa, to the junior college that decides not to
let him play basketball, and she goes off to UMass, and they don't
see each other for a long while. He has time to sort out what's essential, what he needs, *now*, sooner than he ever dreamed. When
they come home for Christmas, he asks her to come over, calls her
to his room and asks her to close her eyes. When she opens them,
he's on his knee, asking her to marry him, and she says yes. And
later, when she asks him when, he says, "As soon as we're done
college."

More and more now, Jaywana finds herself daydreaming of
a future. There is no city or people there, just her and Richie in
a house surrounded by land and trees as far as the eye can see, a
place where no one can touch them. Why the two of them against
all odds? She can't explain. "I don't know what made me stick
through it with him," she says. "All I know is that nothing anybody can ever say or do can pull me apart from him."

X

Here is death. Now, wait a minute—no one is going to be foolish
enough to blame Richie Parker's 15 minutes in the stairwell or the

administration of Mesa Community College or even the media for the death of a coach's father, but every event in life is chained to the next, and how do you ever separate the links?

This was supposed to be the year that Rob Standifer gave his father, Bob, a gift—perhaps the last one—in exchange for the gift his father had given him. All Rob's life his dad had awakened at 3 a.m. and reported to work three hours early at a construction company, logging 12- to 14-hour shifts. It didn't matter how badly his dad felt, with his bad back, his diabetes or his weak heart. Work made his father feel good, and his father had a knack of passing that feeling all around. The lesson Rob took into his bones was the old American one: Outwork everyone and you'll succeed in life.

And it seemed true. As a kid Rob was always the first one on the basketball court as a point of pride, shooting 1,000 shots a day, and sure enough, he found himself playing for the Mesa Community College team that nearly won the junior college title in 1987, finishing third in the national tournament in Hutchinson, Kansas. He worked for nothing as a high school assistant and then for next to nothing for five years as an assistant at Mesa, and he was rewarded with the head-coaching job two years ago. He was only 27, but his dream, to coach a major-college team, was no longer quite so far away.

The pantry was bare his rookie year, but Mesa went 15–15. Then, doing it his dad's way—his typical off-season day ran from 7 a.m. to 10 at night—he ran the summer league, organized a computerized scouting system, cultivated his high school coaching contacts, recruited at hours when other coaches relaxed, pushed his players through an exhaustive weight-lifting program and then nurtured them at night with so many phone calls that his friends called him Ma Bell. He was single and on fire. "I could be a maniac," says Rob, "and I was."

The pantry filled fast. Twice in the summer league in 1995 his players whipped a team with four former Arizona State starters on it, and Rob's target was clear. He was going to take his father and his team back to Hutchinson and this time win the whole damn thing.

Richie? He would sure make things easier. Rob had seen him
play in the annual summer tournament at Arizona State, which
Richie's New York City club team, Riverside Church, traveled to
each year. Just like all the other coaches, Rob was struck by the
distance between Richie and the world's image of Richie. Just like
all the other coaches, he got that same feeling in the pit of his stomach when he saw a talented high school player—if you didn't get
him dunking *for* you, he might soon be dunking *on* you. Besides,
Rob knew Ernie Lorch, the Riverside director, and already had
taken a few of Lorch's kids at Mesa. And so Rob, too, was drawn
in. Mesa would be Richie's safety net, the faraway junior college
where he could go to heal himself and play ball if all the Division
I scholarship offers went up in smoke.

And because there was so much smoke, and Richie kept
hoping and waiting for the next Division I chance, his decision
to go to Mesa occurred at the last minute, just a few days before
the start of school last August. And because Richie waited, Rob
had to wait, and by the time he found out Richie was coming,
there was no chance for cool heads to sit and debate this and
perhaps construct a plan. Rob told the story of Richie Parker
to three women—his mother, his girlfriend and his girlfriend's
mother, and they all agreed with him. "What Richie did was flat
wrong," Rob says, "but are you going to be part of the problem
or part of the solution?" And he insists—*are you crazy?*—that of
course he notified his superiors, two of them, about Richie and
his baggage.

But the Mesa athletic director, Allen Benedict, says he was
told nothing of Richie's past, that all he got was a 9 p.m. call from
Rob telling him that a great player was coming from New York.
The next morning, while Richie was at 30,000 feet heading west
across the heart of America, the junior college president was on
the phone with Benedict, saying, "Why did a reporter from the *New
York Post* just call me . . . and who is Richie Parker?" And then
the National Organization for Women was checking in, and cameras were peering inside the gym for a peek at Richie, and a TV
truck was pulling up to Benedict's house. "Whether you do some-

thing wrong or not isn't the point sometimes," says Benedict. "It's the perception."

Rob was called in to a meeting less than two weeks before the first practice and forced to quit. Richie called Rob, nearly in tears at what he had wrought.

As for Richie, he could stay, but he couldn't play basketball. College athletics, Mesa president Larry Christiansen reasoned, are like a driver's license—a privilege, not a right. What the westward trip and the open spaces had done for so many others, they couldn't do for Richie Parker.

Richie had to decide, then and there, what was most important in his life. He chose to stay at Mesa, take courses and learn who he was without a basketball. He would work the shot clock at games, like one of those earnest guys in glasses that no one ever notices, and by the end of the year the administrators at Mesa would all say good things about him.

Rob had to tell his father the terrible news, that his son had lost his job and his dream. He knew his dad was on the edge of the cliff—doctors had said that if not for the zest that Bob derived from his work, his heart would've likely given way three or four years before—so the son tried to shrug and keep his face a blank, so he wouldn't give his father that nudge. Bob was devastated, but as with all his other pain, he tried to keep it inside. He was bewildered, too. The ethic he had passed on to his only child—outwork everyone and you'll succeed—had failed, been displaced, it seemed, by a new one: Image is everything.

Rob didn't eat for three days after that, unless you count the antacid medication. He wouldn't even show his girlfriend, Danelle Scuzzaro, how badly this hurt and how alone he suddenly felt.

On the fourth day after he was let go, he picked up a diamond ring at the jeweler's and took Danelle to dinner. Afterward, he dropped to his knee—cesium is the damnedest thing—and asked her to marry him. She said yes, and thank God.

Two weeks later, at 5:15 a.m., he got the call from his mother. His father's heart had stopped. He was 61. It might well have happened then anyway. "What happened to me didn't kill him," says Rob, "but it didn't help."

There was only one thing to be said for the timing. All the tears Rob had held back after losing his job could finally come out, and they did . . . again . . . and again . . . and again.

XI

Wait a moment. What about the reporter from the *New York Post*—isn't he here too? Sure, just a moment, he's still on the telephone. Gosh, look at him, just a kid, wouldn't even pass for 25. Just started at the *Post*, covering high school sports, when suddenly—*whoa!*—he has his teeth into the story of his life, and his incisors are wonderful.

Look at Barry Baum rolling out of bed in his Manhattan apartment and running, literally, to the newsstand at the corner of 79th and Broadway to check if the *Daily News* has scooped him on the Parker story. That has actually happened before, so Barry knows that sinking feeling. See him getting that 10 a.m. call from his editor, groggily picking up the phone—a medic on call in a tabloid war. "So what's goin' on with Parker today?" his editor demands. And Barry says, "I'll let you know," then shakes off the cobwebs and begins working the phones, looking for a tip. He loves this part, the detective work. And the most amazing thing keeps occurring. Because there's such an innocent charm about Barry, people *want* to help him.

Some high school scout or basketball junkie with his ear to the streets keeps slipping him the name of the next university showing interest in Richie, and then Barry plays his role, just as the university administrators and the coaches and the women's groups and the loved ones do. He becomes the Bunsen burner, the heat that agitates the cesium and fluorine molecules into rapid movement, more-violent collision. He leaps to call the university president and the campus women's center to ask that 64-megaton question—"How do you feel about your school recruiting a sex felon?"—and if they say they don't know who Richie Parker is, so they can't comment, he faxes them a pile of his Parker stories, and suddenly they have a comment. And all at once the coach and the athletic director are being called onto the president's carpet, and then there's a follow-up exclusive story to write when they all abandon Richie, and there's no time to consider all the layers, all the moral nuances, because the editor's on the phone barking, "O.K., hurry, rewrite that for the second edition!"—just like in the movies. And then street vendors are snaking between the cars bottlenecked at the bridges and tunnels leading into the city the next morning, catching drivers' eyes with thick SEX FELON headlines, and every person who contributes his 50 cents confirms the *Post* editor's instincts and becomes another link in the chain.

"There were nights when I couldn't sleep, an adrenaline I had for a long time," says Barry. "I'd lie in bed, realizing I'd come to New York and made an impact on one of the biggest stories of the year."

Hadn't his editor at the *Post* told him, "We're going to put your name in lights," when he hired Barry in August 1994? Wasn't that music to his ears? Even as a little kid in Brooklyn Heights, he had dreamed of busting back-page stories for the New York tabloids. At 15 he talked his way into becoming the Knicks ball boy by rat-tat-tatting 10 letters to the team trainer, and then he parlayed that job into his own cable-TV show in Manhattan, *Courtside with Barry Baum*, by convincing the station of the wonderful access to big-name Knicks that a precocious 16-year-old ball boy had. He appeared on the televised dating show *Love Connection* three times, and when one of his dates sniffed about Barry's making the wrong turn on their evening out, he brought down the house by sniffing back, "Get a load of Miss Rand McNally, never made a wrong turn in her life!"

And then suddenly the kid who grew up calling *New York Post* and *Daily News* columnists with kudos and beg-to-differs is being lauded for his own back-page *Post* scoops on New York radio talk shows, being asked to appear on the all-sports station, WFAN, and invited to speak at a journalism symposium at Madison Square Garden with a poster board full of his Parker stories. Adrenaline, yes, but anguish, too, stuff you don't talk about when you're a guest on WFAN. Because the nasty phone calls to Barry's desk have begun, people hissing, "Leave Richie Parker alone!"

Then, when he's a guest on a radio talk show one day, a caller says, "Don't you see what you're doing? This is a black kid who comes from nowhere, and you're a white guy who probably comes from a lot of money." Barry blinks. "It hits me," he says. "That's true. I've always had everything, and I'd never even thought of the race factor." New York City high school coaches, his contacts, start saying, "C'mon, Barry, back off. What are you trying to prove?" Even his own father, Bruce, finally says, "Leave him alone already, Barry," and that stings.

"That even someone who knew me that well wouldn't realize that I'm just trying to do my job . . . ," he says. "I mean, don't give me credit for keeping Richie Parker out of college, but don't blame me for it either. And the more people tell me to *stop* reporting a story, the more it means it *is* a story, right? But I keep wondering about Richie. All that time, I couldn't talk to him because his lawyer wouldn't let me, so I couldn't feel him. Finally they let me. You know, it changes things once you talk to him. Before that he was an object, and it was easy to write, 'Richie Parker, sex felon,' because I didn't know him. He was the predator and the girl was the victim, right? I talked to him at a Rucker League game last August, and he actually smiled at me. A smile is a big thing.

"Look, I've never had a problem with Richie playing college basketball. It's not the colleges' job to punish him further. He should be allowed to play—but not without students and their parents being notified, maybe by a letter from the university administration. You know, like Megan's Law, notifying people that a sex felon is in their neighborhood. It's funny. It's like *I've* become Megan's Law for these universities. I'm the one who tells them he's coming. It was amazing how quickly it played out with Oral Roberts. I reported that the school was interested, the story breaks across the country, the TV reporters arrive on campus—and the school announces it has already pulled out! It was like the fire trucks coming, and there's no fire, the local residents have already put it out. These universities have no backbone! Every university president I talk to, except for maybe Stephen Trachtenberg, it's like talking to the same guy. Every one of them says, 'I can't believe my coach did this and that isn't what we stand for and blah-blah-blah.' I'm convinced there's only one college president in the United States: He just keeps changing his name!"

One major-college coach, off the record, asks Barry what will happen if he takes the risk on Richie. What's Barry supposed to do, lie? He tells the truth, the coach says thank you and backs off and—*poof!*—the chance is gone, the chemical reaction begun and finished before anyone ever even smelled it occurring. And it begins to dawn on Barry: "Somehow, I'm *in* this story. I'm not just the observer. People are making decisions based on my reporting. There I am, twenty-five years old and playing the part of deciding if this kid's going to get into college or not, and maybe, if he's good enough, even into the NBA. I have no agenda or angle at all, but he'd probably be playing now if I hadn't called Utah or GW or. . . .

"So where is the line? I've never been taught that line. I keep wondering, Am I doing the right thing? But I shouldn't have to make that choice. I started compiling a list in my mind of all the people whose lives I've affected, the people who have gotten fired, all the universities. And it tears me apart, because the last thing I want to do is hurt anyone. But I know if I stop reporting it and the *Daily News* gets the story, which you know they will, then my editor will call me and say, 'What's goin' on with Parker? What happened? Where are the words?' and what am I going to say? I can't win. So people blame me. It's like *I* was the one in the stairwell."

He stares off at the wall, catches his breath. "And it's not over yet," Barry says. "It's not over until I find out where Richie Parker's going."

XII

One day about a month ago Richie Parker stepped into an airplane in Arizona. The plane rose, and he looked through the window one last time at the desert and flew back across America, back home, with no idea what would happen next. "I've learned I can survive without basketball," he said last month. "I've learned how the real world is and that I'm stronger than I knew I was. There's less fear now. I know myself more. I trust people less, but that doesn't make me sad. Just more aware of things. I can still live a good life." And he said a lot more, but it would be improper to let him do it here, for it might mislead the reader into thinking this was a story about Richie Parker.

This land is vast, and it contains so many kinds of people, and that is its grace. Two weeks ago Gale Stevens Haynes, the 45-year-old provost of the Brooklyn campus of Long Island University—and the black mother of three teenage daughters—offered Richie Parker a basketball scholarship to her Division I school. She didn't pull the offer back when the *New York Post* reporter found out, and Richie accepted it. When asked why she did it, she said, "Unless there's an island that I don't know about, where we send people forever who have done something wrong, then we have to provide pathways for these people so they can rejoin society. If we don't, it can only explode. It can only explode in *all* of our faces."

A Letter from South America

M̲y first pass on a basketball court in one of the world's poorest countries was too hard and too late—six skips, and the ball had rolled into the riverbed. I ran after it, saved it from the sad trickle that is the dry-season river and was about to return to the court, when out of a shack constructed of branches, plastic and scraps of aluminum came tumbling a small boy, crying desperately. From inside I heard a man's shout, a little girl's shriek and the sounds of a father beating his daughter. I stared for a moment, absently tossing the ball toward the court.

As I turned, about to rejoin the game, I saw a player from the other team passing the ball inbounds to the man I was supposed to be guarding. He walked in for a layup. So *that's* how you play here, I thought.

Inside I felt myself turning cold and hard. Now I had the ball at the top of the key. I faked right, drove left, the lane opened and the sun came out and I strolled in, double-pumping for the sheer hell of it. Make it, take it. Now I was dribbling on the left side of the basket, doing something 5' 11" former high school point guards

This story first appeared in 1986.

only do to their little brothers, backing slowly to the hoop, posting up my man, with each step feeling nothing behind me but the thin Andean mountain air. I wheeled, shot, missed, rebounded and scored. Playing offense in the Third World was a joy: no defense!

I came back the next day and the day after, reveling in my dominance. Then I began to grow frustrated. To me, basketball is one of the holy things; once, in a dirt-driveway pickup game in the Ozark mountains, I swarmed my wife so furiously on defense that when she exploded out of her crouch, her head crashed into mine, leaving a preposterous lump on her forehead, a purple moon around my eye. Where was such seriousness here?

They loitered on defense, they giggled at air balls. They lost track of the score. Part of me admired this happy-go-lucky approach to sport—but that part was in my head, and the game was in my blood. "*¡Defensa!*" I began imploring my teammates, "*¿Dónde esta tu hombre?*" ("Where is your man?") I stopped taking pleasure from my strolls to the basket—I began passing off instead. And still, every time I raced out of bounds after a ball or stooped to tie my shoelaces, the other team shook off its nonchalance, exploited my disadvantage and scored, indifferent to my protests in sputtering Spanish.

At the heart of my frustration stood Fortuna, a short, dark boy who played in a jacket on 80-degree days, took siestas on defense and, grinning, chucked 35-foot shots from his hip every time he touched the ball. Instead of scolding him, his teammates fed him the ball. "Fortuna! Fortuna!" they serenaded every one of his heaves, following the ball's arc with giddy delight. Every now and then, the ball grazed the rim or the backboard. I wanted to strangle Fortuna.

Some days, in no mood for such blasphemy, I avoided the pickup games and practiced my shot. My eyes had time to wander. More shacks were being built on the riverbed, and not all of them belonged to families. Abandoned children were congregating inside them, selling cocaine in order to live, smoking it in order to forget. One day the police swooped down and flushed them out of the shacks: drug users, gasoline sniffers, venereal-disease sufferers—none of them older than 15.

I stopped shooting and indifferently watched a game of three-on-three. Mostly I was staring at the riverbed. As my wife and I discovered soon after beginning a year of volunteer work—she in a hospital, I teaching English—rotting garbage and excrement were everywhere; there was no adequate disposal system, so people dumped their garbage in the closest empty space. Pigs, sheep, dogs, cows and donkeys nosed through it for useful morsels. Taxi and bus drivers wheeled their vehicles into the sorry river to wash them; amid lorries and livestock, women washed their clothes and men washed their hair. People, even animals, moved at a slow, resigned rhythm.

Something about poverty here was very different from poverty in the U.S., on the court just as on the riverbed. No one's poverty made him burn. People let fate glide past them instead of moving their feet and grunting to try to stop it; they found short-cuts, quick inbounds passes while the opponent or the authorities weren't looking. Here, that seemed to be the only way to survive.

I looked up and saw Fortuna chucking another 35-footer, everyone giggling, the ball caroming toward the river. That was three months ago, and I haven't played basketball since.

Still, I needed to sweat, to extend, to feel my body move. I had played sports since childhood—many things I could sacrifice to live in South America for a year, but this was not one of them.

Why not jog, I thought. Certainly I would attract attention here, running along sidewalks full of women bent beneath the weight of babies, roosters, kindling, sugar and flour; people dedicated to avoiding a single superfluous step. But in this I was experienced. I had run through Tunis while entire busloads of Arabs reached out the windows to pound the sides of the bus and hoot at me. I had jogged through a zoo in Shanghai, where a hundred Chinese turned their backs on the pandas in order to stare at the white-skinned, brown-bearded animal loping by.

I woke up early and hit the road, maintaining an easy stride out of respect for the altitude. I ran alongside the traffic, swallowing the fumes of automobiles with no pollution-control devices, trying not to stumble over sidewalks buckled by the knuckles of tree roots, blinking away the sting of the dry-season dust roiled up by passing buses and trucks. I came to an intersection, glanced each way and stepped onto the road. A horn blasted, a bumper brushed past my thigh. Stop signs were nonexistent, traffic lights rare. Drivers simply hit their horns just before each intersection and crossed by intimidation or the grace of God. Fools who jogged—let *them* hit the brakes.

I searched for quieter streets, shaded lanes where the people with a little money lived. The dogs lived there, too. Every few houses, just when my mind was beginning to lose itself in the motion, a German shepherd or Doberman pinscher—keepers of the status quo, guardians of the gap—would hurl itself at a fence, barking ferociously, its muzzle protruding between the bars, its teeth gnashing, unable in its fury to distinguish between a trotting have and a thieving have-not. My breath hitched, my legs trembled, my feet leapt into the gutter. The activity designed to prevent my having a heart attack at 66 was bringing one on at 33.

Human beings are adaptive miracles. I threw in my lot with the mad dogs, the autos and buses, doubled my wits at intersections and continued my jogs. An awareness began to set in about the people I was running past, more unsettling than the intensity of the starers in Tunis or Shanghai. *There were no starers.* Nowhere should I have felt myself more an object of curiosity; nowhere had I stirred less. No one looked at me, waved at me, honked at me, hooted at me. Invisibly I weaved my way through them, a spirit among the dispirited. Did the extremes of poverty take curiosity from a man, too?

Here and there I passed a few children kicking around a soccer ball, but far fewer than I had expected. Mostly they played marbles or killed time. Why didn't destitution drive them to the courts, the fields, the boxing rings? Why didn't it ferment athletes as it did back home?

I concluded, at first, that poverty was simply a heavier and blunter instrument here than on the playgrounds of Harlem or West Philly—it bludgeoned desire instead of whetting it. Then I found myself stopping to chat with the children on the streets. Who were their heroes? I asked them. Who did they want to be like when they grew up?

"Rambo," they said.

"Chuck Norris."

"Bruce Lee."

"What about athletes?" I said. "Which ones do you admire most?" A few mentioned Pelé, a few others Maradona. The rest remained silent. I began to list other athletes I had supposed to be known by 13-year-olds worldwide—Larry Holmes, John McEnroe, Carl Lewis. They stared back blankly.

They had no role models here; they had no ladder. No high school, university or professional leagues, except for soccer, where the average player earned $4,000 a year and knew better than to keep reminding children that they could do it, too. They had no concept of sports as a ticket out of hell. Few of the children even realized exercise might prolong their lives. Few looked as if they felt that was something to strive for.

Weeks passed. Jogging grew more joyless. I had run the dirt roads of black townships in South Africa, past crumbling, over-crowded tenements in Bombay, some days observing, some days dreaming, but every day having fun. Why was it different here?

One morning I ran past a neighbor whom I knew to be a teacher. I began to calculate. The $40 it cost to buy my sneakers was two months' income for him. I ran by a post-office employee trudging up the steps to his work; the price of my jock was his weekly salary. I passed a nurse walking toward the hospital; *one* of my sweat-soaked socks was twice her daily wage. In Africa and Asia I was a one-week visitor. Here I was living for a year, talk-ing to people, entering their homes, reading, learning. Here I *knew.*

I spun around a corner and felt something strike my chest. The arm of a wrinkled beggar, outstretched. He reeled against a wall. I stopped, put my hand on his shoulder, apologizing. He extended his open palm.

I tried to explain and turn away. He tugged on my $15 warm-up jacket and mumbled. Finally I pulled free. The men who sleep on sidewalk grates in New York City—they know not to beg from joggers.

Sports are a luxury. The activity I once considered to be a necessary function, as natural as the breathing in of oxygen and the breathing out of carbon dioxide, I now saw as one for people who could dream where it might take them, for people with spare time, energy and money.

I went to a sporting goods store to buy a basketball net for some kids who shot now and then at a crooked rim. The price was the equivalent of $12. I asked about a decent soccer ball: $27. A regular pair of sneakers: same cost as in the U.S. A canister of tennis balls: $7.50, three times what it costs back home. How could they possibly afford it?

I bought the tennis balls anyway and went to my closet for the racket I had brought from home. The town's clay courts were isolated, enclosed by a fence and bushes.

I had taken up tennis only a year before. My wife, a former university player, thrashed me regularly. I cursed my mistakes, praying no one nearby knew English, but still I paid dearly. One morning a powerful forehand stroke, all on its own, missed the ball and hit my mouth, which bled for an hour and swelled to the size and color of something you could float down the Snake River.

Every time I played, I noticed an odor. It wasn't my forehand. Just beyond the fence lay a pile of garbage where men gathered to pick through the scraps for food and to defecate. My curses mocked me. While I fretted over my second serve, men a few feet away gnawed on potato peels.

I pushed that from my mind, consoling myself with the teaching I was doing, and slowly my game improved. One afternoon I trailed my wife by only 5–4. Never had I won a set from her— here, perhaps, was my chance. She hit a ball low and deep to my backhand, I swung and hit the ball off the rim of my racket and high into the air. It soared over the fence and landed where it belonged—in the pile of garbage.

"*Chico,*" I called to the little boy scavenging there for food. "*¿Puedes lanzarme la pelota?*" ("Can you throw me the ball?") If we lost this ball, we would be down to only one.

The boy picked it up, looked at me, then turned and began to run. *That little sonofa....* I dropped my racket, raced for the gate and tore after him.

He ran two blocks, turned a corner and scrambled over a fence. My God, I hadn't seen spunk like this since I had arrived. I chased him through a lot and back onto the street, the green ball pumping in the little brown hand at his side. As I was closing the gap, my feet slowed beneath me. He had a $2.50 ball in his hand, half his dad's weekly salary.... Now he could toss it against a wall with his friends. My feet came to a stop. I turned and walked back. A man could play tennis with one ball.

As Time Runs Out

He entered the arena with his wife on his arm and a container of holy water from Lourdes in his black leather bag. His back and hips and knees ached. That was the disease, they told him. His ears rang and his stomach turned and his hands and feet were dead. That, they said, was the cure. Each step he took brought a rattle from his bag. Twenty-four tablets of Advil were usually enough to get Jimmy Valvano through the day.

He braced himself. No doubt someone would approach him this evening, pump his hand and say it. Strangers were always writing it or saying it to him: "We're pulling for you, Vee. You can do it. Nobody thought you had a prayer against Houston in that national championship game in '83, and you pulled that off, right? Keep fighting, Vee. You can do it again."

No. Not in the same breath. Not in the same sentence, not in the same paragraph, not in the same magazine or book could the two be uttered: a basketball opponent and a cancer eating its way through the marrow and bone of his spine. A basketball opponent and death. *No.* In their fear of dying, people didn't make it larger

This story first appeared in 1993.

than it was. They shrank it, they trivialized it. Vee versus meta-static adenocarcinoma. Vee versus Phi Slamma Jamma. Go get 'em, baby. Shock the world, Vee.

No. No correlation, baby, he longed to tell them. *None.*

The cameras, the reporters, the microphones awaited him inside the Civic Center in Tallahassee. A brand-new season. Iowa State at Florida State, 46-year-old Jimmy Valvano's first game back as an ESPN college basketball analyst since he had learned last summer that he most likely had a year to live.

He tried to quicken his pace. His left leg wouldn't let him. Four or five times each day he dabbed his finger in the holy water and made the sign of the cross on his forehead, his chest, his back, his hips and his knees. Then he poured a little more into his palm and rubbed the water deep into his hands and feet.

When he was coach at North Carolina State, Vee used to pause at this point, just as he entered the arena. Having delivered his pregame talk, he would leave the locker room on the lower level of Reynolds Coliseum in Raleigh, mount the steps that led to the court, and stand on the top one, still unseen by the crowd. For a moment he would not be an actor at the heart of the drama. He would be a spectator absorbing the immensity, the feeling of it all—the band blaring fight songs, the crowd roaring, the cheerleaders tumbling through the air, the players taking turns gliding to the glass for layups. And he would think, God, I am lucky. What do other people do when they go to work? Go to an office, sit at a desk? I get *this!*

Yes, here was Vee's gift, the gift of the select, to be in the swirl and at the very same moment above it, gazing down, assessing it, drinking in all of its absurdity and wonder. It enabled him to be the funniest man and most fascinating postgame lounge act in sports; it enabled him to survive the scandal at North Carolina State that stripped him of his reputation and his job. Even during his most harrowing moments, part of Vee was always saying, "God, in a year this is going to make a great story." Exaggerate this detail just a little, repeat that one phrase four or five times, and it's going to have 'em howling. Even in the darkness after he had been forced to resign, he looked down at himself lying in bed and

thought, Boy, that poor son of a bitch, he's really taking a pounding. But he'll be back. Give him time. He'll be fine.

That was what cancer had stolen. The fear and the pain and
the grief swallowed a man, robbed him of detachment, riveted him
to *himself*. "I can't do it," he said. "I can't separate from myself
anymore."

He tightened his grip on the black leather bag and walked
under the lights.

It flooded through him whenever he walked onto a basketball court—the jump shots with crumpled paper cups he took as a
little boy after every high school game his dad coached, the million three-man weaves, all the sweat and the squeaks and the passion so white-hot that twice during his career, having rocketed off
the bench to scream, he had blacked out, and five or six times every
season the backside of his suit pants had gone *r-iii-p!* He wore
Wolfpack red underwear just in case, but it didn't really matter.
A guy could walk around in his underwear at home; Vee was at
home. Maybe here, for two hours tonight, he could forget.

He looked up and saw a man striding toward him. It was the
Florida State coach, Pat Kennedy, who had been Valvano's assistant at Iona College. Kennedy leaned toward Vee's ear and opened
his mouth to speak. Those who had been in a bar at 1 a.m., when
Vee was making people laugh so hard that they cried, those who
had seen him grab the deejay's microphone at 2 a.m. and climb on
a chair to sing Sinatra, those whose hotel doors he had rapped on at
3:30 a.m. to talk about life and whose lampshades he had dented
with his head when their eyelids sagged ("Had to do something to
wake you up! You weren't listening!") . . . they could not fathom
that this was happening to him. Vee was a man with an electric cable
crackling through his body; he might walk a couple of dozen laps
around an arena after a big win to let off a little hiss, or wander the
streets of a city until dawn after a loss. He was the kind of guy you
wanted to cook dinner for or show your new house to, because that
would make it the all-time-greatest dinner, the all-time-best house,
terrific, absolutely *terrific*—and Vee *meant* it. And now Kennedy's
mouth was opening just a few inches from Vee's ear, and there were

a thousand thoughts and feelings scratching at each other to get out—
"Every day with you was an exciting day. Every day you had ten
new ideas. Every day you left me with a smile on my face, saying,
'Boy, that Valvano's something else.' And you left me thinking I
could do more with my life than I'd ever thought before. Certain
people give life to other people. You did that for me"—but no words
would come out of Kennedy's mouth. Instead he just kissed Vee.

This was what Valvano missed most after his coaching career ended in April 1990. Nobody kissed a TV analyst, nobody
hugged him, nobody cried on his shoulder. Vee used to astonish
the directors who hired him to give those dime-a-dozen, $50-a-
pop guest speeches at their summer basketball camps in the
Poconos back in the '70s. The directors would look back as they
strolled to their offices after introducing him, and they would see
a guy in a floppy Beatle haircut pulling a white rat—a *real* white
rat, gutted and stuffed by a taxidermist and mounted on a skate-
board—toward the microphone and roaring to the kids, "What
kind of a greeting is *that?* Look how you're sitting! I come all the
way here and what do I get? A coupla hundred crotch shots? I'm
supposed to stand up here and give a good speech staring at a
coupla hundred sets of jewels? Whadda we have here, a bunch of
big-timers? I want *rats!* Let's try it again. You only get out of life
what you demand! I'm gonna come to the microphone all over
again, and this time I want a standing O, and once I get it you can
bet I'm going to give you the best damn speech I possibly can!"
The camp directors would look back again and see a couple of
hundred kids on their feet, cheering wildly. Look back a few minutes later and see them crying. Look again and see them carrying
Valvano from basket to basket to cut down the nets and chanting,
"VEE! VEE! VEE!" And for the rest of those camps, the directors and counselors would have to peer in every direction each time
they opened a door or walked down a path, because Vee had convinced a few hundred kids to leap from behind walls and bushes
in front of them, to sacrifice their bodies like True Rats, to shuffle
in front of the big-timers and *take the charge!*

He didn't recruit kids to his college program; he swept them
there. He walked into a prospect's home, and 15 minutes later he

had rearranged the living room furniture to demonstrate a defense, had Mom overplaying the easy chair, Dad on the lamp, Junior and his sister trapping the coffee table. Where the hell else was the kid going to go to school? In the 30 games Vee coached each season, the 100 speeches he eventually gave each year, the objective was the same: to make people leap, make them laugh, make them cry, make them dream, to *move* people. "Alive!" he would say. "That's what makes me feel *alive!*"

And then one day last spring he was playing golf on a course in the hills overlooking the Mediterranean in the north of Spain. He had weathered the scandal at N.C. State. He had won an ACE for excellence in cable-television sports analysis. He had turned down an offer to coach at Wichita State and signed contract extensions with ABC and ESPN. He had time, finally, for long dinners with his wife, for poetry readings and movies with his 12-, 20- and 23-year-old daughters. He had an assignment to do sideline commentary on a World League football game in Barcelona; he had a tee time on the course just north of the city. "How beautiful it was that day," he would remember. "How happy I was. . . ." And then he felt an ache in his testicles. That's how death comes. A pang in the crotch when a man's standing in the sun gazing across the green hills and the bluest goddam sea in the world, deciding between a three-wood and an iron.

He laughed at all the inevitable aching-testicle jokes; the doctor was almost sure it was just an infection or perhaps referred pain from the lower-back ache Vee had been feeling. He was still laughing, in the MRI tube last June at Duke University hospital, joking through the intercom with the nurses about the heavy-metal music they were pumping into his headphones as they scanned his spine to see if he had damaged a disk, when the radiologist glanced at the image appearing on his screen, and suddenly the laughter stopped and the nurses fell silent. And the dread, the sick dread began to spread through his stomach as the radiologist quietly said, "Come with me, Coach." And then: "Let me show you a picture of a healthy spine, Coach. . . . Now look at yours."

The vertebrae in his spine were black where the others were white. And the dread went up Vee's chest, wrapped around his ribs and his throat, but he squeezed out another joke: "You forgot to use the flash."

No laughter. "Coach, this is just how we see it in the text-book. . . . Coach, I'm ninety percent sure this is cancer."

The world spun, and he asked a dozen questions that couldn't be answered yet, but the look on the radiologist's face said this was bad, very bad. Vee walked into the waiting room and told his wife, Pam, and they held each other and cried and drove home, where his oldest daughter, Nicole, was helping his middle daughter, Jamie, with a Music 100 class project. They were banging on a piano key, beating a wooden spoon against a pot, a pencil against a wine bottle and two candlesticks against each other when the door opened and their dad said, "I've got cancer. I'm going to die. . . . I don't want to die. . . . I'm sorry. . . . I'm *sorry.*"

It was still incomprehensible five months later. His sockets were a little deeper, his olive skin wrapped a little more tightly around his skull, but the 35 pounds he had lost made his body seem fit, trim. His hair, against all medical logic, had survived massive chemotherapy. He lived in a land where people vanished when they became terminally ill. Most people who saw him walking through airports, stepping in front of cameras and cracking jokes about his plummeting weight ("Hey, I'm the quickest analyst in the country now—there's not an announcer who can go around me!") assumed his cancer was in remission. It was not. "How you doin', Coach?" they would call.

What could he say? "Hangin' in there," he usually replied. "Hangin' in there."

The crowd at the Civic Center caught sight of him now. The Florida State band rose to its feet, waved a sign—WELCOME BACK, BABY!—and chanted, "JIMMY VEE! JIMMY VEE! JIMMY VEE! . . ."

It was a Friday night. On Monday morning, as he did every two weeks, he would walk into the basement of the oncology center at Duke and sit with a hundred people who stared into the nothingness, waiting hours for their turns. His name would be called and a nurse would say, "Veins or port?" and he would say,

"Port," which meant that his veins had collapsed from being pierced by so many needles, and that the four vials of blood the doctors needed today would have to be drawn from the lump over his left breast, where a plastic access valve had been surgically inserted. He would remove his shirt, and a nurse would swab the lump with disinfectant and squirt it with ethyl chloride to numb it, flush out the tube inserted inside his superior vena cava with saline solution, take his blood and send him back to the waiting room while the lab ran tests. He would wait another 45 minutes, murmuring something now and then to Pam or a word of encouragement to nearby patients, then he would go to the office of a doctor who tried to be cheerful but who saw 40 cancer patients a day, and then he would be sent to the third floor to lie down again and have Velban, a cell killer, pushed into his veins through the port in the hope that it would kill as many cancer cells as healthy cells. Finally he would limp out clutching Pam for support, his body bent as if beaten with a bat, and you could count on it, somebody would ask him for his autograph, and you could count on it, he would smile wanly and say, "Sure."

". . . JIMMY VEE! JIMMY VEE! JIMMY VEE!" He put the headphones on and turned the sound up so he could hear the producer's cues over the ringing that was always in his ears now, and then he stepped onto the court to tape an introduction to the game. He could feel it now, surging up through the hardwood, into his deadened feet—the *thump, thump, thump* of basketballs as the two teams pounded through layup drills. Everything had a beat, a lovely chaos with an old, familiar rhythm. The players were grinning and slapping five with him, the fans were waving paper and pens at him, the band was blaring the theme song from *Rocky*, the cheerleaders were tumbling through the air, and Vee's right foot was tapping. In one breath he looked into the ESPN camera and told the audience how Iowa State would have to use its speed and *stick the jump shot* to win, whereas Florida State would have to *pound it inside.* In the next breath he turned to the boom mike and the interviewer on his right to answer her question about the cancer consuming his spine, and with the horn section and the backflips and the crowd's roar all around, he fell into that same easy metaphor and delivered it in that same hoarse, hyped voice. "I'm not happy to *be here.* I'm just happy to *be!* Even as we speak the good cells are going after the bad cells. You gotta encourage 'em. Good cells . . . *go get 'em!* That's what's going on right now! . . . *It's hoops time! Let's play some hoops!*"

"I'm helpless! I make no decisions! I have no control! I'm totally at the mercy of the disease and the treatment! I'm not a dad! I'm not a husband! I'm a *freak!* I can't do anything! I just lie there and they stick needles into this lump in my chest and pour poison in my body, and I don't believe in it. I'm a *freak!*"

He couldn't cry *that* into a microphone to the million and a half people listening at home and watching in bars, but it was right there, at the back of his tongue, at the base of his brain, welling up and wanting to spill. It did, sometimes. There was no reason to hide it, no reason anymore to hide anything. There were days that he passed huddled in his bathrobe in front of the television, flinching from the pain, curling up in sorrow and wondering how in God's name he would summon the strength again to make the quip that would put everyone around him at ease, to tell the world in that hoarse, hyped voice, *You gotta get it into the middle, it's the only way to beat a trap defense!* as if there were a hundred thousand more tomorrows. There were days when Jamie, who had taken off her junior year at N.C. State to help him through this horror, would shout, "Get up! Go talk to your doctor! Go see a priest! Don't just lie there! You've given up! Get up! Yell at somebody! Yell at *me!*"

"Can a doctor or a priest take the cancer out of my body?" he would ask.

"I don't know! I just want you to *do* something! Yell, fight, punch! Even if it's all for nothing. So we can say, 'There's *Dad.*'"

The old Dad, the Charge of the Light Brigade Dad, son of a man who had a booming voice and an ear-to-ear grin and a yellow-pad list of things that Vee's team needed to get right to work on . . . but didn't they understand? How could Vee allow himself to hope? If Vee liked a movie, he saw it five times. If Vee liked a song, he transcribed every word, memorized it, sang it twenty times a day and talked his kids into singing it with him a half dozen more times on the way to the beach. Vee couldn't throw half or three-quarters of his heart into anything; he had to throw it all. Didn't they know how dangerous it was for a man like him to throw all of his heart into a hope as slender as this? Vee was a dreamer. Vee had no life insurance. A man whose lows were as low as his highs were high couldn't hope too hard, couldn't lean too far, because the next downturn in his condition or the next darting away of his doctor's eyes could send him whirling down a shaft from which he might never escape.

Besides, where were the hooks to hang his hopes on? Doctors couldn't even find the origin of his cancer—they were guessing the lungs, even though he had never smoked more than an occasional cigar. With his kind of cancer, there were no tumors to X-ray, no reliable way to chart the course of the disease. "You'll know when it's getting worse," they told him. "You'll know by the pain." So he would wake up each morning and ask himself the terrifying question: Is there more pain?

Get up! Yell! Fight! Punch! He tried. He refused to put on the gown when he checked into the hospital every sixth week for massive doses of chemotherapy. He refused to take the prescription pain pills. He talked to God out loud. He marched into the salon and ordered them to buzz off all of his hair—*he* would take it off, not the chemotherapy. The same way, in the last minute of a tie game when the other team had the ball, he flouted convention and ordered his players to foul and risk handing the opponents the game-winning free throw—*Vee* wanted the rock at the end; *Vee* wanted the last shot. He refused to sit there, cringing on defense, waiting for fate to happen to him.

But the joke was on him. The hair grew right back and never fell out. Every tactic in this new war came back at him turned upside down. Every stoking of his fever to live increased his horror of death. And he would remember that astonishing flood of emotional letters that dying people had written to him after N.C. State had shocked Houston nine years earlier, people thanking *him* for giving them a reason not to give up, and he would sit there, shaking his head. Could he explain all that to TV viewers during the next timeout? Could he let everyone know that he only had to see his three daughters walk in the house in order to cry now, that a TV commercial showing a dad accepting a bowl of cereal from his little girl, hugging her and saying, "I must be pretty special for you to bring me bran flakes," brings tears to his eyes because they're just so goddam happy and lucky?

Iowa State guard Justus Thigpen's jump shot was descending a good foot in front of the rim, a fine opportunity for Vee to say, as he had with a slow, stupefied shake of his head two days earlier at home, "*Justus Thigpen!* Can you believe it? Who knows how much time I have left, and I've been sitting here poring over *Justus Thigpen's* stats in the Iowa State basketball brochure. I'm sitting here reading, and I quote, that 'Justus Thigpen was twice selected Big Eight Player of the Week' and that 'he scored eleven points at Kansas and seventeen points in ISU's overtime win on ESPN versus Colorado.' *What the hell am I doing?* The triviality of it just clobbers me. You get this sick and you say to yourself, Sports means nothing, and that feels terrible. God, I devoted my whole *life* to it."

He might say *that* to a million and a half people. He *could* say that. He was a man who converted feelings to thoughts and thoughts to words with stunning ease—solid to liquid, liquid to gas; it was beautiful and terrible, both. Sometimes he would look at his daughters or his wife and say, "God . . . I'm going to miss you," and it would rip their hearts in half. What were the rules after you had dragged out of the doctor the fact that only a few patients with metastatic adenocarcinoma diagnosed in its late stages, like Vee's, lived more than two years, and most were gone within a year? Did you tell the people you loved all the things that were banging at the walls of your heart, or did you keep them locked inside to save your family the agony of hearing them? Nobody taught you how to do this; what were the rules?

Maybe it was time now for the TV camera to focus on his hands, the left one balled and the right one wrapped around it, desperately trying to squeeze some feeling into it as Bob Sura zinged in a 21-footer and Florida State's lead swelled to 50–31. Perhaps Vee should tell all the viewers and listeners, even if it wasn't what they had tuned in to hear: "I'm being deprived of my senses. I can hardly taste food anymore. I can't hear. I can't feel. My wife will have to button my shirt soon because I won't be able to feel the buttons between my fingers. It's got my feet and my hands and my ears . . . but it doesn't have my mind and my heart and my soul. And it's not *going* to. I'm going to fight this as long as I can. I'm going to keep doing what I love.

"I'm going to have to miss some games because of chemotherapy. I don't think you're going to see John Saunders in the studio saying, '*Live! From room 401 at Duke University Hospital, it's Jimmy Valvano!*' because I'm going to be at the sink throwing up. I don't want to be wheeled to the microphone to do games, but I *will*. I'll keep doing this until my mouth doesn't work, until my brain doesn't function."

Maybe he should tell them what he does some days at home in Cary, North Carolina, how he removes his shoes and walks barefoot in the grass. Just to feel. How he puts his hands around the trunks of the pine trees and closes his eyes. Just to *feel*.

Here was a story he could tell. Goddammit, the Seminoles were up by 21 at halftime, let him tell it. It was the one about a 23-year-old coach at Johns Hopkins University who was on a bus ride home from Gettysburg, Pennsylvania, with his players, exuberant over his team's 3–0 start. A 23-year-old coach who had plotted his life on an index card: five years, high school head coach. Five years, small-college head coach. Five years, university assistant coach. Five years, small-university head coach. Ten years, big-time-university head coach. A 23-year-old who didn't know he was going to compress the first 20 years of the plan into 13, who didn't realize he was going to have his dream, live his Pocono camp speech, cut the NCAA title nets at 37 . . . who didn't know his life might already be half over. His players called him to the back of the bus. "Why is winning so important to you?" they asked. "We've never seen anything like it. You're irrational."

"Because the final score defines you," he said. "You lose; ergo, you're a loser. You win; ergo, you're a winner."

"No," the players insisted. "The participation is what matters, the constancy of effort. Trying your very best, regardless of whether you win or lose—that's what defines you."

It took 23 more years of living. It took a rampage in his office at home after a 39–36 N.C. State loss to Virginia in 1982, lamp busted, chairs toppled, papers and books shoved everywhere. It took charging through a locker room door so hard that it knocked out the team doctor. It took the pregame talk of his life and the coaching jewel of his career, the 1983 NCAA championship upset that helped rocket the Final Four onto the level of the World Series and the Super Bowl. It took a couple of dozen Christmases when his wife had to buy every gift and decorate every tree. It took bolting up from the mattress three or four times a night with his T-shirt soaked with sweat and his teeth rattling from the fever chills of chemotherapy and the terror of seeing himself die again and again in his dreams—yes, mostly it took *that* to know it in his gut, to say it: "They were right. The kids at Johns Hopkins were *right*. It's effort, not result. It's *trying*. God, what a great human being I could've been if I'd had this awareness back then. But how can you tell that to any coach who has a couple kids and a mortgage and fifteen thousand people in the stands who judge him only by wins and losses? Do you know, that 39–36 loss to Virginia was ten years ago, but I could never let go of that game until I got sick. Now it doesn't bother me at all.

"But I can't sit here and swear I'd do everything differently. I wouldn't trade those years. Nobody had more fun than me. How many people do you know who've had their dream come true? You're looking at one. That was my creative period, my run, my burst of energy. . . ."

Start his own company, JTV Enterprises? *I can do that.* Write his own newspaper column, his own championship-season book? *I can do that.* Broadcast his own daily radio commentary, his own weekly call-in radio program and local TV show in Raleigh? *I can do that.* Sell the advertising time for his own radio and TV shows? *I can do that.* Commission an artist to paint an NCAA championship-game picture each year and sell the prints to boosters of the school that wins? *I can do that.* Commission a sculptor to produce life-sized figures of the greats of sport for teams to showcase outside their stadiums? *I can do that.* Write a cookbook? (He didn't know where the plastic bags for the kitchen trash can were.) *I can do that.* Make 10 Nike speeches, 20 alumni-club speeches, 25 to 50 speeches on the national lecture circuit and a dozen charity speeches a year? Host his own sports talk show on ESPN? *I can do that.* Take on the athletic director's job at N.C. State as well as coach basketball? Are you sure, Vee? *I can do that.*

This was not for glory, not for money. There was none of either in the AD's job, for God's sake. It came from a deeper, wider hunger, an existential tapeworm, a lust to live all the lives he could've lived, would've lived, should've lived, if it weren't for the fact that he had only one. A shake of the fist at Death long before it came knocking, a defiance of the worms.

"Girls! Dad's in the living room!" his wife called upstairs one night.

"Which channel?" a daughter shouted back.

"Live!" Vee hollered up. "In person! Downstairs! I'm actually here!"

Home at 1 a.m. Wide-eyed in bed at two, mind still grinding, neurons suspicious, even back then, of sleep. *"Inside! Get the ball inside!"* A daughter standing in the hall in her pajamas, hearing him cry it out in his sleep. Up at 5 a.m. for the two meetings before the breakfast meeting. Blowing out of his campus office at 4 p.m. to catch a plane. Day after day, year after year. "A maniac," he said. "I was an absolute maniac, a terrible husband and father. Everybody in the stands went, 'Awwwwwww, isn't that cute?' when my little girl ran across the court in a cheerleader's outfit and hugged me before every home game, but for twenty-three years, *I wasn't home.* I figured I'd have twenty years in the big time, who knows, maybe win three national titles, then pack it in at fifty-three or fifty-four, walk into the house one day, put on a sweater and announce: *'Here I am! Ozzie Nelson's here! I'm yours!'* I always saw myself as becoming the all-time-great grandfather. Leave the kids with me? No problem. Crapped his pants? Fine, I'll change him. Vomited? Wonderful, I'll clean him up. I was going to make it up to them, all the time I'd been away." His eyes welled. "God. . . . It sounds so silly now. . . .

"But I didn't feel guilt about it then. My thinking always was, I would make a life so exciting that my wife and kids would be thrilled just to be a part of it. But I remember one Father's Day when I happened to be home, and nobody had planned anything, nobody even mentioned it. How could they have planned anything? I'd probably never been home on Father's Day before. I might've been in Atlanta giving a Father's Day speech or in Chicago receiving a Father of the Year award, but you can bet I wasn't at home on Father's Day. Finally I asked them what we were going to do, and my daughter Jamie said, 'Dad, we spent all our lives being part of your life. When are you going to be part of *ours?*' It hit me like a punch in the stomach.

"But it went on and on, that insatiable desire to conquer the world. I was an arrogant son of a bitch. But it wasn't just arrogance. I kept thinking of those lines from 'The Love Song of J. Alfred Prufrock':

> *And indeed there will be time*
> *To wonder, "Do I dare?" and, "Do I dare?"*
> *Time to turn back and descend the stair,*
> *With a bald spot in the middle of my hair—*
> *(They will say: "How his hair is growing thin!")*

"I *wanted* to dare. I wasn't afraid to show my bald spot, my vulnerability, by trying new things. I'd go to bed after watching TV on a Saturday night, and my mind would be saying, '*I* should be the host on *Saturday Night Live*. I can do that.' I look back now and I see the truth in the Icarus myth. You know the story about the boy who's so proud of his wings that he flies too close to the sun, and it melts the wax and he falls and dies? What enables us to achieve our greatness contains the seeds of our destruction.

"Every season I had bronchitis, bad colds; twice I had pneumonia. The night we won the NCAA, I was sick as a dog. I was the Mycin Man all season—erythromycin, clindamycin. I wouldn't rest. I'd just pop the antibiotics and keep going. Who knows? Maybe I put my body in a position to get this. I've been reading books about cancer. They say it often occurs if your immune system is lowered, and then you have a trauma. . . ."

Yes, a trauma. To hell with that basketball game; it was going to end just as it began, a Florida State blowout. Here was a man who lay awake every midnight, chewing on mortality—let him talk. Let him wonder out loud if a book published in 1989, and the 15 months of investigations and media barrage it set off, was his bullet . . . and then try *not* to wonder, try to shut that midnight whisper down and ignore the connection between cancer and personal trauma, because otherwise he would have to blame a few people— a writer, a local managing editor—for this nightmare he was living, and he would have to hate, and hatred and blame were the worst detours a man could take when he was locked in mortal combat to live. "I can't do that," Vee would say. "I've got to fill these days I have left with love and laughter and forgiveness. But I *wonder. . . .*"

January 7, 1989, the first headlines. A book entitled *Personal Fouls*, by Peter Golenbock, was about to appear, accusing Valvano and his staff of fixing grades, hiding drug-test results from authorities, diverting millions of dollars from the alumni club to the players and paying the players off with automobiles. One publishing house rejected the book; another one bought it, and the hammer blows began in earnest, usually starting with the *News and Observer* in Raleigh and then ringing throughout the country, banging at the core of who Vee was. He called press conferences, he dug up graduation statistics, he demanded hearings by the North Carolina State Board of Trustees. But the Icarus arc was now at work—his glibness becoming proof, to his critics, of his guile; his gargantuan appetite for life proof of his greed.

The NCAA investigation lasted eight months. In the end the investigators found no million-dollar diversions, no automobiles, no grade-fixing, no hidden drug tests. They found two punishable violations—players had sold complimentary tickets and complimentary sneakers—and the NCAA placed N.C. State on two years' probation, declaring it ineligible for the 1990 NCAA tournament. Dave Didion, the lead investigator, wrote Valvano a letter. "I wanted to let him know that he had cooperated with me more than any coach I had ever worked with," said Didion, "and that not everyone thought he was evil. I wanted to let him know that if I had a son who was a prospect, I would be proud to have him play for Jim Valvano. He wasn't the smart-ass egomaniac I'd anticipated. Yes, the graduation rate of his players was not good . . . but no one cared to look at the overall graduation rate at N.C. State. Yes, he probably shouldn't have recruited some of the kids he did. But if he hadn't, he'd have ended up playing against them and getting his brains beaten out by them, because everybody else wanted those *same* kids."

Then came the final blow: allegations of point-shaving a few years earlier that involved former N.C. State forward Charles Shackleford. No one believed Valvano had knowledge of it, and nothing would ever be proved, but the hammering had to stop. In April 1990 he was forced to resign. "The pain of that—having my mother, my brothers, my wife, my children reading the things that were written about me," he said. "I felt physical *pain*. There were things I should've done differently, but I knew I hadn't done anything *wrong*. The insinuation that I didn't care about the kids. . . . I *hated* that. To be lumped with coaches who cared only about winning and nothing about education. . . . I *hated* that. I majored in English, not P.E. I had two daughters on the dean's list. All but perhaps two of my players at Johns Hopkins, Bucknell and Iona graduated. I didn't change. I'll take responsibility, but that's different from blame. I didn't admit the kids to N.C. State who didn't graduate—our admissions office did. In hindsight it's easy to say who shouldn't have been recruited, but who knew beforehand? Sometimes kids from worse backgrounds, with worse high school grades, did better than kids from decent homes, with decent grades.

"Maybe I trusted the kids too much. The school wanted me to force education down their throats, and I wouldn't do it. They wanted me to say, 'You don't go to class, you don't play. I take away ball.' What does that tell a kid? That *ball* is more important than education! My approach was, If you don't study, you pay the consequences. You flunk out. I tried to excite them about learning. I had Dereck Whittenburg read *King Lear* and then go to the chalkboard and do a pregame talk on it. I wasn't one of those coaches telling them to learn but never reading a book myself. I *lived* it. They saw me reading Shakespeare on buses. They saw me trying things outside of sports all the time.

"I guess I was unrealistic to think I could change kids. I should've said to them, 'I love you, but I don't trust you yet. You have to do this and this your first two years here, and *then* I'll trust you.' And there's no way around it—I didn't have as much time to give them after I became athletic director. I tried to do too much. They couldn't just walk into my office at any time of the day, like before, and talk. It was a little less each year, especially for the thirteenth, fourteenth, fifteenth players. But each time, the change was imperceptible to me. It happens without your realizing it.

"And now I'm fighting to live, and the irony of having people think of me as a man who cared only about winning and athletics . . . it overwhelms me. I'm looking for a reason to hope, a reason to live, and the only thing that helps me do that is my education, my mind. If I survive this, or even if I just wage this battle well, it will be because of what I grasped from reading, from understanding the world and my place in it, from learning to ask the right questions and to grasp all the alternative treatments for this disease—from *academia*, not from athletics. People think a sports background helps you fight death. Are you kidding? Athletes and coaches are taught that they're special. You're *nobody* when you're a cancer patient. You're *nobody*.

"I want to help every cancer patient I can now. For some reason, people look to me for hope. I'm feeling half dead, and they're coming up to me in the hospital for hope. I don't know if I can handle that, but it's the only conceivable good that can come out of this. If the Clinton administration wants someone to raise money for cancer research, I'm here. If I survive, I'm going to work with cancer patients one-on-one and help them find a way to hang on, like so many people are trying to do for me. Half a million people die of cancer every year in America, one out of every four of us will get it, and there's no moral outrage; we accept it. I'm all for AIDS funding and research, but how can the government give ten times as much per AIDS patient as per cancer patient? Barbra Streisand isn't singing for cancer, Elizabeth Taylor isn't holding a celebrity bash for cancer, and yet every time I go into that cancer building at Duke, it's a packed house! If it means more doctors, more space, more money, we've got to get it, because millions of people are going to find out that this is one hell of a way to go."

The basketball game was nearly over now. Vee's mind and tongue were still flying, the jokes still crackling, but a deep fatigue was coming over his body. He looked across the court and saw his wife speaking to a woman beside her, saw his wife smile. And he thought: It's so good to see her smile, but how many times have I seen her crying lately? What's going to happen to her? Will she be all right? He would take a deep swallow of air the next day as he remembered that moment, that look across the court at her as the coaches shouted and the players panted and the fans roared. "You see, I had it all planned for our twenty-fifth anniversary, last August sixth. I was going to give her three gifts: the deed to four acres where she could build her dream house, a big diamond ring, and a nice trip, just the two of us on a beach. She'd lift me up when she heard it and I'd cut the nets, a standing O. . . . *Goddam.* What did she get instead? A sick husband in a hospital bed getting Mitomycin, Cisplatin and Velban dripped into him. She got to clean me up when I vomited. *That's* love. I'd told her, 'We're going to get old together, Pam.' Probably the nicest thing I'd ever said to her. 'We're going to get old together.' . . . *Goddam.* . . . *Goddam.*"

The game ended, and then he did something he had never done before. He thanked the hundred fans who had gathered to wish him well, said no to the coaches who asked if he would like to go out . . . and went back to his hotel room with his wife. She fell asleep, and he lay there at 1 a.m., alone, hungry for food and wine, hungry for the conversation he was missing, and the laughter. He ordered a pizza, stared at the TV and cried.

He jumped from his seat one day not long ago. The backside of his pants didn't rip—they weren't that tight anymore. A paragraph had leapt into his eyes from a book he was reading. "That is why athletics are important," wrote a British sportswriter named Brian Glanville. "They demonstrate the scope of human possibility, which is unlimited. The inconceivable is conceived, and then it is accomplished."

"That's *it!*" cried Vee. "*That's* why we strive! That's the value of sports! All those games, they mean nothing—and they mean *everything!*" His fist clenched. He hadn't poured himself into emptiness for 23 years, he hadn't devoured Justus Thigpen's stats for nothing, he hadn't. The people who compared his upset of Houston to his fight against cancer were right!

"It's what I've got to do to stay alive," he said. "I've got to find the unlimited scope of human possibility within myself. I've got to conceive the inconceivable—then accomplish it! My mom's *convinced* I'm going to get better. My mom's always right!"

In early December, when the pain grew so fierce he had to call off a weekend of studio work for ESPN, he had a local shop print up 1,000 small cards. He had hundreds of people across the country calling him, writing him, encouraging him, but he needed more. VICTORIES, it said on each card. "Valvano's Incredible Cancer Team of Really Important Extraordinary Stars."

"See?" he said. "I'm going to make a *team.* I'm going to give a card to everyone I meet as I go around the country doing games. On the back of each card are the requirements of my players. One, they have to say, 'Jimmy Vee, you will make it.' Two, they have to say it out loud—it's important to verbalize. They can call my office number and if I'm not there, leave a message on my answering machine: *'Jimmy, don't give up!'* And three, they have to do something to improve their own health, whether it's mental, spiritual or physical.

"My own team—everybody can join. This is it, baby, my ultimate pregame talk. I *need* this one, *gotta* have it. Gotta have so many people calling my answering machine each day that they can't get through. Gotta have people all over the country opening their windows and shouting it out: 'JIMMY VEEEEEE! DON'T GIVE UP!'"

Jim Valvano died three and a half months after this story appeared.